W9-BAP-652

Register Your Book

at ibmpressbooks.com/ibmregister

Upon registration, we will send you electronic sample chapters from two of our popular IBM Press books. In addition, you will be automatically entered into a monthly drawing for a free IBM Press book.

Registration also entitles you to:

- Notices and reminders about author appearances, conferences, and online chats with special guests

- Access to supplemental material that may be available

- Advance notice of forthcoming editions

- Related book recommendations

- Information about special contests and promotions throughout the year

- Chapter excerpts and supplements of forthcoming books

Contact us

If you are interested in writing a book or reviewing manuscripts prior to publication, please write to us at:

Editorial Director, IBM Press
c/o Pearson Education
800 East 96th Street
Indianapolis, IN 46240

e-mail: IBMPress@pearsoned.com

Visit us on the Web: ibmpressbooks.com

IBM® Rational Unified Process® Reference and Certification Guide

IBM® Rational Unified Process® Reference and Certification Guide

Solution Designer

Ahmad K. Shuja

Jochen Krebs

IBM Press
Pearson plc

Upper Saddle River, NJ • Boston • Indianapolis • San Francisco
New York • Toronto • Montreal • London • Munich • Paris • Madrid
Cape Town • Sydney • Tokyo • Singapore • Mexico City

Ibmpressbooks.com

IBM Press Program Managers: Tara Woodman, Ellice Uffer
Cover design: IBM Corporation

Associate Publisher: Greg Wiegand
Marketing Manager: Kourtnaye Sturgeon
Publicist: Heather Fox
Executive Editor: Chris Guzikowski
Senior Development Editor: Chris Zahn
Managing Editor: Gina Kanouse
Designer: Alan Clements
Senior Project Editor: Lori Lyons
Copy Editor: Gill Editorial Services
Indexer: Cheryl Lenser
Compositor: codeMantra
Proofreader: Lori Lyons
Manufacturing Buyer: Anna Popick

Published by Pearson plc
Publishing as IBM Press

IBM Press offers excellent discounts on this book when ordered in quantity for bulk purchases or special sales, which may include electronic versions and/or custom covers and content particular to your business, training goals, marketing focus, and branding interests. For more information, please contact:

   U.S. Corporate and Government Sales
   1-800-382-3419
   corpsales@pearsontechgroup.com.

For sales outside the U. S., please contact:

   International Sales
   international@pearsoned.com.

This Book Is Safari Enabled

The Safari® Enabled icon on the cover of your favorite technology book means the book is available through Safari Bookshelf. When you buy this book, you get free access to the online edition for 45 days. Safari Bookshelf is an electronic reference library that lets you easily search thousands of technical books, find code samples, download chapters, and access technical information whenever and wherever you need it.

To gain 45-day Safari Enabled access to this book:

- Go to http://www.awprofessional.com/safarienabled.

- Complete the brief registration form.

- Enter the coupon code 37F2-7QUE-SEWB-JUER-834S.

If you have difficulty registering on Safari Bookshelf or accessing the online edition, please e-mail customer-service@safaribooksonline.com.

Library of Congress Cataloging-in-Publication Data

Shuja, Ahmad K.
 IBM rational unified process reference and certification guide / Ahmad K. Shuja, Jochen Krebs.
   p. cm.
 ISBN 0-13-156292-4 (pbk. : alk. paper)
 1. Electronic data processing personnel—Certification. 2. IBM software—Examinations—Study guides. 3. Computer software—Development—Examinations—Study guides. I. Krebs, Jochen. II. Title.
 QA76.3.S466 2007
 005.1–dc22

                    2007038771

   ISBN-13: 978-0-13-156292-9
   ISBN-10: 0-13-156292-5

Text printed in the United States on recycled paper at RR Donnelley in Crawfordsville, Indiana.

First printing December 2007

To my ever-loving family, to my father, Pir Shuja-Ul-Mulk, who made me all that I am today and to my lovely daughter, Zara Kamran Shuja, who is the joy and happiness of my life.

—*Ahmad*

To Melanie, my wonderful wife and biggest supporter.

—*Jochen*

Contents

Part II   Unified Method Architecture (UMA)

Chapter 3   Basic Content Elements   **63**

Chapter 4   Basic Process Elements   **71**

Part III   **Rational Unified Process: Content and Process Elements**

Disciplines

Chapter 5   **Business Modeling**   **81**

Chapter 6   **Requirements**   **93**

Chapter 7   Analysis and Design   **111**

Chapter 10   Deployment   157

Preface

The Rational Unified Process® (RUP®) is the most mature iterative-incremental software development process on the market. It has a long tradition in the industry that can be traced back to the 1990s when different methodologies merged into this unified approach. This maturity is not only expressed by the age of the process and its updates throughout the years but also through a certification process that complements this IBM® process product.

With the increasing number of users, training courses, and adopters of RUP, the demand for certification has received more and more attention. The interest in certification has come not only from specialists who like to distinguish their skills from others, but also from organizations that use certification to filter candidates and establish a certain skill standard. These trends have raised a tremendous number of questions about the certification process, its administration, and its content in Internet forums and e-mail exchanges.

With the release of RUP 7.0 and a brand-new method authoring tool (IBM Rational® Method Composer) came a new certificate called **IBM Certified Solution Designer – IBM Rational Unified Process**. This book includes the new RUP process framework, authoring capabilities, and, of course, a strong focus on the new RUP certification.

We hope that this book will introduce the latest RUP for newbies, provide a new reference for everybody transitioning from a previous version of RUP, and serve everybody who is interested in receiving the RUP certificate.

Content and Structure of the Book

With those three groups of readers in mind, we have arranged the chapters in this book accordingly to allow you easier navigation of the reference material and preparation for the certification examination.

In Part I, "Introduction," Chapters 1 and 2 introduce the RUP and the key principles of business-driven development.

- Chapter 1: Welcome to the IBM Rational Unified Process and Certification

  This chapter serves as foundation for the rest of the book. It discusses in detail some of the core RUP concepts and provides an overview of the new process architecture and the key principles of business-driven development. Finally, it introduces iterative development using an architecture-centric approach and discusses some of the implementation-specific scenarios.

- Chapter 2: Key Principles for Business Driven Development

  Chapter 2 takes a closer look at each of the key principles and discusses successful patterns and how to implement them in a RUP project. It also discusses so-called anti-patterns, which are signals in a project when one or more of these principles have not been followed.

In Part II, "Unified Method Architecture," Chapters 3 and 4 cover the Unified Method Architecture (UMA).

- Chapter 3: Basic Content Elements

  This chapter covers the UMA element types that are used for describing RUP content, such as work products, roles, and tasks. These are the elements that contain language from the RUP pages.

- Chapter 4: Basic Process Elements

  In contrast to the previous chapter, this chapter discusses the UMA elements that are used to arrange content elements, such as to activities or delivery processes.

In Part III, "Rational Unified Process: Content and Process Elements," Chapters 5 through 14 lay out the reference material for RUP 7.0.

The chapters are organized into two subgroups: Disciplines and Process.

- Disciplines

  Chapters 5 through 13 introduce the RUP 7.0 content discipline by discipline in the following sequence: Business Modeling, Requirements, Analysis and Design, Implementation, Deployment, Project Management, Change and Configuration Management, and Environment. The content presents the work products, roles, and tasks being used in the RUP for large project configuration.

- Process

  Chapter 14: Phases, Activities, and Milestones

  This chapter covers the process elements used in RUP 7.0 that align RUP content with the various phases and activities, including their milestones.

At the end of Chapters 1 through 14 are sample questions that help you assess how well you learned the material in the chapter. The content and format of the sample questions also help to prepare you for the test-taking experience.

In Part IV, "Tailoring and Tooling," the two chapters introduce tailoring approaches and the necessary RUP tooling to get the job done.

- Chapter 15: Tailoring

   This chapter focuses on various tailoring and adoption strategies of the RUP.

- Chapter 16: Tools

   This chapter is especially important for process engineers who need to customize the out-of-the-box RUP process to their own needs. We will discuss the IBM Rational Method Composer (RMC) and MyRUP, which provide two alternative approaches.

The final three chapters are important for readers who are interested in the RUP certification. Part V, "Certification, Examination, and Practice," includes the following chapters.

- Chapter 17: The Value of RUP Certification

   This discusses the motivations to pursue and the benefits of earning the RUP certification.

- Chapter 18: Sample Examination

   This chapter has an examination like the real one to give you a chance to test your knowledge of the RUP before you decide to attempt the real examination. The exam content and format conform closely to the type of questions, question categories, and structure of the questions in the actual exam.

- Chapter 19: Before, During, and After the Examination

   The final chapter of this book has tips and tricks before you take the examination, during the examination, and after you have achieved the certification.

Finally, the Appendix, "Answers to Sample Questions," includes the correct answers for all the questions at the ends of the chapters and the questions in Chapter 18, "Sample Examination."

Audience

Obviously, the overall audience for the book is those who are interested in RUP certification. But the two segments of this book target different subaudiences. The reference segment, which serves as the latest collection of RUP content and tooling, is useful to process engineers, project managers, and members of the program management office (PMO). In addition, each of the disciplines chapters provides value to many different roles participating in the software engineering effort—business analysts, testers, programmers, and architects. The part on business-driven development will provide motivation for line managers and senior management who consider adopting RUP. The last part of this book (certification) will be useful for all RUP experts who are interested in achieving the new certification, but it also provides details for decision makers who are interested in including this certification in their culture.

If you are new to the RUP, we recommend studying the reference material a few times, before approaching the certification, examination, and practice material. Professionals with a strong RUP background can read through the new reference material once and go straight to the final three chapters. We recommend that you do not memorize the sample examination but try it only once or twice (with your attempts spaced apart) prior to the actual examination.

Final Thoughts

We wish you luck in your pursuit of the certification and in your use of RUP in your projects. If you work through the book carefully, internalize the material, and apply it, you should be successful in your attempt to earn the certification and also in your software development projects.

Acknowledgments

We'd like to thank all those people who helped review the manuscripts and give general feedback or other assistance for this book. Those people include Russell Pannone, Nayna Malavya, Per Kroll, Peter Haumer, Mike Perrow, and Jeff Smith.

Thanks to the entire Addison-Wesley team, especially Bill Zobrist, Chris Guzikowski, Chris Zahn, and Karen Gill, who helped not only shape the vision of this book, but did a tremendous job in editing the chapters during crunch time.

A very special thanks goes to Denise Cook (IBM) and Brian Lyons (NumberSix), who provided vital and detailed feedback on each chapter and gave us the opportunity to see RUP from even more angles. Unfortunately, Brian, who was a big proponent of the RUP certification, did not get the chance to see the final product on the shelf.

About the Authors

Ahmad K. Shuja, www.shuja.info, is an accomplished IT manager and professional who has worked at some of the major financial services (Citigroup Inc., Merrill Lynch & Co., and others) and management consulting organizations (Ernst & Young Inc. / Cap Gemini Ernst & Young Inc., and others) around the globe. He has a proven track record of successfully enabling organizations to build and manage high-quality, software-intensive products and services efficiently and effectively. Ahmad provides advisory and consulting services in IT strategy and planning, IT Service Management (ITSM) and governance, program and project management (PMO) transformation and operations, software engineering processes and agile software development (RUP, XP, SCRUM, and others), enterprise architecture, and business process management. In addition, he offers training and mentoring services across a wide range of IT disciplines.

Ahmad holds the degrees Master of Science in Management of Technology from the Massachusetts Institute of Technology (MIT Sloan School of Management), Master of Science in Computation (Mathematics and Software Engineering) from the University of Oxford, and Master of Information Systems from the University of Toronto. He also holds numerous professional certifications, including Project Management Institute (PMI) Project Management Professional (PMP), Software Engineering Institute (SEI) Certificate in Capability Maturity Model Integration (CMMI), IT Infrastructure Library (ITIL) Service Manager (ITIL Master Certification), and Certified RUP Specialist, to name a few. Ahmad can be reached directly at ahmad@alum.mit.edu.

Jochen (Joe) Krebs, www.jochenkrebs.com, is an active member of both the Agile Alliance and the Scrum Alliance. He also is a member of the Agile Project Leadership Network (APLN) and spearheads the local chapter in New York City. He is an IBM Certified Specialist – Rational Unified Process and an IBM Certified Solution Designer – Rational Unified Process 7.0. He is also a Certified ScrumMaster (CSM) and a Project Management Professional (PMP®). Joe frequently publishes articles with a focus on project management and requirements engineering, and he speaks at conferences and companies. He received his MSc in Computing for Commerce and Industry from the Open University and teaches regularly at New York University (NYU). In his current role, he is responsible for successful adoption of agile development practices in a large investment bank in New York City and provides agile mentoring services through http://www.incrementor.com. He is currently working on his new book, *Agile Portfolio Management*, to be released in 2008.

Prior to taking on his current responsibilities, Joe codeveloped the latest RUP certification examination and authored content for RUP using the Rational Method Composer. In addition, he contributed to the OpenUP project within the Eclipse foundation.

Throughout his career, Joe has taught more than 1,000 professionals in the USA and Europe. The topics have included project management, requirements engineering, object-oriented analysis and design, Smalltalk, Java™, agile development processes, and the RUP.

PART I

Introduction

CHAPTER 1

Welcome to the IBM Rational Unified Process and Certification

By Ahmad K. Shuja

This chapter is about RUP's breadth and not its depth, so this introductory chapter will be mile wide and inch deep in terms of content. It introduces some of the core concepts that the RUP is founded on but does not go into detail about its different parts. It does, however, discuss the most important aspects of the RUP as they relate to software development. This chapter provides an overview of the book content.

An Overview of the Rational Unified Process

The IBM Rational Unified Process, also known as the RUP, is a process framework for successful iterative-incremental software development. In the software engineering domain, there are a number of development methodologies that organizations have successfully adapted and adopted to meet specific business needs. These range from traditional waterfall development to more agile ones. Figure 1-1 shows some of the more famous methodologies and where each can be positioned with respect to agility and discipline. Note that the up-front goals modeling component may not be directly associated with any given software development methodology but is there to ensure alignment between new software products or releases and the business strategy.

At its core, RUP is defined by the following three central elements:

- Key principles for business-driven development
- A framework of reusable method content and process building blocks
- The underlying method and process definition language

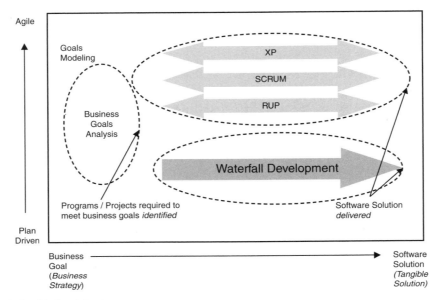

Figure 1-1   Methodologies map

Key Principles

RUP focuses on six key principles in software engineering (formerly known as *best practices*). These principles, which are easy to memorize because they start with the letters *A* through *F*, constitute the foundation of the RUP:

- **A**dapt the process.
- **B**alance stakeholder priorities.
- **C**ollaborate across teams.
- **D**emonstrate value iteratively.
- **E**levate the level of abstraction.
- **F**ocus continuously on quality.

The key principals are not sequential; in fact, you will see in Chapter 2, "Key Principles for Business-Driven Development," that the principles actually reinforce each other. For example, the principle of demonstrating value iteratively supports the principle of focusing continuously on quality. Similarly, other key principles support and drive one another. Chapter 2 explains all six key principles in detail and discusses their inter-relationships.

A Framework of Reusable Method Content and Process Building Blocks

A **process framework** can be defined as an incomplete support structure in which another process can be organized and developed. Therefore, you need to finish a process framework before you can apply it to specific projects within an organization. Similarly, you need to finish the RUP skeleton and its libraries to fit the organization.

The RUP framework is defined by a family of method plug-ins from which, based on the unique business needs as well as the context (technical and management complexity), organizations are able to create their own method configurations and tailored processes. RUP provides an architectural foundation and wealth of material from which a process definition can be constructed, therefore enabling the adopting organization to configure and extend that foundation as desired.

A few factors influence the configuring and tailoring of RUP:

- Project complexity

  In most cases, the more complex and technical the project, the greater the formality and control required to ensure its successful completion and timely delivery. This formality normally involves greater plan-driven development and more discipline. The term commonly used in RUP to determine the level of formality and control that is required within the process is **ceremony**. Figure 1-2 shows the relationship between complexity and ceremony. Accordingly, the level of ceremony affects the number of artifacts and details of the workflow descriptions.

- Organizational maturity

  Less mature organizations might require more discipline than more mature ones.

- Organization culture

  Culture plays an important role in the successful adaptation and adoption of the process.

- Regulatory compliance and policy requirements

  Some industries, especially financial and healthcare, might require more controls, which in turn require a high ceremony process and more artifacts.

- Development type

  The type of software development, such as green field versus COTS based, affects the process.

- Organization size

  The size of the organization determines how to customize the RUP to enable successful development and timely delivery of the software solutions.

These factors lead to one or more RUP flavors meeting the specific needs of an organization. IT organizations commonly develop multiple RUP instances to meet the needs of different types of projects. That approach satisfies the need for different levels of ceremony for small or large IT projects. In Part IV, we discuss Rational Method Composer, which can be used for effectively and efficiently customizing and publishing various flavors of RUP. We include some further discussion within Chapter 13, "Environment." Even though hundreds, if not thousands, of RUP customizations have been performed, they are based on the original RUP process framework, which is the subject of this book and the certification.

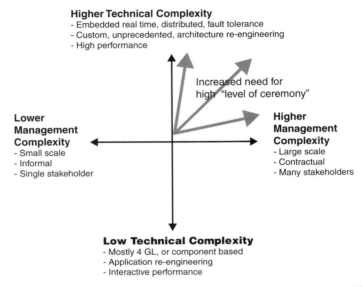

Figure 1-2 Complexity and ceremony (source: IBM Rational Unified Process v7.0)

Architectural Views

RUP represents the software architecture in multiple architectural views. Each architectural view addresses concerns specific to stakeholders in the development process. These stakeholders might include users, designers, managers, and maintainers. The architectural views capture the major design decisions by presenting the software architecture in terms of how components connect to produce useful forms (Perry & Wolf, 1992).

The typical set of views in the RUP, called the **4+1 view model**, is composed of the following.

- Use-Case view

  This view provides a basis for planning the technical content of iterations. It is used in the Requirements discipline.

- Logical view

  This view provides a basis for understanding the structure and organization of the design of the system. Logical view is used in the Analysis and Design discipline.

- Implementation view

  This view captures the enumeration of all subsystems in the Implementation Model, the component diagrams illustrating how subsystems are organized in layers, and hierarchies and illustrations showing important dependencies between subsystems.

- Process view

  This view illustrates the process decomposition of the system, including the mapping of classes and subsystems on to processes and threads. The Process view is used in the Analysis and Design discipline.

- Deployment view

  This view illustrates the distribution of processing across a set of nodes in the system, including physical distribution of processes and threads. This view is used in the Analysis and Design discipline.

Method and Process Definition Language

A unified method architecture (UMA) meta-model provides a language for describing method content and processes. UMA is an architecture to conceive, specify, and store method and process metadata. UMA clearly separates Method Content definitions from their application in delivery processes. It does this by defining the reusable core Method Content in the form of general content descriptions and the project-specific applications in the form of process descriptions. Basic elements of UMA are shown in Figure 1-3. We will discuss UMA is greater detail in Part II, "Unified Method Architecture (UMA)."

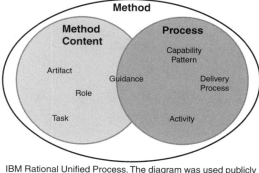

IBM Rational Unified Process. The diagram was used publicly in a *Rational Edge* article in 2006.

Figure 1-3 The basic elements of UMA

An Overview of the RUP Architecture

This valuable section offers a concise explanation of the RUP architecture. It starts with the popular hump chart, shown in Figure 1-4, which illustrates the overall RUP architecture. This figure contains information on phases, iterations, milestones, disciplines, their inter-relationships, and the lifecycle concept. This section focuses primarily on establishing a foundation from which you will be able to achieve the most value from this book. This foundation will enable you to clearly appreciate the relationships between different components of RUP architecture, as illustrated in Figure 1-4. By the end of this section, you will look at the RUP hump chart differently; you will be able to discuss why some disciplines should be there in your organization's specific rollout of

RUP and how phases, iterations, milestones, and disciplines are related. This chapter also discusses the importance of disciplines, phases, and iterations in iterative and incremental development. Let's now discuss these components in a little more detail.

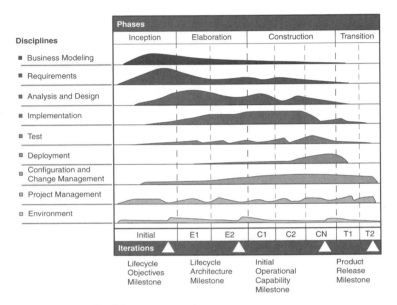

Figure 1-4 The Rational Unified Process overview

Phases and Milestones

The RUP provides an iterative and incremental approach to developing software. This iterative and incremental development happens within iterations that occur within a structured lifecycle consisting of phases and milestones. The RUP has four sequential phases: Inception, Elaboration, Construction, and Transition. Each of them plays a central role in managing iterative[1] and incremental development projects using RUP. Each phase concludes with a major milestone, as shown in Figure 1-5. The following sections provide a brief discussion of each phase. The focus in this section is to clarify, at the process framework level, the difference between the traditional waterfall lifecycle and the iterative and incremental development lifecycle as implemented by the RUP.

Overview

As discussed earlier, phases are made up of iterations, and both phases and iterations are important concepts to grasp for building a concrete understanding of the RUP. Disciplines play an important role in designing the iterations carried out within each phase. Although we do discuss disciplines later, let's briefly see how the RUP defines the term *discipline*. According to the RUP, "a discipline is

---

[1]   Iterative development is an approach to building a product (software or any other product) in iterations. Each iteration is a small project with its own clear deliverables. In software projects, most iterations end up with an executable build.

a collection of related activities that are related to a major area of concern." Based on which phase you are in, each iteration contains activities from across different disciplines. For instance, earlier in the RUP lifecycle, although there is a focus on the development of an executable build as early in the lifecycle as possible, there is a greater need to build an understanding of the business problem or opportunity. Therefore, this need, as shown in the hump chart, requires more activities from the Business Modeling and Requirements disciplines to be performed earlier in the RUP project lifecycle.

Iterations are designed and executed with certain goals in mind. Depending upon which phase the iteration belongs to, the iteration goals are aligned to accomplish the respective milestone. For example, iterations for the Elaboration phase are designed such that its objectives are achieved and the Lifecycle Architecture milestone is accomplished. Therefore, achievement of each iteration goal moves the project closer to achieving the respective objectives of that phase. This concept is presented in Figure 1-6. Each iteration has its own respective goals and is designed such that collectively, the iterations are executed within a given phase. These iterations achieve respective objectives of a milestone.

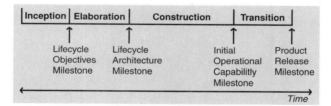

Figure 1-5 The phases and milestones of a RUP project

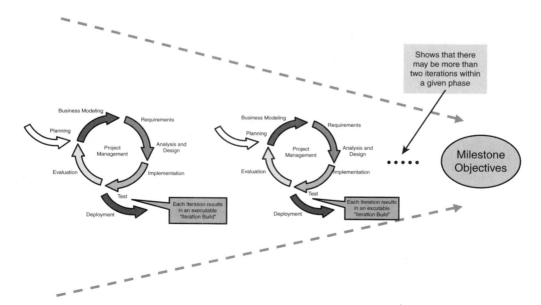

Figure 1-6 Iterations achieve objectives of phase milestone

Phases need to end with accomplishment milestones, as shown in Figure 1-5. Each milestone provides a critical decision point, or a go or no-go. Chapter 14, "Phases, Activities, and Milestones," discusses in detail all four phases and their respective objectives and evaluation criteria. Here, we will briefly review these phases. Please note that phases are executed in a sequence, as shown in Figure 1-5.

Inception Phase

The main goal of the Inception phase is to achieve concurrence among all stakeholders on the lifecycle objectives of the project. The following are the primary Inception phase objectives:

- To establish the project's scope and boundary conditions
- To identify the critical use cases of the system
- To exhibit and demonstrate one candidate architecture
- To estimate the overall cost and schedule for the project
- To produce detailed estimates for the Elaboration phase
- To estimate the potential risks
- To prepare the support environment for the project

The RUP is risk driven; the highest risks are identified earliest, and efforts are made to mitigate or address those risks as early in the project lifecycle as possible instead of pushing them forward. The Inception phase plays the most critical role in the project and will result in the first release of the product. In such cases, significant business and requirements risks need to be carefully managed. Accordingly, for new releases or enhancements of existing products, the Inception phase becomes much shorter. The Lifecycle Objectives milestone concludes the Inception phase. At that point, a major decision is made on whether to proceed with the project or cancel it.

Elaboration Phase

The main goal of the Elaboration phase is to baseline the architecture of the system to provide a stable basis for the bulk of the design and implementation effort in the Construction phase. The architecture evolves based on the most significant requirements and assessment of risks. To evaluate the stability of the architecture, one or more architectural prototypes may be developed. This architectural prototype is the executable architecture. The Elaboration phase objectives are as follows:

- To stabilize the architecture, requirements, and respective plans
- To sufficiently mitigate risks to predictably determine project cost and schedule
- To address all architecturally significant risks
- To establish a baselined architecture
- To produce an evolutionary prototype of production-quality components
- Optionally, to produce throw-away prototypes to mitigate specific risks such as design trade-offs, component reuse, and product feasibility

- To demonstrate that the baselined architecture will support the requirements of the system at a reasonable cost and in a reasonable time
- To establish a supportive environment

The Lifecycle Architecture milestone concludes the Elaboration phase, establishing a managed baseline for the architecture of the system and enabling the project team to scale during the Construction phase.

Construction Phase

The main goals of the Construction phase are to clarify the remaining requirements and complete the development of the system based on the baselined architecture. Construction phase objectives can be briefly summarized as follows:

- To minimize development costs through optimization of resource utilization by avoiding unnecessary scrap and rework and by achieving a degree of parallelism in the work of development teams
- To achieve adequate quality as rapidly as is practical
- To achieve useful executable versions (alpha, beta, and so on) as rapidly as practical
- To complete the analysis, design, development, and testing of all required functionality
- To iteratively and incrementally develop a complete product that is ready to transition to its user community
- To decide if the software, the sites, and the users are ready for the deployment of the solution

The Construction phase concludes with the Initial Operational Capability milestone, which determines whether the product is ready to be deployed into a beta-test environment.

Transition Phase

The overall goal of the Transition phase is to ensure that software is available for its users. It can span several iterations and includes testing the product in preparation for release and making minor adjustments based on user feedback. This feedback focuses primarily on fine-tuning the product, configuration, installation, and usability issues. All the major structural issues should have been worked out much earlier in the project lifecycle. Following are the primary objectives of the Transition phase:

- To validate the new system against user expectations (by beta testing)
- To train the end users and maintainers
- If applicable, to roll out the product to marketing, distribution, and sales teams
- To fine-tune the product by engaging in bug-fixing and creating performance and usability enhancements
- To conclude the assessment of the deployment baseline against the complete vision and the acceptance criteria for the product

- To achieve user self-supportability
- To achieve stakeholder concurrence that deployment baselines are complete and are consistent with the evaluation criteria of the vision

The Product Release milestone concludes this phase. A decision is made whether the objectives of the project were met.

RUP Phase Workflows

Each phase in RUP has a workflow, which describes the sequence in which activities from across various disciplines can be performed to achieve the objectives of the respective phase milestone. Chapter 14 explores in detail phase workflows and other process elements.

RUP Phases versus Waterfall Phases

RUP phases differ from traditional waterfall SDLC phases. In most cases, those who have been using the waterfall process equate RUP phases to traditional waterfall phases of Requirements, Analysis and Design, Implementation, and so on. The most common expression I hear when training software development teams on RUP is, " ... so it means that Inception is really about understanding and gathering requirements, Elaboration is really about architecting and designing, Construction about coding, and Transition about testing." I hear similar comments when I'm trying to help organizations adopt the RUP. The fact is that the phases in the RUP do not equate to those in the waterfall lifecycle. As discussed earlier, depending on which phase you are in, activities will be performed across multiple disciplines. The key differences can be summarized as in Table 1-1.

Table 1-1   Waterfall Phases versus RUP Phases

Waterfall Phase Characteristics	RUP Phase Characteristics
In any given phase, the activities are performed from a single area of concern. For example, during the Requirements phase, all activities related to requirements gathering and analysis are performed. No code is produced and no testing is carried out.	In any given RUP phase, depending on which phase it is, there will be activities from across multiple disciplines. For example, during the Elaboration phase, activities performed normally span all the core disciplines, including Requirements, Analysis and Design, Implementation, Test, and others.
Not all phases result in an executable deliverable. In fact, only Implementation and Test phases may produce executable deliverables.	With the exception of early Inception iterations, each iteration within each phase produces an executable deliverable.
A given waterfall phase employs a subset of team members who are skilled to perform related activities. This might lead to less than optimal resource utilization.	Producing an executable deliverable at the end of most iterations within RUP phases requires activities from across multiple disciplines to be performed and therefore engages the entire team.
Most waterfall phases result in document-based deliverables.	Most iterations within RUP phases result in an executable deliverable.

The later section "Iteration Maturity Levels" discusses different iteration patterns that have worked well for certain organizations.

Discipline

This section covers the important aspects of disciplines in the RUP. However, before we get into all the RUP details, let's see what the term *discipline* means and how and why it is one of the core components in the RUP.

Meaning of Discipline

According to the Merriam-Webster dictionary, the term **discipline** is defined as follows:

- From Latin *disciplina* teaching, learning, from *discipulus*
- To bring (a group) under control
- A field of study
- A rule or system of rules governing an activity

As you can see, the term *discipline* has been historically used in relation to learning, teaching, controlling, and governing. Discipline is also defined as a controlled behavior expected to produce a specific improvement. Furthermore, it is defined as a pattern of behavior made up of a set of rules and methods. The next section demonstrates how most of these definitions of *discipline* apply to RUP in one form or the other.

Briefly, in RUP, a discipline is defined as a categorization of activities based on similarity of concerns and cooperation of work effort. A discipline is a collection of activities that are related to a major "area of concern" (or "a field of study," as discussed earlier) within the overall project. In RUP, an **activity** is a process element that supports the nesting and logical grouping of related process elements, such as a descriptor[2] and subactivities, thus forming breakdown structures. The grouping of activities into disciplines is mainly an aid to understanding the project from a traditional waterfall perspective; that is, in a traditional waterfall project, your phases are called Requirements, Analysis, Design, Implementation, Testing, and so on. Therefore, within a waterfall project, you focus on a single discipline and associated artifacts for that discipline. For instance, when you have finished the Requirements phase of a waterfall project, you will gain final approval from the customer and move on to the next phase which, in most cases, is Analysis. In the RUP, although it is more common to perform activities concurrently across several disciplines at any given point during the life of a project (for example, certain Requirements activities are performed in close coordination with Analysis and Design activities), separating these activities into distinct disciplines is simply an effective way to organize content, which makes comprehension and learning easier. In addition, because the skill-sets needed to perform the tasks in one area of concern are probably similar, logical grouping of these activities simplifies the way different roles are organized. This enables us to align a small set of roles along discipline lines.

---

[2] According to the RUP, "A Descriptor is a Process element that represents a Method Content Element in the Process. The Descriptor provides the ability to override or add to what is in the original Method Content Element. Descriptors include Role, Task, and Work Product Descriptors."

The Role of Disciplines in the Software Engineering Process and the RUP

According to one of the historical definitions, the term *discipline* is a field of study that allows us to learn about that field in detail. Software engineering can be considered one of the many disciplines of engineering. In the RUP, however, a discipline refers to a specific area of concern (or a field of study, as mentioned earlier) within software engineering. For instance, Analysis and Design is one of the disciplines in RUP, which is itself a field of study and requires dedicated learning and distinct skill-sets. In addition, disciplines in RUP allow you to govern the activities you perform within that discipline. A discipline in RUP gives you all the guidance you require to learn not only when to perform a given activity but also how to perform it. Therefore, disciplines in RUP allow you to bring closely related activities under control.

We will see in detail how these related activities are governed and performed in an organized manner, not in isolation and not haphazardly. In fact, a recommended sequence should be followed to achieve optimal performance and maximize productivity and predictability. Note that although disciplines propose a recommended sequence of activities, these are truly performed in parallel with activities from other relevant (based on where you are in the project lifecycle) disciplines. When I was engaged in enabling one of the financial institutions to adopt RUP, I had to have separate sessions and workshops with System Analysts, Business Analysts, Project Managers, and others. During those sessions, the discipline workflows really proved helpful from the perspective of the involvement of a given role and the related activities to be performed across the RUP lifecycle. The workflows helped the people with given roles appreciate the effort that was required within their discipline.

A clear understanding of these relationships between roles and disciplines and the appreciation of how different roles from across different disciplines collaborate throughout the project lifecycle is important. It is crucial that you establish a clear understanding of this concept right from the beginning, and it will be helpful as you become immersed in the iterative development world. To ensure that you understand this well, Figure 1-7 shows the activities that are performed during an iteration within an Inception phase. Please look carefully at the activities in this figure and then compare it to the hump chart shown in Figure 1-4. You will be able to appreciate the relationship between the height of humps and the activities as they are aligned for each discipline.

The benefits provided by separating the RUP activities into various disciplines are summarized as follows.

- Makes the activities easier to comprehend.
- Proves useful when customizing a given discipline to meet the specific needs of the project or when defining a set of organizational standard processes. For a detailed discussion on RUP customizations and tailoring, please refer to Part IV of this book, "Tailoring and Tooling."
- Enables different roles to better and more effectively appreciate their responsibilities (in terms of the tasks/activities that they are responsible for) on a given project.
- Allows Project Managers to more effectively monitor and control these activities.

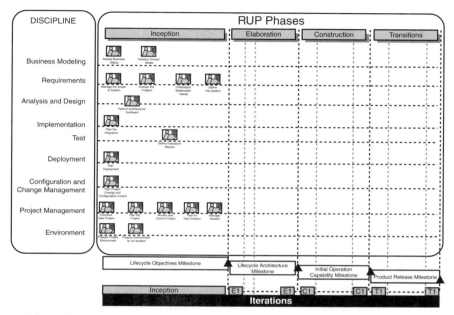

Figure 1-7 Inception iteration activities

Therefore, a discipline in RUP is a collection of activities that are related to a major area of concern or field of study. Each activity is further decomposed into subactivities or one or many tasks. Tasks require an input artifact or artifacts for their successful execution, and these in turn produce or refine some form of output artifact(s). Note that these artifacts can include both document-based artifacts and executables. Each task has an associated role (or roles) responsible for performing that task. To provide additional support and guidance, each discipline in the base RUP offers a set of standard template artifacts related to that discipline. These artifacts, as well as the process, can be (and should be) customized/tailored for a given project or organization.

Discipline Workflow

RUP models the *when* as workflows, and each discipline in RUP has a workflow. Like other workflows, a discipline's workflow is a semi-ordered sequence of activities performed by specific roles to achieve a particular goal. This semi-ordered nature of discipline workflows emphasizes that they cannot present the nuances of scheduling "real work," because they cannot depict the optionality of activities or iterative nature of real projects. Yet, they still have value as a way for us to understand the process by breaking it into smaller areas of concerns.

Keep in mind that the RUP framework, which these workflows are part of, constitutes guidance on a rich set of software engineering principles. It is applicable to projects of different size and complexity, as well as to different development environments and domains. This means that no single project or organization will benefit from using all of RUP. Applying all of RUP will likely result in an inefficient project environment, where teams will struggle to keep focused on the important tasks and struggle to find the right set of information. Thus, as discussed earlier in this chapter, it is recommended that RUP be tailored to provide an appropriate and customized process for developing software. RUP tailoring and related tools are discussed in greater detail in Part IV of this book.

It is important to understand that the sequence of activities in each of the workflows is based on best practices. It should not, by any stretch of the imagination, be taken as a mandatory sequence. As an important component of tailoring the RUP framework, these workflows should be customized to suit project or organizational needs. This customization might require redefining some of these sequences.

Discipline Work Breakdown Structure

According to the Project Management Institute (PMI), the project's work breakdown structure (WBS) provides the relationship among *all* the components of the project and the project deliverables. WBS, according to PMI, is a deliverable-oriented hierarchical decomposition of the work to be executed by the project team to accomplish the project objectives and create the required deliverables. It organizes and defines the total scope of the project. Each descending level represents an increasingly detailed definition of the project work.

You will see that the RUP adopts a slightly different view of WBS. Discipline WBS in RUP represents the *activities*-oriented hierarchical decomposition of the project effort specific to the respective discipline. Each descending level represents an increasingly detailed definition of the project work. In the RUP, the WBS provides *mostly*[3] four descending level of details. These levels include Discipline, Activity, Sub-Activity/Task, and Step. Activity is a process element that supports the nesting and logical grouping of related process elements such as descriptor and sub-activities, thus forming breakdown structures. Task is a unit of work that a role may be asked to perform. Step is a content element used to organize tasks into parts or subunits of work. Note that it is at the Task level that RUP associates the roles and the artifacts produced, modified, or used. These levels are expressed visually in Figure 1-8.

Role

In RUP, a **role** is a definition of the behavior and responsibilities of an individual, or a set of individuals working together as a team, within the context of a business organization. RUP uses the concept of role to model the *who* of the software engineering process. This describes a role played by an individual or team within the project. Each role may be realized by many individuals or teams, and each individual or team may perform many different roles. For instance, Project Manager and Process Engineer are two different roles defined in RUP. On a smaller project, these two

---

[3]   Sometimes you will see additional levels of decomposition. For instance, in some cases, activities are further decomposed into activities, which in turn are decomposed into tasks. The business modeling discipline is a good example in which a few activities have their own activity model.

roles may be performed by a single individual. On a larger project, there might be more than one individual performing the Project Manager and Process Engineer roles. The important point to note here is that whoever is performing any given role needs to have the right skill-set to perform the activities defined in RUP. We will see what primary roles are associated with a given discipline and for which they are primarily responsible. As shown in Figure 1-8, a role performs a task.

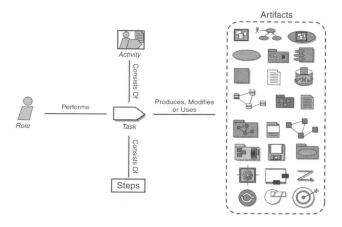

Figure 1-8 Level of activity decomposition

These individuals or teams adopt specific roles when they perform certain activities; therefore, for any activity, RUP can tell us the roles that participate in that activity. Activities may be broken down into finer levels of detail as needed. RUP also provides complete guidance and best practice details on *how* to perform each activity and task.

Discipline Artifacts

Related to each activity are the artifacts, which are either produced or refined depending on when the activity is performed during the project lifecycle. An **artifact** is a work product that is produced, modified, or used by a task and defines an area of responsibility. For any nontrivial development effort, especially where large development teams are involved, the artifacts are most likely to be subject to version control and configuration management. In the RUP, artifacts are generally not paper documents. Note that Figure 1-8 (just for illustrative purposes) shows just a subset of artifacts. Therefore, artifacts are inputs and outputs to the activities performed throughout the project lifecycle; they may be source code, executable programs, standards, documentation, and so on. Part III, "Rational Unified Process: Content and Process Elements," discusses key artifacts of RUP disciplines in detail.

The Hump Chart—Putting Phases, Iterations, Milestones, and Disciplines Together

The reality is that a mini-waterfall project exists within each iteration of the RUP project.

Having discussed phases, iterations, milestones, disciplines, and other key concepts, let's revisit the famous RUP hump diagram shown in Figure 1-4 to put these together and discuss the interrelationships in more detail.

The horizontal axis represents iterations and the progress of a RUP lifecycle. As discussed, every RUP project is divided into four significant phases called Inception, Elaboration, Construction, and Transition. We will discuss the four RUP phases in greater detail later in this book. The dashed lines between the phases are called **milestones**, which mark checkpoints in RUP. These milestones present a go/no-go decision by project management when artifacts have reached a specified state. The word *sign-off* or *freeze* does not exist for RUP artifacts, but artifacts need to reach specific states depending on the time in the RUP project lifecycle reflecting the level of their maturity. For example, the first draft risk list is developed during the Inception phase and is refined during the entire project lifecycle.

The vertical axis, called **disciplines** (called **workflows** in earlier versions of RUP), defines the activities performed during an IT project. The RUP has nine disciplines. Six of them are directly linked to software engineering activities and are also known as **core** disciplines. These are as follows:

- Business Modeling
- Requirements
- Analysis and Design
- Implementation
- Test
- Deployment

The other three are also called **umbrella** activities (also known as **supporting** disciplines), because they are concerned with the overall management and structure of a RUP project:

- Configuration and Change Management
- Project Management
- Environment

We will discuss these disciplines in greater details in Part III of this book.

Iteration Maturity Levels

So far, we have discussed the basics of the RUP. With this brief introduction, let's try to develop a clearer understanding of iteration design evolution. Our goal in the following discussion will be to gain insights into how industries have implemented the RUP and iterative development. We will discuss how different companies have adapted and adopted the RUP and have gone through a true lifecycle of successfully evolving and institutionalizing the new methodology. You will notice how the returns in incremental and iterative development investments increase with the increasing level of organizational maturity. We will also explore how the design of iterations evolved as organizations matured over time. Before we get into all these details, note that, at its core, the focus shifts as we progress through the project lifecycle. This is demonstrated in Figure 1-9.

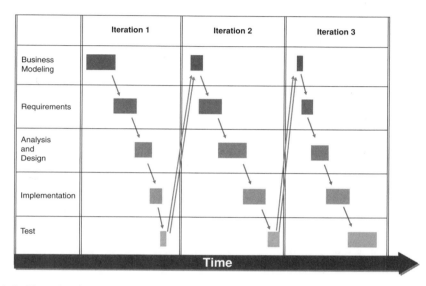

Figure 1-9 Changing focus across the RUP lifecycle (from RUP material)

The relative size of a given box aligned with iteration and discipline respectively shows the level of focus or effort. For instance, during Iteration 1, the primary focus is on Business Modeling, whereas during Iteration 3, the primary focus is on Test activities. Regardless of how iterations are designed, the focus potentially stays somewhat consistent with this figure. With this in mind, let us now look at the iteration maturity lifecycle pattern that I have most frequently encountered in my years of consulting and related professional experiences. As we discuss this, please keep in mind that where an organization starts depends on a number of factors, including organization size, culture, complexity, iterative development experience, and structure. Organizations evolve their processes as they mature and as teams become more experienced with agile-like iterative and incremental development methodologies. I will refer to these different maturity levels as *iteration maturity levels*.

Iteration Maturity Level 1—Incremental Mini-Waterfall

How do you change culture? The change cannot happen overnight, especially if you are dealing with global organizations that span multiple cultures. In addition to project-specific complexities, we need to take into account other factors such as organizational size and differences in execution models. Cultural change requires behavior change, and behavior change is driven by evolving organizational processes. Sponsorship from the senior management becomes absolutely critical. Over time, the integral of all these small incremental process changes impact the team's behavior and enables the team to embrace the new culture and achieve the desired results.

Cultural change is not the topic of discussion here. However, it plays an important role in the way software development organizations are able to enhance their productivity and improve product quality by adapting and adopting the RUP. Enabling large, mature waterfall-based software development organizations to embrace a somewhat revolutionary approach is challenging. In situations like these, such organizations need to take baby steps, demonstrate value, embrace and institutionalize processes, and proceed forward. Big bang may work, but with potentially large disruption.

"Mini-waterfall" may be that first approach that you would like such organizations to take. Get them to think about producing incremental builds and executables as early in the project lifecycle as possible. Don't underestimate the challenges surrounding controls and checks even in the iterative and incremental development world. It will require well-structured management. This is especially true for those organizations that are regulated heavily by industry and other government bodies. Such organizations need to ensure compliance with those regulatory requirements, perhaps by introducing controls throughout the project lifecycle.

The need for such controls is one reason that waterfall development found its way into these organizations and is still there. Waterfall development clearly separates discipline-based phases, which enables management to review and provide the necessary approvals before projects are allowed to proceed further. For example, the Requirements document needs to be reviewed, approved, and frozen prior to analysis, design, or implementation efforts. Such control requirements are best achieved through waterfall development. Some organizations even have their SDLC (Software Development Lifecycle) team report into the compliance department. Both end up with conflicting goals—SDLC wants efficiencies, whereas compliance requires maximum controls. When the waterfall approach is completely embedded in organizational cultures, incremental adoption might be a reasonable option. Let's see what we mean by this mini-waterfall like approach.

Figure 1-10 presents a unique but supporting perspective to the RUP hump diagram shown in Figure 1-4. Let's see how.

Figure 1-10 takes the RUP process framework and presents the way it might look like if it is applied to a green-field type of project (custom development from the ground up). For the sake of our discussion and simplicity, we will only look at a subset of RUP disciplines and will assume that the project consists of six iterations named I1 through I6. Dark gray, light gray, and white represent the focus levels. The figure presents a simplistic view of the way iterations are executed, the relationships with other iterations, and the phases.

Note that each iteration shown in Figure 1-10 resembles a mini-waterfall project. What does that mean? It means that, depending on the goals and objectives of a given iteration and where in the RUP lifecycle it is taking place, the degree of effort (also termed as **focus**) on activities from across different disciplines will shift. As you progress through the lifecycle represented in Figure 1-10, the focus shifts from being analysis driven in the early iterations to implementation, testing, and deployment in the later ones. This change of focus happens primarily because of knowledge gained about the business and the problem. Later iterations might be characterized by few refinements to the business model and requirements and greater focus on implementation and testing. This change in focus across the life of a given project is driven primarily by effectively and efficiently managing risks. Each iteration converges on project goals.

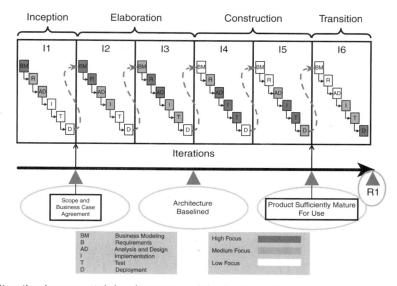

Figure 1-10 Iterative-incremental development and the Rational Unified Process

Let's look at the specific case represented in Figure 1-10. The Inception phase consists of only one iteration: I1. Because it is the first iteration, the focus is on performing Business Modeling to gain enough understanding of the business domain to proceed further. Note, however, the medium effort being invested in the Requirements and Analysis and Design disciplines and the low effort made in the Test and Deployment disciplines.

It works like this. Although you might be learning more of the business domain and associated business processes, it is important to understand the stakeholder needs by having requirements workshops and producing a use-case model and supplementary specs while analyzing the problem. You can also develop a prototype, depending on your understanding, and strategize about testing and deployment. Earliest iterations might not require executable deliverables. However, each iteration should have specific goals that are evaluated at the end.

In iterations I2 and I3, the focus shifts to more designing, programming, and testing while refining the vision and the environment. Iterations I4 and I5 focus on programming and testing, with minor requirements changes. As shown in Figure 1-10, iteration I6 focuses on beta testing, doing some final programming and documentation, and deployment. One element that remains consistent throughout the RUP lifecycle is that each iteration takes the project closer to its stated goals.

By now you should understand that in this specific iteration pattern, iterations are more like mini-waterfall projects, each with its own goal(s), which ultimately help to get the overall project closer to meeting its goals. The next big question that senior managers, who are more concerned with financial aspects of the project, have is about gaining some control over the life of a project and not losing control from iteration to iteration. This is known as **time-boxing**. Few companies would allow you to continue iterations and refinement and never close the project. Any statement similar to "A project plan is continuingly evolved throughout the project lifecycle" is hard to sell to senior managers.

To address these and similar challenges, we need to do time-boxing at the project, phase, and iteration levels. As you continue through the RUP lifecycle, from one iteration to the next, note the four major milestones, as mentioned earlier:

- **Lifecycle Objectives milestone**—Scope and business case agreed
- **Lifecycle Architecture milestone**—Architecture baselined
- **Initial Operational Capability milestone**—Product sufficiently mature for use
- **Product Release milestone**—Product release

Based on the complexity and size of the project, an iteration can be anywhere from 2 to 6 weeks long, and respective phases can be composed of different numbers of iterations. Iterations are logically grouped to meet key milestones at the end of each phase. These milestones mark the accomplishment of clearly specified phase objectives.

Iteration Maturity Level 2—Incremental Mini-Waterfall with Feedback Loops

After firms perform at the mini-waterfall level, the next level is to further refine the iteration design such that feedback loops exist. These feedback loops are shown in Figure 1-11.

Such feedback loops enable the continuous evolution of not only the iteration builds but also the continuous refinement of the related artifacts. This builds traceability and consistency across all artifacts starting with the vision and continuing to the executable code. More and more tools are being developed to support such a model.

Iteration Maturity Level 3—Optimizing Iterative and Incremental Development

At this level, organizations are not only building higher quality products but are also optimizing their resource utilization. As shown in Figure 1-12, at any given point during an iteration at this maturity level, the following steps might be taking place.

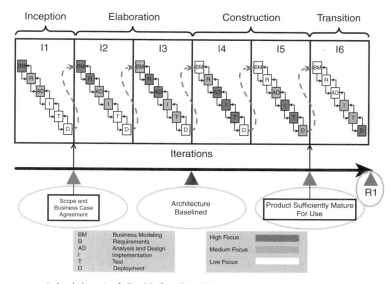

Figure 1-11 Incremental mini-waterfall with feedback loops

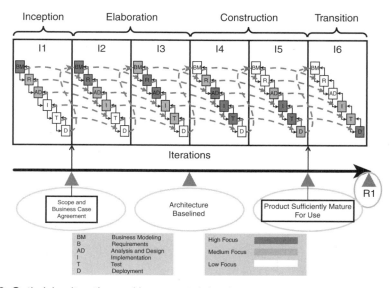

Figure 1-12 Optimizing iterative and incremental development

1. Artifacts that are required by activities/tasks within the same iteration from across other disciplines are produced/refined. For example, architecturally significant use cases need to be identified before the related Analysis and Design activities can be performed, code is required before it can be tested, and so on.

2. Artifacts that are required by activities/tasks within the following iteration might be produced/refined.

3. Artifacts might be refined based on feedback.

Greater efficiencies and higher productivity as a result of such concurrent and iterative and incremental development will most certainly require strong management, a mature and experienced team, and a well-integrated tool suite.

Evolution of the Rational Unified Process

Now that we have a clearer understanding of the RUP architecture, let's discuss how the RUP evolved over the years. RUP often comes across as an overloaded term. For example, many believe that the IBM Rational Unified Process is inseparable from the Rational Unified Process product. Others think that the IBM Rational Unified Process requires other IBM Rational software to function. This section briefly discusses the evolution of RUP and will try to separate myths from realities.

The first version of RUP was released in 1998, but it was heavily influenced by its predecessor, known as **Objectory**™, which dates back to 1988 (see Figure 1-13). With its long history, RUP as an iterative development process has a proven track record unparalleled in the IT industry.

No other modern software engineering process has a higher adoption or success rate than RUP, which is attracting more and more organizations. The RUP story has continued, especially after IBM Rational announced the accomplishment of another milestone in October 2005, which fundamentally changed the distribution, configuration, and deployment of RUP.

This is not a RUP history book, and this history is not important for your certification. However, a brief discussion of the most recent RUP-related decisions will help you understand where the RUP journey might go. This may, in fact, further inspire you to achieve the RUP certification.

In October 2005, IBM Rational donated a subset of the RUP process framework, now known as the Basic Unified Process (BUP),[4] to the Eclipse Foundation. This framework was modified as part of the Eclipse Process Framework project, and the resulting extensible process is named the Open Unified Process, or OpenUP. The distribution of a subset of RUP through an Eclipse project will allow all interested parties to adopt the concepts of RUP as an open-source process framework. This donation will also encourage software engineers to use BUP and develop open-source process enhancements for RUP.

---

[4]   http://www.eclipse.org/proposals/beacon/

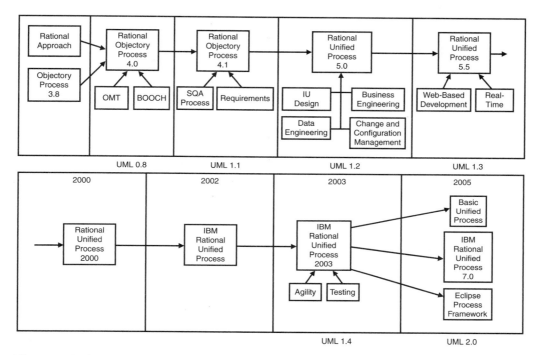

Figure 1-13 RUP evolution

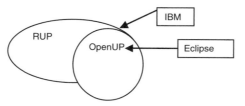

Figure 1-14 OpenUP content

Another significant milestone is the development of the IBM Rational Method Composer[5] (RMC), the new Eclipse-based product to configure and distribute customized processes like OpenUP or RUP. This product will supersede the previous IBM Rational proprietary RUP tools (Rational Workbench, RUP Modeler, and RUP Organizer), which were used to customize RUP. As with the process donation, the basic capabilities of RMC were donated to Eclipse; the resulting tool, Eclipse Process Framework composer, is available free as an open source application.

---

5   http://www-306.ibm.com/software/awdtools/rmc/

Figure 1-15 shows that the BUP knowledgebase is now in pieces available as open source, whereas the IBM RMC is a tool for authoring and publishing BUP or RUP. The clear separation between the framework and tool will encourage a distribution of the concepts of iterative software engineering in the industry, whereas the tool will help process engineers to tailor it.

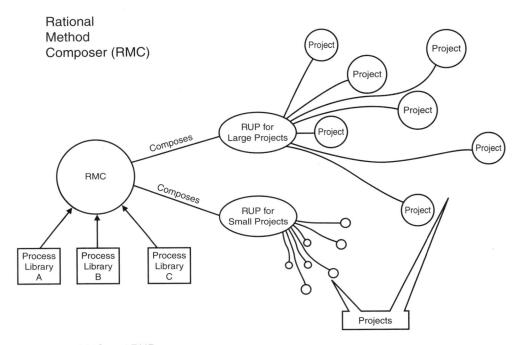

Figure 1-15 RMC and RUP

Why would IBM Rational take such a step? IBM originated the Eclipse foundation and promoted open source development for years. It is the logical next step to do the same thing with a software engineering process, which ties all the concepts under one umbrella. Although IBM has gathered and organized the process for more than a decade, the donation to Eclipse will spread the message through the open source community with one goal in mind: improving the industry's IT processes.

IBM Rational as a division inside IBM delivered software engineering tools to the IT industry for many years. Focusing on the RMC and the integration with the IBM Rational Portfolio Manager (RPM) and promoting the open source process framework will strengthen the role of IBM Rational in this space while the industry benefits from the donation.

Challenges in Identifying RUP Solution Designers

Implementing RUP requires dedication, determination, sponsorship, and expertise. Related to expertise, if you need a RUP Solution Designer, you will appreciate the significant challenge of finding a RUP expert. It is not easy to identify a RUP expert. RUP encompasses a range of disciplines (both Core and Supporting), each of which has a specialized and a dedicated field of study. For instance, there is a Project Management discipline, which focuses on project planning, risk management, monitoring progress, and metrics. Institutions such as the Project Management Institute (PMI) are dedicated to the growth of project management as a profession and provide related certifications such as the Project Management Professional (PMP). Can we then say that a PMP can be a good RUP Project Manager? Probably! However, this person will certainly need to have experienced the iterative and incremental development supported by the RUP. Otherwise, this might turn into a project in itself to mentor a PMP to become a RUP Project Manager. We have seen organizations failing to implement the RUP process due to lack of their Project Managers' iterative and incremental development experience. In short, professionals who aspire to become strong RUP Solution Designers need to have a range of technical and managerial skills to succeed. Such individuals are not easy to find. And when you indeed think you have found them, it is hard to gauge their depth and breadth of knowledge.

You will be able to appreciate the uniqueness of the RUP Solution Designer Certification and the importance of achieving it if you really have such a rare skill-set. With the RUP Solution Designer Certification, your name will be among those few professionals who have been and will be in great demand. With this certification, software engineers and managers can now register after successful completion at http://www-304.ibm.com/jct09001d/member.nsf.

Past, Present, and Future of RUP Certification

In the past, when IBM Rational owned the process and the certification process, individuals were advised to visit the two-day training course PRJ270, Essentials of Rational Unified Process version 2, directly from IBM Rational. Originally thought of as an official measure for future RUP instructors, the certification followed the content of the course. The course was not a prerequisite to achieve certification (and it still is not), but the student book and the course content contained valuable information for preparing for the certification exam. Over time and because of the acquisition of Rational by IBM, the RUP certification came to be seen from a different perspective. Being part of a series of official technical certification exams, the RUP certification became exposed to a much broader audience.

Our goal was to compile a resource to allow RUP professionals to not only use RUP in their daily work as a reference, but also to gain the knowledge required to successfully achieve the RUP Certification. This book, combined with the IBM Rational RUP course (the aforementioned Essentials of Rational Unified Process) and real-world experience will enable you to achieve your RUP Solution Designer Certification, hopefully in the first attempt.

With the increasing awareness and adoption of iterative-incremental software engineering processes through the open source community, the RUP Solution Designer Certification will undoubtedly distinguish experts from casual users. This certification will not only give you the industry recognition of being a RUP Solution Designer, but you will also promote the process in a manner similar to that of an ambassador. This book does not replace the RUP training course by any means, and we do not guarantee that you will pass the exam on your first attempt. But if you follow the guidelines provided in this book, practice with the sample questions, and appropriately use the references to other RUP resources, you can prepare yourself for a successful examination. We dedicated the entirety of Part IV of our book to the actual examination and its logistics.

Summary

This chapter introduced some of the most critical components of the RUP process framework. It covered the history and evolution of RUP and its certification program from its origin until today. It also looked ahead into a possible future of RUP. Using some basic RUP terminologies, this chapter mapped RUP concepts to the structure of the book. Now that you have read this chapter, try to name a few key principles, disciplines, and RUP phases and approach the exercises. By the end of this book, you will have internalized them.

One key lesson for waterfall methodology practitioners is that compared to the waterfall approach, iterative-development can be seen as many mini-waterfalls. As is apparent from Figure 1-7, another important take-away is that activities from numerous disciplines are performed in parallel in any given iteration and not sequentially.

Sample Questions

The correct answers to these questions can be found in the Appendix, "Answers to Sample Questions."

1. In the Rational Unified Process, which of the following provides the means of assessing the progress of a project?
    a. Discipline
    b. Project Management
    c. Milestone
    d. Project Management tools

2. In the Rational Unified Process, which of the following contains activities from numerous areas of study?
    a. Iteration workflow
    b. Phase workflow
    c. Discipline workflow
    d. Project workflow

3. Which of the following is true about RUP disciplines?

    a. Enable the project manager to plan the project in a traditional waterfall fashion more effectively

    b. Represent activities that compose areas of concern in a project

    c. Correspond directly to RUP roles

    d. Are implemented one at a time in serial fashion

4. Which of the following is a key component of the RUP discipline? (Select all that apply.)

    a. Activity

    b. Role

    c. Artifact

    d. Phase

5. In the RUP, which of the following is true about the Work Breakdown Structure? (Select all that apply.)

    a. The RUP Work Breakdown Structure is a deliverable-oriented hierarchical decomposition of project effort.

    b. The RUP Work Breakdown Structure provides relationships among all the components of the project and project deliverables.

    c. The RUP Work Breakdown Structure is an activity-oriented hierarchical decomposition of the project effort.

    d. The RUP Work Breakdown Structure enables the project manager to more effectively plan the sequence in which activities should be performed.

6. Which of the following is a unit of work that a role may be asked to perform?

    a. Task

    b. Activity

    c. Workflow

    d. Work Unit

7. Which of the following is true about the relationship between the RUP Work Breakdown Structures and the RUP Workflows? (Select all that apply.)

    a. The RUP Work Breakdown Structure presents an activities-oriented hierarchical decomposition.

    b. The RUP Work Breakdown Structure presents a deliverable-oriented hierarchical decomposition.

    c. The RUP Work Breakdown Structure contains the tasks that are presented in RUP workflows.

    d. The RUP Work Breakdown Structure activities can be repeated across various RUP discipline workflows.

8. Which of the following is true about a workflow diagram for a discipline? (Select all that apply.)
   a. It shows the sequence in which activities should be performed.
   b. An activity within a workflow can consist of a workflow.
   c. A workflow is made up of tasks.
   d. RUP has more than one workflow for each discipline.

9. Which of the following is true about tasks? (Select all that apply.)
   a. One or more tasks can be carried out within any given activity.
   b. Tasks can be repeated across different activities within a discipline.
   c. Roles are not responsible for performing tasks. Instead, they are responsible for performing activities.
   d. Tasks produce, modify, or use an artifact.

10. Which of the following is true about a role? (Select all that apply.)
    a. A role is a definition of the behavior and responsibilities.
    b. An individual can assume a role.
    c. A role can be a set of individuals working together as a team.
    d. The role and the person performing it are interchangeable.

11. Separating the RUP activities into different disciplines provides which of the following key benefits? (Select all that apply.)
    a. Makes the activities easier to comprehend
    b. Proves useful when customizing a given discipline to meet the specific needs of the project
    c. Enables different roles to better and more effectively appreciate their responsibilities on a given project
    d. Allows project managers to more effectively monitor and control these activities

12. In RUP, a discipline is defined as which of the following?
    a. A categorization of tasks based on similarity of concerns and cooperation of work effort
    b. A categorization of activities based on similarity of concerns and cooperation of work effort
    c. A field of study
    d. A software engineering domain

13. Which of the following is used to describe in detail how to perform a particular activity?
    a. Template
    b. Guideline
    c. Checklist
    d. Concept

14. Which of the following are the key process elements in RUP? (Select all that apply.)
    a. Discipline
    b. Phase
    c. Actors
    d. Template

15. Which of the following is true of a discipline in RUP? (Select all that apply.)
    a. Gives you all the guidance you require to learn when to perform a given activity
    b. Should not be tailored because doing that affects the integrity of the discipline
    c   Provides all the guidance you need to learn how to perform a given activity
    d. Produces documents

16. What important information does the RUP hump diagram present? (Select all that apply.)
    a. Illustrates the varying degrees of focus across different disciplines in the development and evolution of the solution across the project lifecycle
    b. Shows the relationship between RUP phases and RUP disciplines
    c. Shows the roles responsible for performing activities within a given discipline
    d. Provides guidance on the number of iterations to be managed within any given phase

17. Which of the following is a discipline in RUP? (Select all that apply.)
    a. Deployment
    b. Environment
    c. Development
    d. Production

18. Logical grouping of related activities into respective disciplines enables you to do which of the following? (Select all that apply.)
    a. Define the roles for each discipline.
    b. Structure the tasks performed by these roles.
    c. Define artifacts that are produced or refined by these roles when they perform the related activities.
    d. Define the sequence in which these activities should be performed.

19. An artifact is a formal work product that is produced, modified, or used by a task, defines an area of responsibility, and is subject to version control. Which of the following is true about artifacts? (Select all that apply.)
    a. An artifact can be a model, code, or a document.
    b. An artifact is a work product.
    c. An artifact can be a mandatory or optional input into an activity.
    d. An artifact can be output of an activity.

20. Which of the following enables you to assess the quality of a particular artifact?
    a. Checklist
    b. Checkpoint
    c. Guideline
    d. Template

21. Which of the following views is used in the Analysis and Design discipline?
    a. Deployment view
    b. Use-Case view
    c. Analysis view
    d. Physical view

References

IBM Rational Unified Process v7.0.

Perry, D., Wolf, A. (1992). Foundations for the study of software architecture, *ACM SIGSOFT Software Engineering Notes*, 17(4): 40–52.

Chapter 2

Key Principles for Business-Driven Development

By Ahmad K. Shuja and Jochen Krebs

When the George Washington Bridge (GWB) was completed in 1931, it consisted of only one level. This bridge handled the traffic at that time more than sufficiently, and it was a beautiful piece of construction. History shows, however, that the builders could not have anticipated how much more traffic this bridge would need to carry. Today when you approach the GWB, you must decide between taking the upper or the lower level. With the bridge slowly reaching its capacity, the builders added a new level just below the existing one, to meet the growing traffic needs.

The situation at the GWB project bridge is something that occurs in software engineering quite often. Even though engineering disciplines are similar in many ways, some major differences distinguish them. Let's take a look at some of these differences in more detail.

When civil engineers prepare and submit their plans to the community, the plans usually consist of high-level and detailed drawings in addition to textual information. With no expertise in this field, we can still imagine how the bridge will look, how many lanes it will carry, and if ships will clear underneath. Plans like these are signed off on by stakeholders, such as town planners, who are leaving the structural details to the experts. Creating such mental pictures in software engineering is much more challenging, because the outcome of IT systems is intangible. To make this challenge even more difficult, software engineers have their own visual notations and techniques that are not intuitive for external audiences. Such differences exist because software engineering is unique in the sense that there are few guiding scientific principles, few universally applicable methods, and it is as much managerial, psychological, and sociological as technical. Software engineering is a unique brand in the sense that software is malleable, intangible, and has a discontinuous operational nature; software construction is human intensive; software problems are unprecedentedly complex; and software solutions require unusual rigor (USC, 2003).

A typical sign-off such as that in the traditional engineering disciplines, which triggers the next step in the plan-build-assemble paradigm, is more temporary in software engineering. In fact, according to Larman (2004), software engineering and development projects have been inappropriately associated with a predictable manufacturing paradigm (plan the work, work the plan, or plan-build-assemble) that can be predictably specified and planned (such as mobile phones), rather than a new product development paradigm. Plan-driven methodologies, inspired by other engineering disciplines, do not always lead to predictable results for software development (Fowler, 2005). Software projects that have adopted this approach have had more frequent failures or faced significant cost and schedule overruns (Boehm & Turner, 2003). With that said, modern software engineering processes, such as the RUP, embrace the fact that software is engineered in shorter cycles and with architecture and functionality delivered in shorter segments called increments. Even though it might sound crazy to engineers in other fields, comparing the GWB project to an IT project, stakeholders and software engineers might decide to build one lane at a time or raise the bridge after a few increments to accommodate taller ships. At first glance, that might sound like a lack of planning. That perception is more a result, however, of the misunderstandings of those initial mental pictures. The abstractness and complexity of the software development project make it impossible to pin down from the beginning. Software development activity involves well-coordinated teams working together, each within a variety of disciplines that span the entire software development lifecycle (traditionally known as SDLC). What also makes it more complex is the fact that planning and creating separate pieces and then assembling them later is not as straightforward as it is for some other disciplines of engineering.

Unfortunately, the world does not stop changing after a system is released in its environment. However, the GWB team got lucky by having a structure in place that could carry the additional level. Even with structural engineering expertise, the idea of adding a new level to the bridge sounded like a huge endeavor. If the experts would have said that adding the additional level would have been impossible to implement, people probably would have believed and accepted that fact due to their own assessment. Software engineers, on the other hand, are confronted with changes like this all the time. The difference between software engineers and other people is that the former rarely accept that something is impossible. The reason for this might be buried in the fact that software engineers can deliver in iterations and increments throughout the project, so they believe they can do it after the project is completed too. Iterative-incremental software engineering helps shape the mental picture while driving the project to completion, but architectural changes after a project is completed might be costly if not impossible. RUP, for example, dedicates an entire phase, called Elaboration, to validating the architecture.

Software is reaching more and more parts of our lives—sometimes even heart surgery. Software can enable life support, create games, or support business processes in organizations. The latter are systems used to keep, for example, enterprise resource, customer and customer expectation, marketing and sales, accounts and billing management, and other related processes going. They are systems for accepting parcel delivery or running forecasts in financial portfolio applications. You get the idea. What these applications have in common is that they are usually part of rapidly changing organizations. Just to further emphasize this difference between software and other engineering disciplines, organizations in the same domain compete for the same market, try to open to new markets, or consolidate markets. This is similar to the idea of multiple bridges over the Hudson River competing for traffic with their services and fees. The teams maintaining the systems that tie all these perspectives together are constantly challenged to enforce the latest set of business rules in the IT systems. In some organizations, you can almost feel the frustration of marketing or product management versus the IT team. On the one side you have the team that has the vision and its fruitful implementation in front of it; on the other side is the team that needs to build support beams to hold on to the future lanes and levels.

With these differences in mind, it seems natural that software engineers need to be guided through a different process model than other engineers. IBM Rational describes best practices based on software development techniques. These best practices, which have repeatedly and consistently demonstrated added value, describe a more iterative and incremental approach to software development than the plan-build-assemble process. Inspired and harvested from experience, IBM Rational retrieved six fundamental principles to guide organizations and projects toward success.

- **A**dapt the Process
- **B**alance Competing Stakeholder Priorities
- **C**ollaborate Across Teams
- **D**emonstrate Value Iteratively
- **E**levate the Level of Abstraction
- **F**ocus Continuously on Quality

These six key principles match, in particular, the need when building in a business-driven environment. The principles are the evolution of what were originally called six best practices. The key principles, however, emphasize the value for business-driven development.

All six principles are equally important; they often benefit each other and are easy to memorize (A through F). The remainder of this chapter discusses each key principle in more detail and gives examples of how these key principles benefit each other. Each principle follows the same template:

- A general overview of the key principle
- Its benefits and the patterns of application
- Its anti-pattern

The last point is a negative scenario you can observe in organizations where the key principle is not successfully implemented.

Adapt the Process

The one-size-fits-all principle does not apply to software development. Remember that more is not always better, and less is not always bad. You must appropriately configure the software development process to meet the needs of the project. This process includes the granularity of activities to be performed, the respective input and output artifacts, the roles that are responsible for performing and contributing toward the execution of these activities, the policies and regulations that drive and control the execution of these activities, and so on. Numerous factors can contribute while configuring the process to meet such project needs as the amount of ceremony, precision, and control. Some of these factors include project size, complexity, risks involved, and team structure. Other factors have been discussed in Chapter 1, "Welcome to the IBM Rational Unified Process and Certification," as well as in Chapter 15, "Tailoring." In the Rational Unified Process, the Environment discipline is dedicated to helping with the adaptation of the process. The following sections briefly look at some of the components of the Environment discipline that support the key enablers for adapting the process.

Benefits

When you adapt the process to the project's specific needs, some key benefits result, including lifecycle efficiency and communication of risks.

Lifecycle Efficiency

When the process is adapted, it keeps in mind the project efficiency and effectiveness—deliver higher-quality and lower-cost software solutions. Process adaptation is critical to lifecycle efficiency and is achieved by rightsizing the process to match project needs, adapting the degree of process ceremony to the lifecycle phase, continuously improving the process, and balancing project plans and associated estimates with the uncertainty of a project. Process size and ceremony are appropriately designed to encourage creativity in the earlier phases of the lifecycle, whereas enhancing predictability by having more controls in place is the hallmark of the later phases. In addition, adapting the process ensures that you have the right process for the right project and the right organization. In fact, applying all of RUP will more often than not result in greater efficiencies.

Communication of Risks

RUP, by design, is based on risk. This means that the highest risks are identified and mitigated as early in the project lifecycle as possible. Less control and light formality during the early stages of the project are essential for open and honest communication, which ultimately leads to better identification and management of risks to the project.

You will see in coming sections how these benefits are realized by adapting the process.

Patterns

Part of adapting the process is adopting patterns. **Patterns** in this context are behaviors that enact the key principles of successful business-driven development. Patterns that are specific to adapting the process are outlined in this section.

Rightsizing the Process

What is the process size? Quite simply, the process size incorporates the degree of formality required. Formality includes the number of artifacts and models required, the details necessary within each artifact, the number and formality of reviews needed, and the type and frequency of reporting. More formality means more process, and more process is not always better. To achieve the objectives of a project, you need to correctly configure some form of base process (right sized) to improve the probability of successfully achieving project objectives. Some obvious factors influence the process size. These include the project size, the level of distribution of project resources, the technology complexity, the number of project stakeholders, the need to be in compliance with standards and government regulations, and the phase that the project is in. A larger, more complex, and more distributed project in the later phase of its lifecycle will more likely require a more disciplined process than a smaller project with a more centralized team utilizing a relatively well-known technology.

Figure 2-1 is an overview of factors that are likely to affect the process size. Determining the right size of the project plays an important role in successfully adapting the process and is one of the key enablers.

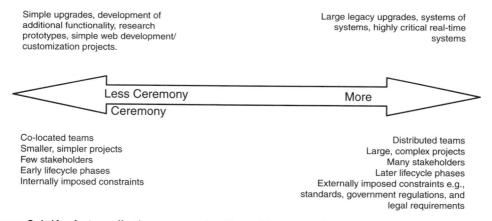

Figure 2-1 Key factors affecting process size (Some ideas taken from IBM Rational training course)

Important Environment Artifacts include Development Process and Development Case. Development Process is a configuration of the RUP that meets the needs of the project. Development Case describes the development process in greater detail. This may include the artifacts that will be produced, who will produce them, when they will be produced, and to what level of detail. We will discuss the Environment discipline in greater detail later in the book.

Adapt Process Ceremony to Lifecycle Phase

Where you are in the project lifecycle greatly influences the required level of ceremony. Earlier in the lifecycle, there is a greater need for creativity. More process means more controls, which can potentially impact creativity in a negative sense. Therefore, earlier in the lifecycle, it is important to keep ceremony at the required, necessary level to encourage creativity. When the vision of the project and the product have been established, some form of proof-of-concept has been completed, and the project enters into the architecture and development phases, the need for more control increases to ensure that the product meets the stated vision in a timely fashion.

Figure 2-2 shows how this relates to the Rational Unified Process.

Rational Unified Process Lifecycle			
Inception	Elaboration	Construction	Transition
Lesser ceremony Light formality More creativity Less precision Focus on big picture Higher uncertainty			Greater ceremony Heavy formality More control More precision Focus on delivery Higher certainty
Continuous Process Improvement			

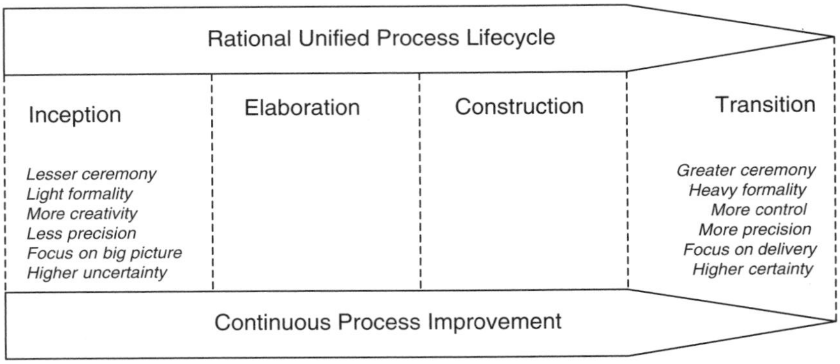

Figure 2-2 Rational Unified Process lifecycle and continuous process improvement

Continuous Process Improvement

As shown in Figure 2-2, the process needs to continually evolve and refine during the RUP lifecycle. It is recommended that process-specific lessons learned for a given iteration, as well as the project, be recorded and subsequently used to further improve the process. Within a project, each iteration results in greater experience, and you should use the results to refine the process for later iterations. Similarly, at the conclusion of a project, review the overall project process and record necessary improvement recommendations for ongoing process refinements. One of the factors that is likely to contribute significantly toward process improvement is the overall culture. All team members should feel responsible for contributing to the improvement of the overall software development process.

Uncertainty-Driven Planning and Estimating

Greater uncertainty leads to greater risks for the successful completion of the project. As shown in Figure 2-2, uncertainty is higher in the early stages of the project. This means that attempts to produce detailed plans and accurate estimates will likely fail. However, as a project progresses, more details are revealed, an architecture is baselined, and the uncertainty decreases, giving way to higher certainty. As uncertainties are resolved, formality becomes more pronounced, and the ability to produce detailed plans and better estimates increases.

Anti-Patterns

Anti-patterns are behaviors that do not support the key principles of business-driven development and can harm software development projects. This section briefly discusses these anti-patterns as they relate to adapting the process.

Early Baselining of Estimates

This behavior forces early estimates to be produced and then scheduled and financial performance to be tracked to those estimates. Any attempts to baseline estimates early in the development life-cycle will most likely result in minimal accuracy and a greater degree of wasted effort than baselining later in the project. Do not attempt to baseline estimates earlier in the project because uncertainty is greater then. Toward the end of the Elaboration phase in the RUP, the architecture is more stable and you can start baselining the estimates then.

Developing Static Plans

As explained earlier, software engineering and related development projects are unlike other engineering disciplines. Buildings can be precisely architected, models created, and principles tested prior to commencing the construction effort. Hundreds of years of knowledge are available to more accurately plan for such projects. That is why it is possible to produce detailed and likely static plans (with an allowance for variation to some degree) prior to initiating the construction effort. However, software development projects are different in the sense that there is a relative absence of quantifiable principles based on hard facts. Consequently, the plans need to be more dynamic and evolving. Such plans go through cycles of refinements based on actual prototyping and executable software releases before they can be baselined. Therefore, it is an anti-pattern to develop precise plans and manage projects by tracking against those static plans.

Using a Static Process

As shown in Figure 2-2, continuous process improvement must persist throughout the software development lifecycle. Each iteration should contribute toward refining the process. It is an anti-pattern to try to always use the same degree of process through the lifecycle. Note that the degree of process does incorporate execution of the project in terms of the iterations (iteration maturity levels are discussed in Chapter 1), the techniques used across the RUP disciplines, and so on. Lessons learned during each iteration play an important role in improving the overall execution of the project by continuously improving the process.

Balance Competing Stakeholder Priorities

Complex decision-making situations are not unique to software engineering. Other disciplines, such as psychology and organizational behavior, have studied decision making thoroughly (Beck, 1999). Classical decision-making models have been mapped to various requirements engineering activities to show the similarities (Beck, 1999). For instance, in your everyday life, you make decisions. The greater the impact of these decisions, the harder it will be to make them. The decision-making process becomes even harder and more critical if others, usually stakeholders, are affected by your decisions. A stakeholder can be defined as someone or something—human or a system—impacted as a result of the new product. Therefore, a stakeholder can include an end user, a customer, a product manager, or a buyer, each with different priorities as far as the product is concerned. With this in mind, balancing competing stakeholder needs is one of the key challenges to objectively manage during the software development lifecycle and requires careful and planned effort. A customer may be primarily concerned about financial investments, whereas end users are primarily driven by the tasks they need to perform without much concern for the cost of delivering the needed functionality. Therefore, it is critical to balance these competing stakeholder priorities by appropriately performing the custom development and leverage existing assets. This section discusses the benefits of balancing competing stakeholder priorities key; principle, relevant patterns; and key anti-patterns.

Benefits

Benefits realized as a result of balancing competing stakeholder priorities include increased business alignment, reduced custom development, and optimized business value.

Increased Business Alignment

Research shows that in software engineering, the ability to satisfy the needs of the customers and users often determines the quality of a product (Carver, Shull, and Basili, 2003). Most software projects have more needs than can be included, so you need to assign priorities based on the needs that will bring the most value to the business. Prioritizing stakeholder needs and managing the software development projects accordingly results in applications that are in greater alignment with the actual business needs.

Reduced Custom Development

The need to have software solutions sooner and at lower costs is leading to shorter software development lifecycles. This means teams need to be able to limit custom development, leverage packaged solutions and internal existing assets, and reuse software designs and solutions in new versions of systems and products. Besides shortening development time, properly handled reuse improves reliability because code is executed for a longer time and in different contexts (Fenton and Pfleeger, 1996). As you might suspect, there is always a trade-off, and this time the trade-off is requirements. The trade-off can be managed smoothly if requirements are appropriately prioritized while achieving alignment with the most important business needs.

Optimized Business Value

When stakeholders' needs are prioritized to build alignment with the business and efforts are invested in shortening time to market by leveraging packaged applications and existing assets, business value optimization follows.

Patterns

Patterns are behaviors that enact the key principles of successful business-driven development. Patterns that are specific to balancing competing stakeholder priorities key principle are covered in this section.

Define, Understand, and Prioritize Business and User Needs

Correct definition, clear understanding, and the right prioritization of the business and user needs are prerequisite to meeting these needs. Understanding the business goals and objectives, relating those to the user needs, and then uncovering those that are high priority are part of the process required to build the product that satisfies these needs. You must appreciate the importance of this stage in the software development lifecycle. This stage is the most challenging to get right and plays the most critical role in shaping the vision for the product. Each stakeholder believes his need is the most important one. Balancing many such "most important" needs, yet meeting the real business need while keeping the costs low and the time to market short, is a challenge that requires strong negotiating and management skills. You can use different types of models to achieve a thorough understanding of the business need. We will discuss more about these models and related concepts in Part III, "Rational Unified Process: Content and Process Elements."

Prioritize Projects and Requirements and Couple Needs with Software Capabilities

Following a thorough understanding and prioritization of the business needs, the next step is to translate those into product requirements. To maximize the overall business value offered by a product, select and prioritize critical requirements so that key stakeholder needs can be met. Of course, you can rectify incorrect decisions later on via change management, but this can be costly because it is significantly more expensive to correct problems later in the development process (Bradner, 1997).

I want to stress here the importance of the term *critical* in requirements. It is similar to identifying architecturally significant use cases that are critical to the business needs. A clear understanding of business needs plays a central role in architecting the right solution to satisfy those needs. Such a prioritization of critical needs is an important step toward delivering business value incrementally early in the project lifecycle and for identifying and mitigating risks. Note that agility is at the core of delivering business value in an iterative and incremental fashion. According to Brooks (1987), the hardest part of building a software system is deciding precisely what to build. No other part of the work so cripples the resulting system if done wrong. Furthermore, no other part is more difficult to rectify later. Research, experience, and leading industry practices have demonstrated that the most effective way of building software-intensive products is to first identify and prioritize the requirements and then determine the optimal requirements set in the early stages of the development lifecycle.

Understand What Assets You Can Leverage

Before you can reuse existing software assets, you need to identify those assets and understand how to reuse them. Software evolution over years makes the reusability hard. How? Well, as software evolves and more and more patches are added to address immediate needs, the complexity of software architecture increases, the documentation becomes outdated, and it becomes difficult to identify which systems or subsystems you can reuse and how. This pattern is about gaining that understanding of the systems or subsystems that can be leveraged as new software applications are being developed.

Balance Asset Reuse with User Needs

This pattern is really about limiting the changes that are made to the legacy system to meet the real user needs. The challenge however, is, making the right choice while balancing shorter-term gains at the cost of longer-term costs. Asset reuse can happen at various levels; you can use an entire legacy system as a component of a new system (provided as a service in service-oriented architecture), or, in the case of a decision being made to redevelop the legacy system, you can reuse artifacts such as requirements. In any event, carefully decide and manage any form of change to legacy systems to ensure that overall complexity does not exceed the necessary limit and future reusability remains an option.

Anti-Patterns

Anti-patterns that apply to this key principle are covered in the following sections.

Thoroughly Document Precise Requirements and Force Stakeholder Acceptance

How do you write precise requirements when the only constant element from the initiation to the closure of a software project is evolving requirements? Identifying true software requirements is a continuing process of learning and refining. Any attempt to document precise requirements early in the software development project and to force stakeholder acceptance almost always results in a product that does not satisfy the real business needs. That is the reason why this is one of the key anti-patterns.

Architect a System Only to Meet the Needs of the Most Vocal Stakeholders

Most of us in the software engineering and development profession have experienced situations where difficult and vocal stakeholders influence the way requirements are prioritized and implemented. Defining, understanding, and prioritizing the business and user needs through use-case driven development and user-centered design enable requirements to be managed objectively.

Collaborate Across Teams

Before discussing the benefits, patterns, and anti-patterns for this principle, let's briefly discuss the core element—communication—which plays the central role in the success or failure of any project. The way that teams are organized determines the challenges they might face to build optimal channels of communication. As a general rule, the larger and more distributed the teams, the greater the importance of communication and the harder it will be to build these channels for optimal communication across teams. Size and distribution of the team will determine how this optimal communication is achieved. People management and a collaborative environment are key enablers to achieving optimal communication. With systems being architected in one part of the world and code being produced in another, dispersion of software teams is becoming the norm in today's business world. This trend is creating a huge challenge in ensuring optimal communication across teams. To make the situation even more complex, effective development requires development teams to closely collaborate with other stakeholders from the business and IT operations. Key characteristics of effective and efficient teams are that they are results-focused, with clear deliverables. Formal communication practices will ensure the required knowledge sharing across teams. Even small projects need optimal collaboration to ensure success.

People issues and collaboration have been the primary focus of agile development practices, and team distribution affects them both. Business evolution and identification of innovative ways to use software applications to create value lead to more complex systems. And as systems become more complex, the need for stakeholders with collaboration skills becomes crucial for project success. This principle of collaboration across teams stresses the importance of optimal communication across team(s). According to Kroll and MacIsaac (2006, Chapter 5, "Collaborate Across Teams"), the following are the four imperatives for effective collaboration:

- Motivate individuals on the team to perform at their best
- Encourage cross-functional collaboration
- Provide effective collaboration environments
- Integrate across business, software, and operation teams

Figure 2-3 shows that these imperatives play a crucial role in ensuring effective collaboration between the core elements of an organization—business, operations, and development.

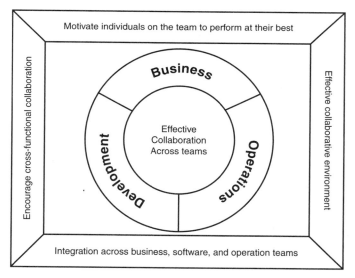

Figure 2-3 Imperatives and effective collaboration

Chapter 1 discussed work breakdown structure. Another breakdown presented by the OpenUP is shown in Figure 2-4. (Note that OpenUP is not part of RUP and its certification.) This is a development-specific breakdown and is composed of Intent, Solution, and Management. This representation has some overlap with what is shown in Figure 2-3. For instance, Management in Figure 2-4 may be composed of managers and leads from all three organizations—Business, Development, and Operations.

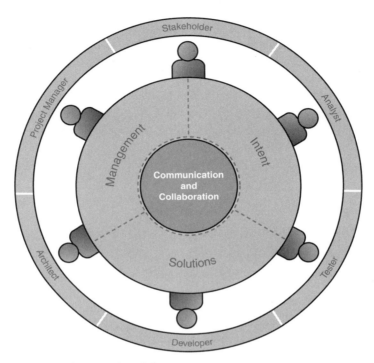

Figure 2-4 OpenUP development breakdown

Benefits

The benefits of collaborating across teams include team productivity and better coupling between business needs, development, and IT operations.

Team Productivity

Understanding what creates a high-performing team is complex. A team is based on effective collaboration to achieve common objectives (Kroll and MacIsaac, 2006). To achieve these common objectives, you need to communicate a consistent message to the team members about the importance of teamwork and individual productivity.

Better Coupling Between Business Needs, the Development, and IT Operations

Building alignment between business and IT development and bridging gaps between IT development and IT operations is essential for building software solutions that provide real and expected value to the business. One of the major benefits achieved by implementing this principle is the better communication and enhanced collaboration between the business, development, and IT operations.

Patterns

This section covers patterns related to this key principle.

Motivate People to Perform at Their Best

To create high-performing teams, you need individual high performers who are also team players. People should feel excited about being on the team. Clear communication of responsibilities, implementation of effective and efficient processes, provision of enabler tools, instillation of the right values, stipulation of organizational clarity, addition of the right people, establishment of trust, establishment of rules of communication, and effective management of knowledge are some of the core ingredients required to build high-performing teams that endure and achieve team objectives.

Create Self-Managed Teams

The notion of self-managed teams, which has gained popularity in the agile community, is based on making a team commit to what it should deliver and then providing that team with the authority to decide on all the issues that directly influence the result (Schwaber and Beedle, 2002). By clearly communicating the responsibilities for the expected results, providing the right training and tools, establishing trust, and giving the necessary authority, you create much more motivation for teams to do a high-quality job.

Encourage Cross-Functional Collaboration

Unlike traditional waterfall methodology, iterative and incremental development requires members from cross-functional areas (Business Modeling, Requirements, Analysis and Design, Implementation, Test, Deployment, and others) to collaborate to achieve the project results. Project management plays the central orchestration role to ensure that cross-functional collaboration is carried out at an optimal level. In most iterations (which are small waterfall projects), functional teams collaborate with each other to meet the iteration objectives. With the exception of some of the earliest iterations, iterations usually end up in an executable deliverable, which requires cross-functional collaboration.

Provide an Effective Collaborative Environment

As discussed earlier, iterative and incremental development projects are communication and collaboration intensive. Web-based collaboration tools—ranging from project management to virtual rooms and whiteboards—and document management tools enable effective collaboration, which reduces the need for meetings and manually managing artifact evolution and other necessary workflow management procedures, such as reviews and approvals. In addition, the collaborative environment automates much of metrics collection, report generation, reminder alerts, escalations, bug tracking, and other related tasks and enables the teams to focus their efforts on creative activities.

Manage Evolving Artifacts and Tasks

You need to manage evolving artifacts and tasks to enhance collaboration, progress, and quality insight with integrated environments. In an iterative and incremental development lifecycle, artifacts from across different disciplines evolve simultaneously. For example, in an Elaboration iteration, although the focus is primarily on building an architectural proof-of-concept, there will be refinements to the requirements and analysis- and design-related artifacts as a result of gaining better understanding. It is imperative that you manage evolving artifacts effectively to enhance collaboration while staying focused on the overall quality.

Integrate Business, Software, and Operation Teams

As businesses evolve, they identify new, innovative, and effective ways of using IT to better enable their core business processes efficiently. Separation between business, development, and operations can produce extensive damage to the project. In fact, as software applications become more complex, there is a growing need for formal methods to simulate the operational needs, including capacity, availability, security, and business continuity management/IT service continuity management. The IT Infrastructure Library (ITIL) offers guidelines on leading-industry practices to integrate business, software, and operation teams through service delivery and service support disciplines.

Anti-Patterns

The following sections discuss the most recognizable anti-patterns or behaviors contrary to this principle that can harm software development projects.

Nurture Heroic Developers Willing to Work Extremely Long Hours, Including Weekends

Nurturing heroic developers hurts the creation of high-performance teams. In fact, to ensure that team spirit is encouraged, recognitions and rewards should be related to team achievements, not heroic developers. We have all experienced cases in which one or two team members work over weekends to help meet project deadlines. Recognizing and encouraging such behavior sends out the wrong message to other team members and should be avoided. If the project is planned, resourced, and executed appropriately, there should be no need for anyone to work long hours and weekends.

Have Highly Specialized Well-Equipped People with Limited Collaboration

As discussed earlier, iterative and incremental software development really requires cross-functional teams to collaborate closely and effectively to successfully achieve respective iteration, phase, and project objectives. High-end specialized tools implemented in a silo'ed fashion will create obstacles that hinder the creation of a collaborative environment. Imagine that requirements engineering is carried out in its own environment, analysis and design is carried out by a separate team using isolated tools, and so on. Different artifact sets belonging to different disciplines need to be evolved simultaneously. If you do not implement tools with cross-functional integration in mind, the teams will be discouraged from collaborating, leading to unsuccessful projects.

Assume That If Just Everybody Does His Job, The Result Will Be Good

Software development is a team sport, and cross-functional teams need to work together as one to achieve the results. "A team of teams" is needed to deliver results.

Demonstrate Value Iteratively

Before the key principles of business-driven development were defined, one of the original RUP best practices was called Develop Software Iteratively. When we compare that best practice to the newly evolved key principle of Demonstrating Value Iteratively, we notice that the focus shifted from software development toward value demonstration while keeping an emphasis on the concept of iterations. Especially for business-driven development, the key principle requires the project team to display (demonstrate) the equivalent worth or return in money (value) in a repetitive approach.

Following this key principle makes it feel natural for projects to enable feedback, embrace change, remove risks early, and continuously adapt plans to align with reality. These are patterns that will lead to the benefits outlined in the following section.

Benefits

Benefits of demonstrating value iteratively include early risk reduction, higher predictability throughout the project, and trust among the stakeholders.

Early Risk Reduction

Value is demonstrated with risks in mind. In an iterative approach, the higher the risk ranking (for example, the cost impact of the risk or its importance to stakeholders), the earlier it is tackled. If the risk mitigation strategy is successful, risks are reduced in an iterative fashion early in the project. Parallel to the iterative development, the risk list is consistently monitored and managed.

Higher Predictability throughout the Project

Reducing the highest risks early while demonstrating high-priority functionality iteratively, the plans are compared to reality more frequently. Predictions and forecasts for future milestones will be more reliable based on the experiences in earlier iterations.

Trust Among the Stakeholders

With each iteration, the project team also demonstrates its own capabilities; for example, the members might show that they are managing requirements, reducing risks, or providing predictable forecasting within the time constraint of the iteration. As the project moves through iterations, stakeholders are more likely to build a trusting relationship with the project team. This trust is the basis for honest communication and higher team morale.

Patterns

The patterns include enabling feedback, embracing change, removing risk, and adapting plans.

Enabling Feedback

Every software project team receives feedback sooner or later. In a traditional sequential process, also known as a waterfall process, business analysts are heavily involved in the earliest stages (requirements), and verification does not come until user acceptance. Between those stages, the IT project team takes over and produces what has been requested (see Figure 2-5). Sometimes, though, things do not work out so neatly. Requirements are commonly misunderstood or incomplete and frequently change.[1] Based on this knowledge, how could a project team deliver a system for which the requirements set cannot be stable?

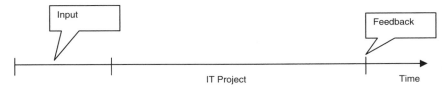

Figure 2-5 Input and feedback in a waterfall project

The Standish Group[2] identified various sources of project failure. It found that the failure of 16 percent of all projects is directly linked to lack of user involvement. Another 8 percent of unsuccessful projects fail because of widely spaced project milestones. Based on the Standish Group's data, an unsuccessful IT project is considered to be one that does not build the functionality that the customer requested. Therefore, the longer the period between the initial input of requirements and the feedback at the end, the higher the likelihood that requirements might change. For example, legal requirements, technology, and sometimes even the customer change between these milestones.

To effectively demonstrate value iteratively, you need to establish a path of enabling and encouraging feedback. Instead of building the entire system in one flow like the waterfall with the big-bang release at the end, iterative development breaks the project into smaller chunks (see Figure 2-6). These chunks, sometimes referred to as **mini-waterfalls**,[3] are now tackled in smaller time-frames, usually 2 to 6 weeks in length, resulting in a demonstrable result.

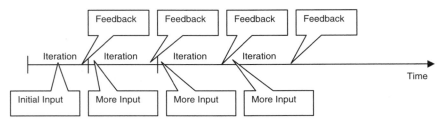

Figure 2-6 Input and feedback in an iterative project

---

[1]   Gause and Weinberg—Exploring requirements.

[2]   Standish Group—Chaos Study.

[3]   Larman, Kruchten, Bittner—How to fail with RUP: Seven steps to pain and suffering.

At the beginning of each iteration, the project team designates certain functionality to that time-box and commits all its resources to the objectives for that period. At the end of each iteration, the team can return to the stakeholders and present the accomplishments. This period is also known as an **increment**, and the technique is also known as **iterative-incremental software engineering**.

Embracing Change

In today's business world, nothing seems to be more constant than change. Through the iterative-incremental approach, feedback is encouraged and welcomed. This feedback can result in change and needs to be proactively managed. One phenomenon, observed at the end of iterations, is called the **Yes, but-syndrome**,[4] where stakeholders commonly agree with the functionality that they see was created in the increment but brainstorm more functionality. Managing feedback does not mean automatically accepting every change but instead understanding the severity and relevance of the change. When you analyze the nature of the change and turn it into a request, rescoping, re-estimating and possibly replanning of future iterations can occur.

Through feedback and change, the customer can shape the direction of the product and can influence important decisions.

Removing Risk

When the content for an iteration is planned, functionality is not the only key aspect of what will be done in the upcoming weeks. Especially during iterations in the Elaboration phase, important functionality related to architectural risks is tackled early, whereas lower-priority risks are deferred to later iterations (for example, iterations in the Construction phase). Assess every identified risk and devise a mitigation strategy. Typical risk mitigation strategies are **risk acceptance** (the project takes on the risk), **risk transfer** (the risk is delegated to someone else out of scope), **risk avoidance** (taking steps that prevent the risk from occurring, such as scope reduction), and **risk reduction** (risks are stepwise reduced, as with iterative development). Execute each strategy according to priority and timing, and reassess it if the mitigation strategy was effectual. Keep in mind that the nature of risk can be diverse; for example, the risk might be technical, business, or programming related. The key principle of demonstrating value iteratively also has a significant positive impact on risk management in the project by removing risks iteratively, with the highest risks removed first.

Adapting Plans

Earlier in this chapter, we compared iterative development to mini-waterfalls. Based on this analogy, we could also see them as mini-projects. With the end of each iteration (mini-project), the project team learned things that it might not have been aware of when entering this iteration. With iterative development, the team has frequent checkpoints to review and adjust the plans. Due to

---

[4]   Leffingwell, Widrig. *Managing Software Requirements*.

the shorter duration of iterations, iteration plans that outline the objectives and goals of an iteration are more stable and less frequently changed than those for a waterfall project. It is the nature of the business that you cannot foresee and plan for all circumstances, but iterative development allows you to incorporate the knowledge into future forecasts. Iterative planning is likely to be closer to the reality, because the plan contains lessons learned from earlier iterations.

Anti-Patterns

This section covers the anti-patterns.

Plan the Entire Project in Detail

When you don't break down the entire project into smaller chunks, the planning process can become time-consuming and less reliable. Although project managers in iterative projects outline roughly the objectives of the following iterations, they plan only one iteration ahead in more detail. Applying the anti-pattern of planning the entire project in detail, you'll waste valuable time maintaining the detailed plans, which are far from reach. In addition, when plans are communicated and change is difficult to introduce, stakeholders lose trust in the team's capabilities.

Rely on Deliverables Other Than Test Results or Demonstrations

The most important outcome of the software engineering process is most likely working software. Stakeholders might also be interested in maintainability and flexibility, but what are these features worth when the system does not function properly? This anti-pattern emphasizes that projects relying on project documentation instead of demos and test results might bet their money on the wrong horse. If you are not getting paid for documentation, trust the test results and the demonstrable software that you see executed in front of you. By definition, an iteration is not complete without executable software that stakeholders can demonstrate and verify. If executable software is not delivered, you either allocated resources to the wrong activities or didn't reduce risks. Trust among stakeholders might be lost.

Elevate the Level of Abstraction

A successful approach to dealing with complexity involves leveraging patterns and services instead of reliving the software experiences and actively reusing components and systems instead of building things from scratch. Proving the architectural capabilities first while managing the complexity is a key criterion for a successful project. With this key principle in mind, the project team will gain two major benefits: improved productivity and reduced complexity.

Benefits

The benefits of elevating the level of abstraction include improved productivity and reduced complexity.

Improved Productivity

With different views and perspectives on the architecture, software engineers are likely to stay focused while keeping the big picture of the overall system. Advanced construction tools with code generation and a consistent use of standardized languages provide a collaboration platform for the project team. Proven patterns and services increase the speed with which solutions are assembled and systems are orchestrated.

Reduced Complexity

Nesting components inside others while loosely coupling them and wrapping components and systems while exposing important services reduce system complexity. Patterns, models, and assets provide helpful instructions for approaching the complexity of a system.

Patterns

This section covers the patterns that help elevate the level of abstraction.

Re-use Existing Assets

Today's IT world is diverse in languages, systems, and business domains. For example, many organizations have similar payroll processes (manual, semiautomatic, or fully automated) even across different domains, such as manufacturing and retail. The businesses have certain differences depending on the domain, but at a high level, the process of recording work, allocating work, calculating pay, reducing taxes, and printing checks is similar. The nuances, such as how the pay is calculated and how much tax is deducted, are more granular details we like to defer to at a later point. In today's IT world, where many systems and products already exist, it's not as necessary to develop and build systems from scratch. Analyzing existing systems and identifying re-use seems like a logical step. Besides a quicker turnaround and faster ROI (return-on-investment), one psychological effect is associated with this approach: the confidence that it has been successfully used before. Sometimes a problem-solution-pair is not as general and as high level. In that situation, the grand solution is assembled from various smaller ones. In the payroll example, you could build a system that records personnel-related information, uses a web service to calculate the tax, and uses an external system (third party) to accept the data and print and send the checks to the employees. This scenario would reduce the risks of incorrectly calculating employee taxes and printing paychecks, while still keeping personnel data within the organization.

This scenario describes re-use on an organizational level, which has enormous strategic value for an organization. But re-use does not stop at this level; you can delegate it to more granular items, subsystems, components, objects, and more, as illustrated in Figure 2-7. The lower the element is in the pyramid, the higher the chances are of re-use. For example, you can use a component clock in a larger variety of systems than an entire payroll system.

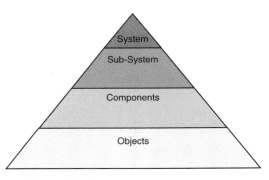

Figure 2-7 Re-usability on different levels

Certain concepts and technologies promote this sort of bottom-up re-use approach. This section takes a closer look at them, in particular patterns and services.

Patterns and Re-Use

Patterns are a part of life, including software engineering. A pattern is a proven template whose use often leads to more success and confidence than working without it. Documenting a procedure does not qualify as establishing a pattern; it would only qualify as a pattern after you'd applied it and proven it several times. For example, a software engineer has difficulties assigning a responsibility to an object. The engineer could use trial and error or consult the GRASP catalog (Larman), which provides solutions to fundamental design decisions. The so-called Gang-of-Four (Gamma, Johnson, Helm, Vlissides) pattern catalog offers 23 additional solutions to common problems in object orientation. These are just two examples from a large repository of catalogs. Patterns also exist for architectures, such as service-oriented architectures (SOA) or tiered-architectures. Patterns are often related to other patterns, which promotes a pattern-driven software engineering (Krebs), which in turn encourages and promotes the use of patterns commonly related to other patterns. With all the publicly available pattern catalogs, individuals and organizations can extend the variety of patterns by defining their own catalogs. The application of patterns brings additional benefits with it; for example, engineers then start communicating in patterns and documenting in patterns.

Patterns also exist on a process level; for example, RUP fulfills all the criteria for a pattern. It has been successfully applied many times before for iterative-incremental software engineering and documented inputs, outputs, and activities.

Services and Re-Use

Like patterns, services appear on different levels. For example, let's consider the example of when you want to know what time it is. Technically speaking, who would you send the question to? You'd probably send it to a clock. A clock can be seen as a service provider, offering a publicly available interface. For object-oriented software engineering, an object clock would expose such a service as public, whereas other services would not be exposed and would in fact be protected from the outside (defining exactly what a second or minute is). In object-oriented systems, objects exchange information through sender-receiver communication, which is similar to service communication.

You can also elevate the level of abstraction by wrapping certain logical grouped objects into a component and offering services on an elevated component level. This allows the sender to send service requests to larger units, without knowing all the internal details of the component. For example, a driver of a car does not need to know all the details of how the car accelerates; instead, he simply presses the gas pedal. Software engineering encourages the same approach, enabling users to use components through the interface, while preserving a highly flexible and maintainable system. That approach requires that one component can be easily replaced by a different component, such as plug and play.

Services can also be provided across system boundaries through inter-system communication. The most popular interfaces include standardized interfaces, such as SOAP. Using the Internet protocol, SOAP standardizes service communication among systems. For example, SOAP provides electronic Internet payment services as well as information exchange. This way, existing systems can request or provide services without exposing their internal details. Systems turn into users for other systems.

Use Higher-Level Tools and Languages

Invoking services for systems within the Internet is complex if you have to write everything at every step from scratch. The good news, though, is that modern languages such as Java offer a vast collection of class libraries to enable more efficient programming. The advantage is obvious; without getting bogged down in the inter-system communication, software engineers can now stay focused on their programming objectives. Equipped with these class libraries, systems are more reliable but also more maintainable because they use reusable assets. With the latest tools, software engineers create a visual design first, for example, in a standard notation like UML, before the design is transformed to code. Reducing this separation between design and code has many advantages. First, the architect and designer do not lose the big picture while working on the implementation detail. Engineers can drill down the architecture from the high level to get more detailed views on demand and vice versa. Second, the visual documentation of the system is generated on the fly while building the system. These visual models can serve as live data when architects present them to other stakeholders, such as senior management.

Focus on Architecture

Imagine one of the nonfunctional requirement states that a system shall process up to X trades for the stock exchange every second. Somewhere in the vision document, senior management states that a system with less capacity than X trades a second would not be considered useful. This requirement challenges the architecture significantly, because the entire success of the system depends on the successful implementation of this requirement. It would be foolish to postpone this requirement to later phases in the project. You need to determine Candidate architectures, based on finding the most promising architecture baselined. To reduce the risk even further, you can build architectural prototypes, using core components with their responsibilities, and interfaces. With sample data, the architecture is validated as proven, and the engineering process continues with one less critical risk on your mind.

Anti-Patterns

This anti-pattern works against elevating the level of abstraction.

Go Directly from Vague, High-Level Requirements to Custom-Crafted Code

During the early days of programming, without the tools and technology available today, programmers approached problems differently. Perhaps programmers specified procedures on paper but implemented the solution directly into code. Once the procedures were programmed, the paper trail of the solution often disappeared or was outdated the minute that changes to the code occurred. Even worse, other programmers had to get their mind around the logical path of the original author, which could require more time and sometimes an entire rewrite of the procedure. The chance of introducing new bugs and problems by touching existing code increased, while the programmer had little perspective on the overall architecture. More serious software engineers today call this practice hacking; it is similar to the idea of an architect who is going to build a family home and shows up with a shovel, ready to dig.

Focus Continuously on Quality

Quality begins with the start of the project, such as when an initial set of requirements is documented. The quality of a system is affected by the quality of the architecture, which is supported by the key principle of elevating the level of abstraction. This principle encourages re-use of assets on different levels. During implementation, code inspection and unit testing ensure that the source code is in synch with standards and style guides. People in the role of testers test the bigger picture, based on use case scenarios or nonfunctional requirements, such as performance and usability. Even though they often identify issues, the responsibility of finding errors must be shared among all team members. One successful way of finding errors is to test often and continuously. Also, the key principle of demonstrating value iteratively goes hand in hand with this principle. This is a perfect example of how these key principles encourage and support each other. The ongoing attention to quality will, in return, benefit the project in two significant ways: higher quality and earlier insight into progress and quality. Let's take a closer look at the patterns that provide these benefits.

Benefits

The following sections outline the benefits that result from a focus on quality.

Higher Quality

Quality is difficult to measure, especially when an ambiguous word like *higher* is put in front of it. No body or no thing is perfect, including IT systems. However, you can establish certain mechanisms to strive for the best quality possible. By applying the following patterns, you activate these mechanisms, leading to a higher quality product than you would get without applying them. Ensuring quality might consume project resources, but to a large degree test automation alleviates this concern.

Earlier Insight into Progress and Quality

The earlier you test, the earlier you learn about the progress you make. Many software engineers test their own code through unit testing, which is an essential piece of the overall testing strategy. A project's value, however, must be aligned with the technical correctness of its components from the point of view of system functionality, which is often expressed in use case scenarios. In an iterative-incremental approach, these components' functionality as expressed in use case scenarios and testing must harmonize with each other. Only tests conducted along the lines of functionality and use cases will expose the project's lack of quality or measurable progress.

Patterns

The patterns that help ensure a focus on quality are presented in this section.

Ensure Team Ownership of Quality for the Product

Establishing quality is a team effort and an ongoing activity. When we use the term *team*, we do not mean a team of testers. We mean the entire project team, including analysts, developers, managers, and, of course, testers. Job descriptions commonly give a rough outline of the work to be performed. That leaves behind a gray area where responsibilities are not as clearly defined and professionals either enlarge their job and grow into the position or they do not. For quality, this no-man's-land of job responsibility has a large impact. It could mean that problem identification is delayed or missed altogether.

In some cases, it might even help to be more distanced from the problem. Sometimes this can lead to useful, out-of-the-box thinking.

Test Early and Continuously in Step with Integration of the Demonstrable Capabilities

The next time you are in the early stages of a project, check the reactions of others when you ask for a test plan or a test script while others talk about high-level requirements. With more and more organizations applying iterative-incremental development, requests like this are more common, but you will still see today some dazzled faces. For example, in eXtreme Programming (Kent Beck), the unit tests are written prior to the code. If you don't know what to test, how would you know what to program? So through iterative-incremental development, there is not only early testing but a continuous testing in each iteration. In previous key principles, we have seen that the most important and riskiest features are implemented earlier. That means for an iterative-incremental cycle, these features get repetitive attention and are tested again and again. In a 12-month project (12 iterations over 4 weeks), how is your confidence level after the eleventh iteration? First, by then only low-ranked risks should be left for the twelfth iteration, so if worse comes to worst, there is still a system with the functionality from 11 iterations to deliver. Second, the highest risks items are mitigated and tested up to 11 times. These two things are significant differences from traditional software engineering, and they positively affect quality and feedback on progress.

Incrementally Build Test Automation

Every iteration introduces some new functionality that requires new test scenarios. However, executing all test scenarios from previous iterations is time consuming and allocates resources who could work on other activities. Yes, it might not be possible to automate every test scenario, but where test scripts are repeated, automated testing tools can support the tester in this activity by triggering a test script, providing input data, capturing output data, and capturing the pass or fail information. It is essential for a project to start early with test automation so that the benefits of repetition provide the biggest bang for the buck.

Anti-Patterns

The anti-patterns include in-depth peer review and completing unit testing before integration testing.

Conduct In-Depth Peer Review

When all the software engineers come together and spend time on design review and testing the design on paper, a major issue might be missed: application testing. Application testing is crucial for the success of the system, because it is commonly noticeable to customers and stakeholders who test the application as a black-box. If you observe this anti-pattern in a project, focus on executable software on an application level and record the results. All intermediate project artifacts have lower priority than testing the results.

Complete Unit Testing Before Integration Testing

Unit testing is important and is usually performed by the person who built the component. However, you need to test components in collaboration with other components and validate the integration. These tests can bring up issues with the component that require significant rework in their messages and methods. As discussed earlier, quality is a team sport, and the components must harmonize even among different software engineers. If you observe this anti-pattern, the application quality might come up short.

Summary

This chapter introduced the six key principles of business-driven development, including their patterns, their benefits, and their potential anti-patterns. On the exam, be prepared to address not only memorization questions about this topic but also how these principles impact RUP disciplines.

Sample Questions

You can find the correct answers to these questions in the Appendix, "Answers to Sample Questions."

1. Which of the following statements is true about the Adapt the Process key principle? (Select all that apply.)
   a. The one-size-fits-all approach does not apply to software development.
   b. The formality of artifacts will drive the quality of those artifacts.
   c. The process should be appropriately sized.
   d. Uncertainty drives planning and estimating.

2. Key benefits of the Adapt the Process key principle include which of the following? (Select all that apply.)
   a. Software development lifecycle efficiency is achieved.
   b. More ceremony is designed into the process.
   c. Risks are communicated in a more effective fashion.
   d. The process is sized correctly for the specific needs of the organization or the project.

3. Which of the following is an anti-pattern related to the key principle of Balancing Competing Stakeholder Priorities? (Select all that apply.)
   a. Balance asset re-use with user needs.
   b. Understand what assets can be leveraged.
   c. Thoroughly document precise requirements and force stakeholder acceptance.
   d. Architect the system only to meet the needs of the most vocal stakeholders.

4. Which of the following are the imperatives in effective collaboration? (Select all that apply.)
   a. To motivate individuals on the team to perform at their best
   b. To encourage functional collaboration
   c. To provide effective collaborative environments
   d. To integrate across business, software, and operation teams

5. Which of the following is a pattern that reflects the key principle of Collaborate Across Teams? (Select all that apply.)
   a. Motivate people to perform at their best.
   b. Create self-managed teams.
   c. Encourage team members to work the most hours.
   d. Manage evolving artifacts and tasks to enhance quality.

6. Which of the following items can be re-used? (Select all that apply.)
   a. Pattern
   b. Iteration
   c. Service
   d. Component

7. What benefits are directly linked to iterative-incremental development? (Select all that apply.)
   a. Higher quality
   b. Less testing
   c. Early reduction of risks
   d. Fewer requirements

8. Which of the following statements about quality is true? (Select all that apply.)
   a. Iterative development encourages continuous quality testing.
   b. Quality is noticeable only to the customer during user acceptance test.
   c. Quality assessment is useful only when done in later phases when requirements are stable.
   d. Elevating the level of abstraction improves quality.

9. Which of the following statements about risks is true? (Select all that apply.)
   a. Risks are managed iteratively.
   b. One risk is assigned to one iteration.
   c. Higher risks are tackled earlier then lower risks.
   d. Always start with low risks first, and then move to higher level risks.

10. Which of the following are key principles of business-driven development? (Select all that apply.)
    a. Demonstrate value iteratively.
    b. Use component architecture.
    c. Elevate the level of abstraction.
    d. Reduce stakeholder priorities.

References

Beck, K. (1999). *Extreme Programming Explained*. Upper Saddle River, NJ: Addison-Wesley.

Boehm, B. W., & Turner, R. (2003). *Balancing Agility and Discipline: A Guide for the Perplexed*. Boston, MA: Addison-Wesley.

Bradner, S. (1997). RFC 2119. Retrieved on August 30, 2006 from the World Wide Web at http://www.ietf.org/rfc/rfc2119.txt .

Brooks, F. P. Jr. (1987). *No Silver Bullet: Essence and Accidents of Software Engineering.* Los Alamitos, CA: IEEE Computer Society Press.

Carver, J., Shull, F., & Basili, V. (2003): Observational studies to accelerate process experience in classroom studies: An evaluation. Proceedings of the 2003 International Symposium on Empirical Software Engineering (ISESE '03), pp. 72–79.

Fenton, N. E., & Pfleeger, S. L. (1996). *Software Metrics: A rigorous and practical approach.* International Thomson Computer Press.

Fowler, M. (2005). *The New Methodology.* Retrieved from the World Wide Web at www.martinfowler.com on September 2, 2006.

Gamma, E., Helm, R., Johnson, R., & Vlissides, J. (1994). *Reusable Design Patterns.* Boston, MA: Addison-Wesley

Gause, D. & Weinberg, G. (1989). Exploring Requirements: *Quality before Design,* New York, NY: Dorset House

IBM Rational Unified Process v7.0.

Karlsson, J. (1998). A systematic approach for prioritizing software requirements. Linköping Studies in Science and Technology, Doctoral Dissertation No. 526. Department of Computer and Information Science. Linköping Institute of Technology, Sweden.

Krebs, J. *The Rational Edge* May, 2006. "Patterns in Action."

Kroll, P., & MacIsaac, B. (2006). *Agility and Discipline Made Easy: Practices from OpenUP and RUP.* Boston, MA: Addison-Wesley.

Kruchten, P. (2000). *The Rational Unified Process: An Introduction.* Boston, MA: Addison-Wesley.

Larman, C., Kruchten, P., & Bittner, K. http://www.agilealliance.org/system/article/file/941/file.pdf

Larman, C. (2004) *Applying UML and Patterns.* Third edition. Upper Saddle River, NJ: Prentice-Hall.

Leffingwell, D., & Widrig, D. (2003). *Managing Software Requirements.* Boston, MA: Pearson Education.

Schwaber, K., & Beedle, M. (2002). *Agile Software Development with SCRUM.* Upper Saddle River, NJ: Prentice Hall.

USC. (2003). *Overview of Software Engineering Principles.* http://sunset.usc.edu/~neno/cs589_2003/Week1.ppt on September 2, 2006.

PART II

Unified Method Architecture (UMA)

CHAPTER 3

Basic Content Elements

By Jochen Krebs

This chapter focuses primarily on the UMA elements that describe the schema elements for the static aspects of a process. These schema elements include artifacts, roles, tasks, and guidelines, to name a few. The elements are usually defined in human languages such as English.

Content revolves around the concept of tasks (with or without steps) that roles perform. Starting a task often requires input, and the result of a task is often output. These inputs and outputs are called work products. If a role requires help, or a task or work product requires more details, you can associate guidance elements to clarify. Content can be large and complex, but categories can help organize such content. Let's take a closer look at roles, work products, tasks, guidance elements, and categories.

Role

Picture a theatre play; similar to the way actors play out a designated role, members of an IT project play out their roles in a project. Sometimes, however, actors play multiple roles, and multiple actors might even share a role when, for example, the same musical is performed in many cities. The same thing happens in IT projects, when people are assigned to specific role(s) or multiple people act in the same role. Examples of roles in RUP include System Analyst and Project Manager. A **role** is defined as a set of related skills, competencies, and responsibilities. The people or tools in the roles perform tasks and produce work products. For some tasks and work products, those in the roles are directly responsible for performing the tasks and producing the work products. For other tasks and work products, those in the roles simply participate in accomplishing what's needed.

Work Product

UMA distinguishes among three different kinds of work products: artifact, outcome, and deliverable. **Artifacts** are tangible and can be nested in other artifacts. For example, a software development plan is an artifact that contains the risk-list artifact among others. An **outcome** is commonly intangible and not reused, which could be a state or result. For example, an outcome could be improved performance or a competed tool installation. A **deliverable** is intended to be value provided to stakeholders internally or externally. A deliverable consists of the other two work products: artifacts and outcomes. Deliverables are intended to package content from other work products to be consumed, for example, by stakeholders.

Work products are produced, consumed, or modified while a task is performed. Only one designated role is responsible for each work product.

Task

A task is an action performed by roles, associated with input and output (work products), and driven by a goal. An example of a goal might be to develop vision. The task describes the work to be performed and commonly an optional set of steps. Tasks usually last between a few hours and a few days and affect only a small number of work products. Because of their granularity, tasks are often repeated in iterations and are often too small for planning purposes.

Step

A step represents the most granular unit of work to be performed. It has a name and a textual description. Steps are useful for breaking down tasks into more granular elements. They define tasks in greater detail and can separate various aspects of the task. Even though steps are typically conceptualized as being sequential, as part of UMA, they are treated as optional and can be executed in any order that works to complete the task. As a general rule of thumb, steps may call upon the performing role to think, perform, or review.

Guidance

The following guidance types are optional elements that can be associated with tasks, work products, or process elements (Chapter 4). The intent behind them is to add more details to a certain element in a particular situation. The type of guidance determines the content of the element. There is no limit on how many guidance elements you can attach to other elements. You can also associate one guidance element with another. The following 14 guidance elements are listed in alphabetical order:

- Checklist

  Like a shopping list, a checklist allows you to specify a set of statements that can be used to check the completion of a set of activities but can also be attached to work products. This guidance is especially useful for reviews and status checks.

- Concept

  A concept guidance provides more context to key ideas used in the referenced element. For example, a concept for discipline might describe the basic principles, motivations, and advantages of grouping elements by disciplines.

- Estimation Consideration

  Each estimation consideration guidance offers additional information about a specific estimation technique. It provides sample situations in which the technique can be applied. Estimation consideration guidance elements usually reference other elements that require cost, schedule, or work-effort estimation.

- Example

  Examples show a practical application of a work product or task. For instance, a project plan template becomes more descriptive when a real example of the artifact is demonstrated. Examples provide a hands-on application of other content elements.

- Guideline

  A guideline element supplies more in-depth information about the referenced element, such as how to execute steps or complete work products. Guidelines are particularly useful for new users who need more assistance to complete their work. A guideline is equivalent, for example, to the instruction shipped with a tax return form. That guideline leads you through the actual form.

TIP

Remember the difference between a guidance and a guideline. **Guidance** is a generic name for all kinds of optional elements attached to process or content elements. A **guideline** is a specific instance or example of it.

- Practice

  Practice guidance elements describe positive, proven strategies that are applied in various situations. For example, the practice of iterative development impacts many tasks, work products, and roles and contributes to the overall success of the project.

- Report

  Report guidance elements describe the standards for predefined forms and layouts of information. They are often used in combination with tool automation when the structure and content of the generated report requires specification. The report guidance also describes the information extracted from work products.

- Reusable Asset

  Assets are useful elements that provide value and quality. If a solution provides value in various situations in a certain context, it can be treated as a reusable asset. A reusable asset might be, for example, a design pattern that can then be directly linked to a tool of choice (such as IBM Rational Software Architect).

- Roadmap

    Perhaps someone wants you to walk her through a process. A roadmap describes exactly such a request. Roadmap guidance elements are associated with activities to guide the user through a complex process, providing a start-to-finish scenario.

- Supporting Material

    Any required guidance elements that do not fit the definition of any of the other guidance elements can be described as supporting material. No specific intent is outlined other than the general purpose of providing a kind of guidance that can not be specified elsewhere.

- Template

    Template guidance elements provide a predefined structure to a work product. They are helpful for creating consistency in a project through the use of similar work products. For example, the various tax forms from the IRS use common templates in their form design.

- Term Definition

    A glossary contains term definitions. This guidance element defines and describes common concepts and puts them in a glossary. The individual terms can then be used in other content element descriptions to provide guidance similar to an encyclopedia. The glossary is automatically generated when the process is published and term definitions are not attached to other content elements like the rest of the guidance elements.

- Tool Mentor

    Many software engineering projects use tools to get their job done more efficiently and productively. Often, tools help in certain situations that are restricted to a task, activity, or work product. Tool mentors provide the technical and conceptual details to the user concerning how to apply the tools to the situation outlined in the process. For example, you could fill out your tax return statement with a typewriter (or pen) or by using the Internet. Two different tool mentors would support the same task depending on the applied context.

- Whitepaper

    This guidance element connects externally published papers to the process, providing a larger scope on the same concepts, different perspectives, and opinions. Whitepapers are commonly written and published independently and appear isolated from the process. Therefore, you can often add and remove them without consequence.

Categories

Categories are useful organizational and structural aids that can be used to group content elements. There are four standard categories: Discipline, Domain, Role Set, and Tool. There are also custom categories, which you can use to group method content of your choice. The four standard categories are defined as follows.

- Discipline

  Discipline categories aid in allocating certain content elements (that is, tasks, capability patterns, and guidance) to a certain area of concern. For example, you can group content related to project management under one umbrella. Content referring to disciplines helps users understand and group the overall complex process.

- Domain

  This category groups content elements based on resources, timing, or relationship. Compared to disciplines, domains can be broken down even further, into subdomains, creating a domain hierarchy. Even though domains often group content elements from the same discipline, such groupings are not limited to intradiscipline content.

- Role Set

  Large projects usually require more than one managerial role (for example, project manager versus deployment manager). Even though both roles are grouped into different domains and disciplines, the roles are associated with management. You can use the role set to categorize these roles and group them as managers.

- Tool Category

  In the tool category, tool mentors are usually bundled together as a unit to provide one view of all the tool mentors used.

Summary

The basic content elements introduced in this chapter bestow a diverse catalog of items that you can use to assemble and define process content. One of the most necessary elements is the work product. With outcomes, deliverables, and a vast list of guidance elements, the process engineer not only can describe the most diverse processes, but also typify each element. This gives the process consumer a chance to distinguish between optional and mandatory content. However, it also provides an expectation of the kind of content nested in each element.

Sample Questions

You can find the correct answers to these questions in the Appendix, "Answers to Sample Questions."

1. Which of the following could be input or output of a task? (Select all that apply.)
   a. Artifact
   b. Role
   c. Outcome
   d. Deliverable

2. A role is a set of related _____, _____, and _____. (Choose three.)
   a. Skills
   b. Competencies
   c. Tasks
   d. Responsibilities

3. Which of the following statements about work products is true? (Select all that apply.)
   a. Work products are always tangible.
   b. Work products are input to tasks.
   c. Work products require a guidance.
   d. Only one role is responsible for each work product.

4. How many performers can a task have?
   a. Always zero, because only steps are performed.
   b. One primary performer and only one additional performer
   c. One primary performer and multiple additional performers
   d. Many primary performers and several additional performers

5. Which of the following is a guidance element? (Choose two.)
   a. Guideline
   b. Checklist
   c. Work product
   d. Discipline

6. Which guidance element(s) can you use to give detail to the structure and layout of a work product?
   a. Checklist
   b. Guideline
   c. Tool mentor
   d. Template

7. Which statement is correct about the role-set category?
   a. Every role needs to be grouped in at least one role-set.
   b. A role set merges two roles into one.
   c. Role sets are optional and can group related roles.
   d. Role sets are predefined categories from the OMG.

8. Which of the following elements is a content element? (Choose all that apply.)
   a. Work product
   b. Role
   c. Task
   d. Activity

9. As a process engineer, you are being asked to deliver content for a solution to a common problem. Which guidance element would you choose?
   a. Checklist
   b. Practice
   c. Reusable asset
   d. Template

10. As a process engineer, you are being asked to deliver additional content to a work product, but none of the guidance elements seem to fit. Which one would you choose?
   a. Supplementary material
   b. Term
   c. Template
   d. Tool mentor

References

Haumer, P. IBM Rational method composer part I: Key concepts. http://www-128.ibm.com/developerworks/rational/library/dec05/haumer/. *The Rational Edge*, 12/05.

Haumer, P. IBM Rational method composer part II: Authoring method content and processes. http://www-128.ibm.com/developerworks/rational/library/jan06/haumer/index.html. *The Rational Edge*, 01/06.

IBM Rational Unified Process v7.0.

CHAPTER 4

Basic Process Elements

By Jochen Krebs

Process elements organize content elements into activities and lifecycles and give the content a sequential structure. These elements help answer questions about when content elements occur, either sequentially or in parallel. The advantage of separating the process elements from the content elements is that process engineers can assemble processes from existing content elements based on the needs of a particular project. You can even structure the process elements in a way that you can reuse them; such process elements are referred to as **capability patterns**. This chapter introduces these elements.

Process Elements

The UMA standardized activities, capability patterns, delivery processes, phases, and milestones arrange content elements in sequences using work breakdown structures. With the UMA, however, you can also arrange work in parallel, as often happens in iterative and agile software engineering process, such as RUP. Grouped in work breakdown structures, process engineers can build hierarchies of process elements in a top-down linear time flow or in a parallel fashion, when activities occur without strict time boundaries. Let's take a look at the definition and intent of the process elements, working through them in alphabetical order.

Activities

Method content (specifically tasks) is bundled into activities, which group a unit of work. In contrast to tasks, activities are not considered method content because they are work breakdown elements. The sequence of the elements in the work breakdown structure orders the activities for execution or parallelism depending on the process authoring. Because activities might contain other activities, the process engineer can create everything from a simple to a complex activity hierarchy, depending on the need. The following four elements are special forms of activities (stereotypes) that provide additional semantics to the activity depending on their purpose.

Iteration

RUP is an example of iterative-incremental software engineering. Iterations are frequently planned and executed throughout all phases. The iteration process element allows process engineers to group activities that are planned to be repeated more than once. Iterations represent a special form of activity.

Phase

A phase element groups process elements into a significant period in a project. Phases are often related to different views or project perspectives. For example, in RUP, the Elaboration phase takes a different perspective and emphasis on a project than the Construction phase does. Phases are not expected to be repeated as activities or iterations are, but they are a variation of an activity concept.

Capability Pattern

Capability patterns are incomplete process fragments that can contain activities and milestones. Grouping common process elements into capability patterns enables process engineers to re-use these process fragments and compose delivery processes from them. If a common pattern, such as plan iteration, is needed in different parts of the delivery process, a capability pattern can be formed and re-used.

Delivery Process

The intent of a delivery process is to publish and deploy what is grouped so the user can eventually consume it. Delivery processes are end-to-end project lifecycles assembled from a set of activities, phases, iterations, capability patterns, and milestones. For example, RUP out-of-the-box is delivered with three delivery processes: classic, small, and medium RUP.

Milestone

Milestones are decision points. They might follow an activity, capability pattern, phase, or iteration to verify a certain situation followed by a decision. Milestones are often associated with metrics that compare a plan with the actual result. The lifecycle objective (LCO) is an example of a milestone in RUP.

Process Package

For organizational purposes, process packages group process elements into folders. These folders are optional and can be used to group solely capability patterns or delivery processes in the style of choice.

Process Diagrams

In addition to work breakdown structures, UMA supports visual representations of process elements. Three diagrams are relevant in the context of RUP. The three diagrams are the workflow diagram, the activity detail diagram, and the work-product dependency diagram. The entire set of UMA elements has a textual and visual representation according to the UMA superstructure. So far, we described the elements mainly textually. By looking at the process diagram, however, we use the visual representation of the elements and focus on the content and intent of the diagram.

Workflow Diagram

The workflow diagram (see Figure 4-1), which is a tailored version of the UML activity diagram, can contain a start and end point, decision nodes, links, activities, synchronization bars, task descriptors phases, and milestones. The workflow diagram provides a high-level overview of the activities and their sequence. The guards allow branching in certain situations, whereas the synchronization bars demonstrate which activities are performed in parallel. The user can drill down into each activity to retrieve an activity detail diagram to get further details on the activity.

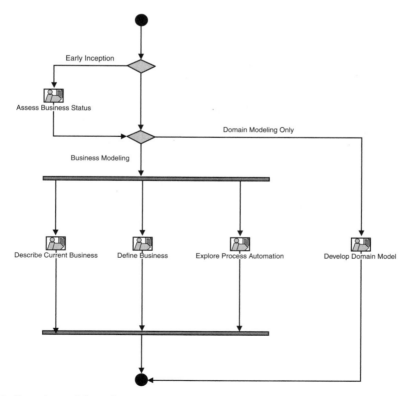

Figure 4-1 Sample workflow diagram

Synchronization bars show possible parallelism among the activities. The arrows on the links show the order between the process elements.

Activity Detail Diagram

The activity detail diagram gives a visual overview of the task descriptors within an activity, the responsible role descriptors associated with the task descriptors, and the input and output work product descriptor. The two diagrams in Figure 4-2 show for each responsible role horizontally (in the example, the Process Engineer and the Tool Specialist) the list of task descriptors in the activity and vertically the flow of work product descriptors. A **descriptor** is basically a reference object inside a process that represents the occurrence of a method content element, such as a task or work product inside an activity. It has its own relationships and documentation that defines the difference between the default implementation and this particular occurrence of the element in the process.

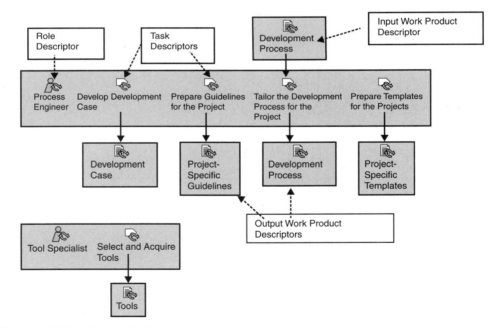

Figure 4-2 Sample activity detail diagram

Work-Product Dependency Diagram

The work-product dependency diagram (see Figure 4-3) illustrates the relationships and dependencies among various work products.

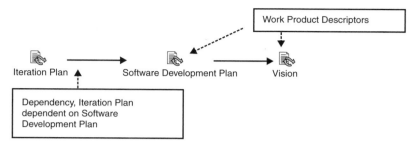

Iteration Plan   Software Development Plan   Vision

Work Product Descriptors

Dependency, Iteration Plan
dependent on Software
Development Plan

Figure 4-3 Work-product dependency diagram sample

Descriptors

To utilize the same content elements in different aspects of process elements (for example, capability patterns), use the common concept called descriptors. These descriptors replace the actual content element (role, task, and work-product) in the context of the activity in which the element was accessed. Therefore, within work breakdown structures, you use role descriptors, task descriptors, and work-product descriptors. The advantage of using descriptors over content elements is that you can adjust the used content element (role, task, or work-product) to the current situation without changing the actual source of the content. Also, a task descriptor, for example, can remove steps from a task, making content elements more versatile when processes are assembled. The user, however, will always be able to track back from the descriptor to the content element to which the descriptor refers. Therefore, all the roles, tasks, and work-products used in Figure 4-2 and Figure 4-3 are actually the descriptors of the element, not the element itself.

There are three kinds of descriptors: Work Breakdown descriptors, Role descriptors, and Task descriptors. Each of them shares the following attributes important for process authoring:

- **isPlanned**—Indicates whether a breakdown element is marked for inclusion in a generated project plan.

- **hasMultipleOccurances**—Indicates whether a breakdown element is generated multiple times, maybe even in parallel.

- **isOptional**—Indicates whether the breakdown element is optional or mandatory when a project is carried out.

Furthermore, the task descriptor contains three additional attributes:

- **isRepeatable**—Indicates whether a breakdown element (for example, a task descriptor) is expected to repeat sequentially over the same set of work-products (for example, an iteration).

- **isEventDriven**—Indicates whether a certain event has to occur before the planned element is performed. Without the event, the work does not need to be done. For example, an event issuing a change request triggers tasks that deal with the change request.

- **isOngoing**—Indicates whether the element has no exact duration and has to be continuously planned for. For example, the Project Management Office might periodically check the compliance of a project to a certain standard.

TIP

Knowledge about the breakdown element attributes is important for process engineers who need to align the content elements with the process depending on a project situation. Questions about the attributes, however, are not part of the exam.

Summary

The basic process elements align the content elements introduced in the previous chapter to a time sequence. This chapter defined the terms activity, phase, iteration, delivery process, capability pattern, and milestone. In addition, it discussed the process package to organize and group these elements. Visualization is an important aspect of reviewing and sharing processes. The workflow diagram, activity detail diagram, and work-product dependency diagram are the potential choices. Last, but not least, this chapter covered the role of descriptors and their attributes. With their help, the process engineer can more easily generate project plans with a variety of flavors of the referenced content element, without actually changing the content element.

Sample Questions

You can find the correct answers to these questions in the Appendix, "Answers to Sample Questions."

1. Which type of process element is used to describe a phase?
   a. Activity Descriptor
   b. Task
   c. Activity
   d. Task Descriptor

2. Which of the following is a process element? (Select all that apply.)
   a. Capability Pattern
   b. Activity
   c. Roadmap
   d. Delivery Process

3. Which of the following is a delivery process in RUP for large projects?
   a. Classic RUP lifecycle
   b. Supporting process with tools
   c. Delivery Process
   d. Capability Pattern

4. Which of the following is a valid descriptor? (Select all that apply.)
   a. Task Descriptor
   b. Role Descriptor
   c. Activity Descriptor
   d. Work-Product Descriptor

5. Which process element can you place in a process package? (Select all that apply.)
   a. Capability Pattern
   b. Activity
   c. Delivery Process
   d. Milestone

6. Which statement is true about descriptors? (Select all that apply.)
   a. Descriptors replace content elements in the work-breakdown structure.
   b. Descriptors point back to their referenced content element.
   c. Descriptors modify the content element.
   d. Descriptors are rarely used.

7. As a process engineer, you are asked to provide a process lifecycle to Project X. You start from scratch to design a process lifecycle for Project X, but then you realize that the process lifecycle of the project you are coming off of, Project Y, is only slightly different. You could re-use aspects of Project Y. To promote re-use, to which element of Project Y would you direct your attention?
   a. Descriptors
   b. Capability Patterns
   c. Work-Product Dependency diagram
   d. Classic RUP Lifecycle

8. Which of the following is a notational element used in a workflow diagram? (Select all that apply.)
   a. Link
   b. Activity
   c. Synchronization bar
   d. Task

9. An activity detail diagram contains which of the following? (Select all that apply.)
   a. Activities
   b. Task Descriptors
   c. Role Descriptors
   d. Milestones

10. Which of the following process elements is a special representation of an activity? (Select all that apply.)

    a. Phase

    b. Activity Detail

    c. Task

    d. Iteration

References

IBM Rational Unified Process v7.0.

PART III

Rational Unified Process: Content and Process Elements

CHAPTER 5

Business Modeling

By Ahmad K. Shuja and Jochen Krebs

Business Modeling plays an important role in analyzing the intended functions of a business and how those functions are realized. In short, business modeling enables a deeper and clearer understanding of the business operations, which constitutes one of the most important inputs into a system's development. In this chapter, you will learn about the most effective way to perform business modeling in an iterative and incremental development lifecycle.

Overview

Does every project require business modeling? No! Do projects benefit from it? Yes! With that said, many subject matter experts (SME) have exactly this information in their heads when they initiate and participate in IT projects. For example, the target organization assessment that describes the current state of the organization or the business goals is often communicated verbally in meetings and announcements. The discipline of business modeling captures that information, and the result is various work products that become accessible to the project team even though they were not included in the initial meetings.

Often, the business vision and its objectives are defined much earlier than IT projects are initiated, which creates a distance between the early business analysis and the vision of the software project. Even though RUP strongly recommends business modeling for projects that start new businesses or re-engineer existing businesses, it is optional for so-called improvement projects. RUP also includes business modeling in the iterative development lifecycle, which reduces the time between defining the business vision and implementing it. As an important side effect, the target organization can draw conclusions from the iterative development effort, which can lead to more optimization in the automation of the business.

Business modeling work products—whether newly created or re-used existing ones—connect the business strategy with software requirements engineering introduced in Chapter 6, "Requirements."

Purpose

The Business Modeling discipline has several purposes:

- To understand problems in the target organization and identify potential improvements
- To ensure customers and end users have a common understanding of the target organization
- To derive system requirements to support the target organization
- To understand the structure and dynamics of the organization in which the system is to be deployed

Business Modeling Discipline Workflow

The Business Modeling workflow is shown in Figure 5-1.

As you can see, you can take several paths through the Business Modeling workflow. The decision is derived from the purpose of the business modeling effort as well as the phase in the software development lifecycle. We will go into more detail concerning these different paths during our discussion later in this section.

The workflow enables us to see various activities performed within the Business Modeling discipline and the sequence in which these should be performed. Please note that this sequence *does not* imply that one activity is completely finished before you can move on to the next one. In fact, each of these activities is performed multiple times throughout the project lifecycle. Every time an activity is repeated, the associated work products are further detailed or refined based on increased knowledge. This sequence is significant from the perspective that you need to achieve certain goals at some level prior to initiation of the following activities. The following sections outline the key business modeling activities.

Assess Business Status

In the early iterations, most likely the first one, you assess the status of the organization and identify areas needing improvement. You do this during the Assess Business Status stage, and based on the results, you can make an intelligent decision regarding the next steps. The goal is to limit the business modeling effort. After you've described the current state, you define the target state in the business vision. This ensures that you clearly understand and can define the problem to be solved or the opportunity to be exploited. Assessing business status involves assessing the target organization, setting and adjusting objectives, identifying and documenting business goals, and analyzing business architecture. The key work product created as a result of this activity is the Target Organization Assessment, which is discussed later in this chapter.

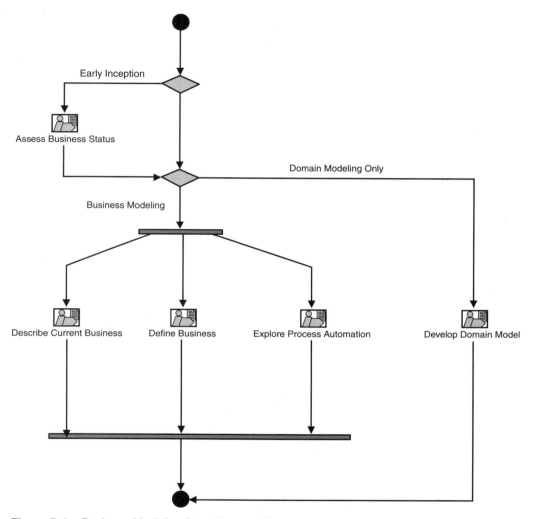

Figure 5-1   Business Modeling Discipline workflow

Describe Current Business

If you establish during the Assess Business Status activity that you will make no major changes to the business processes, and your intention is to develop a software system that will help automate existing business processes, then all that is required is to model those processes and software requirements in subsequent activities. Typically, though, you define or refine the organization structure first, and then you define business goals along with business actors and business use cases, which you should trace back to the business goals that they support. Based on the Business Modeling objectives, you can prioritize the business use cases and then produce the business use-case realizations for the highest-priority business use cases. As you perform these activities, you gain more knowledge about the business and accordingly refine objectives and expectations. Successful completion of this activity involves assessing the target organization, setting and adjusting objectives, identifying business goals, finding business actors and use cases, and performing analysis of the business architecture.

Define Business

This activity defines the to-be business. It involves identifying the business process and refining the business process definitions. If you apply the use-case realization approach, you design business process realizations via use-case realizations. Otherwise, you define business operations. Finally, you refine roles and responsibilities. The Define Business activity consists of the workflow shown in Figure 5-2.

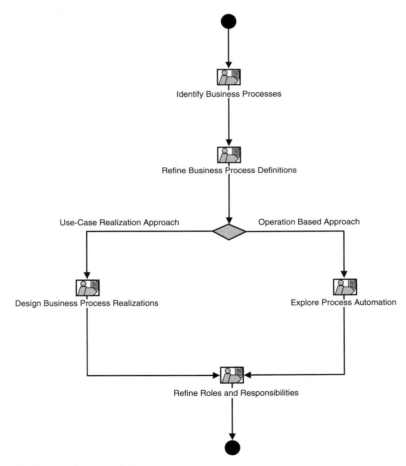

Figure 5-2   Define business activity

You perform the **Identify Business Processes** activity to define business goals that support the business strategy, to outline the Business Use-Case Model, and to prioritize the business use cases that need to be described in detail. High-priority business use cases are then further detailed in the **Refine Business Process Definitions** activity. In this activity, a subset of the business processes are detailed in the form of business use cases and linked to business goals. These business use cases must support the business goals. In addition, these business use cases reflect how the business is actually conducted. If you take the use-case approach, then you can design the to-be business use-case realizations in terms of collaborations of business systems and business workers during the **Design Business Process Realizations** activity. If you select an operations-based approach, then the business subsystems define operations during the **Define Business Operations** activity. Finally, independent of which approach you adopt, you detail the business systems, business workers, business entities, and business events and refine their respective responsibilities during the **Refine Roles and Responsibilities** activity. In addition, you verify that the results of business modeling conform to the stakeholders' view of the business.

Explore Process Automation

This activity explores the automation opportunities for the business processes under consideration; details how software systems that are to be acquired, developed, or deployed will fit into the organization; and produces a business model from which to derive software requirements. Note that automation can range from supporting the effort to improve lead times of business use cases, to reorganizing or sequencing the activities of a business process, to monitoring, controlling, and improving the way of working. As a result of experience gained in exploring process automation opportunities, the team might be able to adjust objectives and expectations to make them more practical. This activity analyzes the business use cases to determine which offer the greatest potential for improvement at the least cost, which is a trade-off between smaller short-term benefits for relatively less effort and potentially huge long-term benefits at a greater cost.

Develop Domain Model

If you determine during the Assess Business Status activity that you don't need full-scale business models and require only a domain model, you can perform the Develop Domain Model activity. A domain model in RUP is considered a subset of the Business Analysis model surrounding only the business entities of that model. This activity identifies all products and deliverables important to the business domain, details the business entities, and provides a common understanding of the concepts found in the business operations and environment.

Work Products

This section briefly reviews the key work products, each of which forms a part of the Business Modeling work products set. The Business Modeling discipline produces the work products described in the following sections.

Business Analysis Model

The Business Analysis model contains the business events, business use-case realizations, business workers, business entities, business systems, and business rules work products. You use this model to communicate to stakeholders the impact on the current organization by performing as-is and to-be scenarios. The scenarios document the existing business process and describe ideal scenarios. This allows you to compare the diagrams and helps System Analysts identify requirements. If automation of business requirements is possible and desired, the system analyst derives system requirements from this model.

Business Architecture Document

The business architecture document presents the business architectures as a set of different views of the architecture. Some sample views include the organization view, the domain view, and the geographic view. Taken together, these views facilitate communication among project team members and stakeholders. The set of views reflect what the business is, how it is and should be performed, and where the business is conducted.

Business Deployment Model

This model depicts how the logical business elements described in the business architecture and Business Analysis model are assigned to physical entities such as localities (geographical units). This work product is commonly needed only in large business modeling efforts.

Business Design Model

This model is a realization of the Business Analysis model. During the realization, abstract elements are made concrete and mapped, for example, from business workers to other humans or systems. This design model answers questions such as those concerned with how the business functions and how it is planned to function in the future.

Business Architectural Proof-of-Concept

This work product describes the approach for a potential solution to satisfy the architecturally significant business requirements. This feasibility could be demonstrated through a prototype, a visual representation, or a simulation.

Business Use-Case Model

The Business Use-Case Model contains business actors, business use cases, and business goals work products. The business goals are derived from the business strategy and aligned with the intent outlined in business use case scenarios and role assignments to business actors. Besides communication with stakeholders, the project manager uses this model for iteration planning.

Business Vision

The scope of the business vision is to describe the objectives and goals of the business modeling effort. For small efforts, such as for business improvement, you might focus on the summary sections in the vision, whereas the full version of the vision elaborates on details important for business process re-engineering and new business modeling efforts. Because of its high-level focus, the business vision is an excellent vehicle to communicate with senior management and reiterate the purpose of the project with all stakeholders throughout the entire project.

Target Organization Assessment

This work product provides insight into the "organization under design" and describes the current status of the organization in which the system is to be deployed. This description includes important information about current processes, skill-sets, tools, market demographics, competition, technical trends, problems, and improvement areas. Target Organization Assessment is utilized to

- Provide the rationale and explain to the stakeholders why it's necessary to change the business processes
- Create a common understanding and motivate people in the target organization
- Provide input to the Development Case and the Iteration Plans

Roles and Responsibilities

Each role within the Business Modeling discipline is described along with a diagram showing the tasks that the role performs and the work products for which the role is responsible. Remember that tasks represent the detailed description of work for the role to perform from a method perspective; tasks are grouped into activities when defining a process.

Business Process Analyst

This role owns the business requirements gathering process. Within a given boundary (the target organization), the Business Process Analyst mainly articulates the business vision and leads the business use-case modeling, among others. Often, the same person performs this role and the role of the business designer. The responsibilities of this role are described in more detail in Figure 5-3.

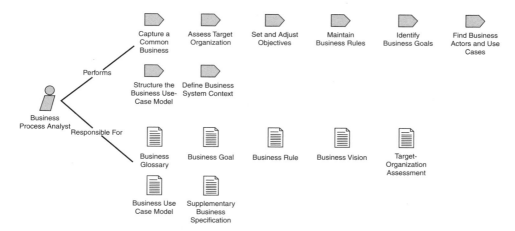

Figure 5-3   Responsibilities of Business Process Analyst

Business Architect

The Business Architect is responsible for describing the statics (structure) and the dynamics (behavior) of a business architecture. Figure 5-4 outlines in more detail the responsibilities of the Business Architect.

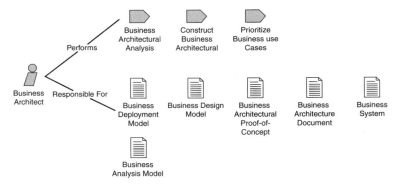

Figure 5-4   Responsibilities of Business Architect

Business Designer

This role develops the business use cases and their relationships and interfaces. That includes the definition of business worker, business entity, business event, and business operations. In larger business modeling activities, business design is split into pieces and assigned to multiple people enacting the role of business designer. Figure 5-5 presents the responsibilities of the Business Designer.

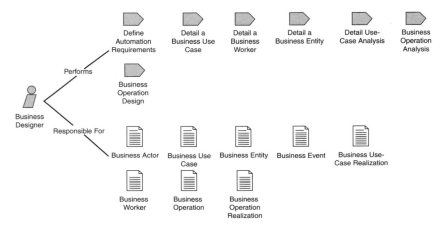

Figure 5-5   Responsibilities of Business Designer

Technical Reviewer

In the context of business modeling, the technical reviewer provides feedback concerning the Business Use-Case Model and the Business Analysis Model. The Technical Reviewer's responsibilities are illustrated in Figure 5-6. Note that the Technical Reviewer does perform reviews across other disciplines as well. However, Figure 5-6 shows only those related to Business Modeling.

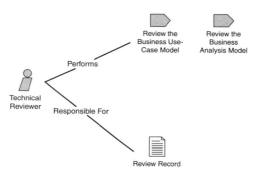

Figure 5-6   Responsibilities of Technical Reviewer

Important Concepts

The Business Modeling concepts are discussed in this section. These concepts are important from both understanding the discipline as well as examination perspectives.

Business Modeling and Software Development

Especially in business-driven software development, automating the business process is essential, because it increases the pace at which information can be delivered and received. These optimizations often lead to decreased internal costs and customer satisfaction. To achieve a competitive advantage, you must align business modeling with software development by carefully analyzing the existing target organization and existing business processes before designing the to-be business. The business vision ties these views together and gives the software engineering team important measures for project success.

If executed independently, business modeling can result in several separate software development projects. When executed in the same lifecycle with the software development project, this discipline provides iteratively refined input for the Requirements discipline. For acceptance testing, the test manager can build test strategies around the business vision and measure against the business design document.

Domain Modeling

A domain model is also referred to as an "incomplete" business analysis model. It describes the information of the business entities, their relationships, and their dependencies. Domain models are created in visual notation, such as UML. They condense the terminology and entities of the business domain and provide valuable input to system analysts whenever business analysis needs to be partially performed on a fast track.

Summary

Even though business modeling is not per-se a software engineering–centric discipline, the RUP for large projects offers business modeling as an optional discipline. The Business Process Analyst and the Business Architect are responsible for defining the present and future business organization and processes. The business architecture document, the business use-case model, the business design model, and the target organization assessment are key work products developed in this discipline.

Sample Questions

You can find the correct answers to these questions in the Appendix, "Answers to Sample Questions."

1. Which of the following statements is true about Business Modeling? (Select all that apply.)
   a. Supports the derivation of software requirements
   b. Is not always mandatory
   c. Aligns the corporate business strategy with software development
   d. Replaces the requirements discipline for business-driven software projects

2. Which work products are part of the Business Use-Case Model? (Select all that apply.)
   a. Business Actor
   b. Business Use Case
   c. Business Worker
   d. Business Goal

3. Which of the following roles is part of Business Modeling? (Select all that apply.)
   a. System Analyst
   b. Business Process Analyst
   c. Business Architect
   d. Test Architect

4. Which Business Modeling activity is performed first?
   a. Explore Process Automation
   b. Develop Domain Model
   c. Describe Current Business
   d. Define Business Vision

5. Which document describes business realization?
   a. Business Goal
   b. Business Entity
   c. Business Architectural Proof-Of-Concept
   d. Business Design Model

6. Who is responsible for the business vision artifact?
   a. CEO
   b. Functional Manager
   c. Business Process Analyst
   d. Business Architect

7. Who is responsible for the Business Design model?
   a. Project Manager
   b. Designer
   c. Business Architect
   d. Business Process Analyst

8. Which of the following role combinations participates in developing the Business Use-Case Model?
   a. Business Process Analyst, Business Architect
   b. Business Architect, Technical Reviewer
   c. Business Process Analyst, Technical Reviewer
   d. Business Process Analyst, Project Manager

9. Which of the following is true of the Target Organization Assessment work product? (Select all that apply.)
   a. Describes current processes
   b. Describes current customers
   c. Describes current tools
   d. Describes current finances

10. Which of the following is correct about the Business Deployment model?
   a. Describes the mapping between abstract and concrete business elements
   b. Describes the mapping between logical and physical business elements
   c. Describes the mapping between logical and rational business elements
   d. Describes the mapping between rational and irrational business goals

References

IBM Rational Unified Process v7.0.

CHAPTER 6

Requirements

By Ahmad K. Shuja

This chapter reviews the activities performed to ensure that the stakeholder requests are captured appropriately and transformed into a set of requirements artifacts. These requirements artifacts enable you to establish the scope of the system to be built and provide detailed requirements for what the system must do. Each of the activities discussed represents a high-level goal to achieve to perform effective requirements management.

Overview

Requirements management is a term describing the activities involved in eliciting, documenting, and maintaining a set of requirements for a software system. It is about discovering what the stakeholders need the system to do for them. Incomplete requirements and lack of user involvement are the two top reasons cited for project failure [Standish 1]. Both of these issues are failures in requirements engineering.

The Requirements discipline consists of activities that ensure effective requirements engineering and management and describes how to create a vision and translate it into a Use-Case Model. The vision in the Requirements discipline defines how the stakeholders view the system in terms of key needs and features.

As shown in Figure 6-1, traceability is critical as we transition from stakeholder needs to features through software requirements to the actual system design and implementation. It is important to note that the purpose of the requirements tracing is to do the following:

- Verify that all requirements of the system are fulfilled by the implementation.
- Verify that the application does only what it was intended to do.
- Help manage change.

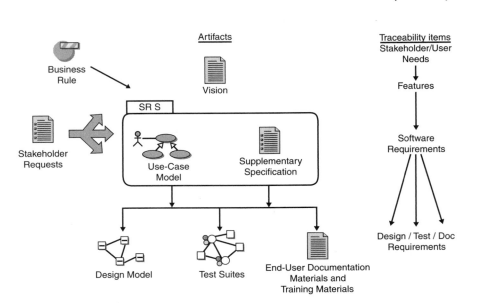

Figure 6-1   From stakeholder needs to final solution

The flow from stakeholder needs to the actual system implementation does not happen in a sequence. Figure 6-1 is intended to show the traceability of the requirements and not the flow of development to realize them. This chapter discusses the evolution of these key artifacts and associated activities in detail.

Purpose

The purpose of the Requirements discipline is to do the following.

- Establish and maintain agreement with the customers and other stakeholders on what the system should do.
- Provide system developers with a better understanding of the system requirements.
- Define the boundaries of (delimit) the system.
- Provide a basis for planning the technical contents of iterations.
- Provide a basis for estimating cost and time to develop the system.
- Define a user interface for the system, focusing on the needs and goals of the users.

Requirements Workflow

The Requirements workflow is shown in Figure 6-2. This workflow enables us to see various activities performed within the Requirements discipline and the sequence in which to perform them. As mentioned earlier, each activity represents a high-level goal that needs to be achieved to perform effective requirements management. Activities can be further decomposed into subactivities or tasks, and tasks can be further decomposed into steps. We will discuss requirements activities and related artifacts as they relate to requirements engineering and management. More details on tasks and steps and a complete discussion of artifacts can be found in the RUP web-based product.

Note that although Figure 6-2 shows the activities in a logical, sequential order, these activities are applied continuously in varied order, as needed, throughout the project. During the Inception phase, the primary requirement goals are to analyze the problem and understand the stakeholders' needs, whereas during later Elaboration and Construction phases of the RUP lifecycle, the emphasis shifts more toward defining and subsequently refining the system definition in terms of the detailed requirements. Note that managing the system scope and ongoing requirements changes is addressed continuously throughout the project.

Each activity area is explored in the rest of this section.

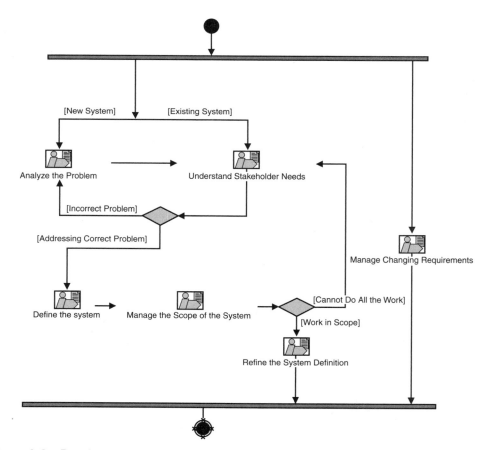

Figure 6-2   Requirements workflow

Analyze the Problem

This activity is especially important if the team is trying to solve a new problem or realize a new opportunity and there is no existing solution in place. Whenever we engage in such a project, we need to understand who the stakeholders are, what the scope (boundaries) of the system is, and what the different constraints imposed on the system are, due to government regulations, end users' unique needs, and others. This activity concludes with an agreement on the problem being solved and proposes a high-level solution.

To ensure that the problem to be solved is understood and that there is an agreement among all the relevant stakeholders, we must carefully identify the stakeholders. Stakeholders can represent different parts of the organization and might have different stakes in the project. It is important to ensure that we all speak the same language. To minimize the potential for confusion or misunderstanding, we can maintain a consistent set of definitions in the **Glossary**, which is maintained throughout the project lifecycle. The **System Analyst** is responsible for **Capturing a Common Vocabulary** and producing the Glossary.

After they're identified, these stakeholders assist in determining the set of features to be considered in developing the software solution. There are a couple of ways to gather these features, one of which is a Requirements workshop. These features, once identified, need to have some form of priority associated with them so that dependencies and work plans can be effectively managed. The information on priority, source, and other related elements is captured in **Requirements Attributes**. The problem or opportunity and the features, which represent the high-level user or customer view of the system to be built, are captured in the **Vision** for the project. The Vision is developed to define the stakeholder's view of the product to be developed, specified in terms of the stakeholder key needs and features. It contains an outline of the envisioned core requirements, so it provides a contractual basis for the more detailed technical requirements. The primary purpose of defining the vision is to correctly scope the project. The Vision document is written from the customer's perspective, focusing on the essential features of the system and the acceptable levels of quality. The Vision should include a description of what features will be included as well as those considered but not included. It should also specify operational capacities, user profiles, and interoperational interfaces. The System Analyst is responsible for developing the Vision. Note that the Business Case and the Iteration Plan, which belong to the Business Modeling and Project Management disciplines respectively, contribute toward the creation of the Vision.

One of the key objectives of the Analyze the Problem activity is to agree on the boundaries of the system. Traditionally, this is called the **scope** of the system. To scope the system and agree on its boundaries, the System Analyst identifies users and systems that will interact with the system being developed. This boundary of the system and the respective users are modeled by the Actor artifact in the Use-Case Model. We have a more detailed discussion of the Use-Case Model in the next section.

One of the other key artifacts required to be produced early in the project is the **Requirements Management Plan**. This plan provides guidance on the requirements artifacts that should be developed, different requirements types (discussed in the next section) that should be managed for the project, the relevant requirement attributes that should be collected, and the approach to requirements traceability that will be used in managing the product requirements. The System Analyst develops the Requirements Management Plan.

Note that the Analyze the Problem activity and the associated tasks help us satisfy some of the patterns associated with the key principle of Balancing Competing Stakeholder Priorities. Specifically, gaining a consistent understanding of the stakeholders' view of the system and prioritizing these in the form of requirements attributes help the project team establish a common goal of the project.

Understand Stakeholder Needs

A requirement is something that we expect the system to meet. According to the RUP, a **requirement** is defined as "a condition or capability to which a system must conform." So where does it originate? Who says that we need to meet this requirement? Who decides which requirements need to be met to achieve maximum business value? Is there a relationship between business vision and the stakeholders' needs? How do we know that the requirement has been met? These are just a subset of all the questions that might come to your mind whenever you think about requirements. In this section, we will try to address most of these and similar questions and concerns.

If this project is an enhancement of an existing system, then the first activity is to understand the stakeholder needs. The assumption here is that if it is an existing system, we will already have a clear understanding of the stakeholders and will need to engage them to understand the evolving needs. However, if this is not an existing system, then the first activity is to Analyze the Problem, which was discussed earlier.

So, at this point in the life of requirements, we know about the stakeholders and we need to gain a deeper understanding of the stakeholder/user needs. Stakeholders/users might have many expectations from the new system or from the next enhanced release of the existing system. Some of these expectations can be mapped directly to features that, if provided by the system, will help meet those needs. Others may be wishes—things that are important, even though we are not exactly sure how the system is going to meet them. The first and most important task is to define and achieve some level of understanding of these requirements. Therefore, this activity addresses collecting and eliciting information from the stakeholders in the project to understand what their needs are.

Defining and understanding any type of request that a stakeholder/user (customer, user, marketing person, sponsor, and so on) might have is one of the essential elements to effectively develop the vision for the project. Note that these requests can also contain references to any type of external sources to which the system must comply. For example, the financial services industry has many regulatory requirements from government agencies—specifically related to information security and privacy in addition to others—that the system has to meet before it can be put into production.

Stakeholder Requests capture all requests made on the project, as well as how these requests will be addressed. Some examples of the sources of stakeholder requests include stakeholder interviews, requirements elicitation workshops, change requests, statement of work, problem statement, laws and regulations, and others. After going through the stakeholder requests the first time and producing the vision, you might need to revisit some of the requests to refine them based on the increased understanding you have achieved. You will encounter these throughout our discussion.

The **Storyboard**™ plays an important role in building a clearer understanding of the stakeholder needs. The Storyboard artifact is a logical and conceptual description of system functionality for a specific scenario, including interaction required between the system users and the system. A Storyboard models and tells a specific story. You can use Storyboards to explore, understand, and analyze the behavioral requirements of the system, especially how the users will interact with the system. You can express Storyboards using visual or textual representations or a combination of both. Some examples of ways to visualize storyboards include paper sketches or pictures, index cards, PowerPoint slides, or screen shots. Requirements attributes describe a repository of project requirements, attributes, and dependencies to assist in managing change from a requirements perspective.

The Understand Stakeholder Needs activity also contributes toward refining the Vision and Requirements attributes. If it is for a new system, you have already started identifying actors and use cases in the Analyze the Problem activity. If this is an enhancement project, you can start discussing the functional requirements of the system in terms of its use cases and actors. Here, you will realize that certain requirements do not fit appropriately within the use cases. Such requirements are documented in the **Supplementary Specifications**.

As you discover additional requirements, managing dependencies through ensuring traceability becomes more and more important. To ensure that dependencies are appropriately managed, the System Analyst is responsible for managing dependencies and refining the Requirements Management Plan, the Requirements attributes, the Vision, and the Glossary.

Define the System

The main purpose of this activity is to begin converging on the scope of the high-level requirements by outlining the breadth of the detailed requirements for the system. As we discuss this activity in greater detail, you will see that most of the tasks to be performed within this activity have already been performed earlier. Why is it significant? Because most of the work products will be further refined during this activity.

By utilizing the information gathered so far about the project, this activity helps achieve alignment across the team in their understanding of the system. High-level analysis of the Stakeholder Requests is performed to ensure that stakeholders' needs are considered as we further define the system. The Vision and the Use-Case Model are further refined. Specifically, in the Use-Case Model, use cases are now outlined. During the Find Actors and Use Cases task, actors and use cases are identified more completely by outlining their content. As a result of a deeper understanding of the use cases, non-use-case-specific requirements are further documented or refined in the Supplementary Specification.

The main emphasis during this activity is to focus on problem analysis and gaining further understanding of the stakeholders' needs. Features identified in the Vision are considered, and key system definitions of the system are produced. As you continue to define new requirements, the Glossary is further refined as additional common terms are identified. Managing dependencies across requirements becomes more critical.

Manage the Scope of the System

This activity ensures that the scope of the system being developed is as explicit as possible and that the main focus is to keep the body of requirements work for a development cycle as manageable as possible. An important concept that contributes toward keeping the body of requirements work manageable is prioritization. In iterative and incremental development, prioritization plays a key role in selecting the features and requirements that are to be included in the current iteration. An associated task is Prioritize Use Cases, which is where architecturally significant use cases are identified and prioritized so that their order of development can be decided.

The Software Architect prioritizes the use cases. For architecturally significant use cases that represent some central functionality, behavioral scenarios are defined to gain clearer understanding. Factors that make use cases architecturally significant include the benefits to the stakeholder, the architectural impact, the risks to be mitigated, the completion of the architectural coverage, and other key objectives and imposed constraints. Prioritize poorly understood and architecturally significant use cases for clarification and stabilization. You can find a listing of significant use cases and scenarios in the use case view section of the Software Architecture Document. Also in that document are significant properties, such as descriptions of the event flow, relationships, use case diagrams, and special requirements related to each use case. The Project Manager uses Requirements attributes such as priority, effort, and cost when planning the iteration. Other areas that are addressed during the Manage the Scope of the System activity include refinements to traceability maintenance and the Vision artifact.

Refine the System Definition

To establish a consensus of the system to be created, this activity further refines and details the requirements. This is achieved through the set of prioritized features of the product often described in the Vision to ensure that the system can be delivered on time and within budget. A more in-depth understanding of the system functionality is achieved during this activity, and the detailed requirements are specified in the form of detailed Use Case, Supplementary Specifications, or Software Requirements Specifications.

Actors that have already been identified and defined are reviewed, and further descriptions are added if necessary. Use cases that have been previously outlined for these actors are further detailed. Note that this activity happens during Elaboration iterations, which is supported by the fact that it actually involves further refinement and detailing of requirements. Also, note that not all actors and use cases are detailed here, only the critical ones. To detail a use case, you need to start by reviewing and refining the scenarios that you will be dealing with in the current development cycle. You can use the outline flow of events that you captured during the Find Actors and Use Cases task to detail the flow of events. Storyboards and the User Interface Prototype are helpful in understanding and detailing the use case flows. Structuring the flow of events and documenting preconditions and postconditions are important aspects of detailing a use case. Structuring the flow of events involves identifying and documenting the subflows into which a use case's flow of events can be divided. To illustrate relationships with actors and other use cases, you can create use case diagrams. The Requirements Specifier artifact details use cases and refines the Requirements Attributes artifact.

Another important objective of this activity is to define the software requirements of the system, which you accomplish by detailing the software requirements. You need to specify all requirements in enough detail that designers, testers, and documentation writers can design and test the system. Review the checklists associated with the work products being produced, and package the requirements for review. To achieve this, document a complete definition of the software requirements to be delivered in the current development cycle. You assemble all requirements work products and supply any additional information. For less formal projects, it may be enough to bundle the relevant reports and hand-generated documentation, with sufficient supporting material. On more formal projects, you can produce one or more Software Requirements Specifications that collect and organize all requirements surrounding the project.

Manage Changing Requirements

This activity ensures that the changes to the requirements are managed in an effective and efficient manner. One key aspect of managing changing requirements is managing the downstream impact of the approved changes as they are implemented.

To effectively manage the changing requirements, you must do the following things:

- Evaluate requested changes and determine their impact on existing requirements.

- Structure the Use-Case Model to improve the overall management of the requirements documented in the use case. The System Analyst is responsible for structuring the Use-Case Model to make the requirements easier to understand and maintain. This includes leveraging commonality among use cases and actors and identifying optional and exceptional behavior.

- Properly manage changes to the requirements attributes and traceability relationships. You identify and document these traceability relationships during the **Manage Dependencies** task, explicitly defining the relationships between requirements and the other work products, such as analysis and design work products, test work products, deployment work products, and so on.

- Verify that the results of the requirements work conform to the stakeholders' view of the system.

Key Artifacts

We have discussed the Requirements workflow and associated activities and mentioned the related artifacts. This section reviews and defines some of the key artifacts.

Vision

The stakeholders' view of the product, in terms of needs and features, is captured in the Vision artifact. Core requirements, which play a central role in providing a contractual basis for the more detailed technical requirements, are envisioned in this artifact.

Glossary

So that important terms are consistently understood across the team, one Glossary is produced for the entire system. It is useful for the project members to understand the terms that are specific to the project.

Requirements Management Plan

Requirements artifacts, requirements types, and their respective attributes are described in the Requirements Management Plan. This plan also specifies the information to be collected and control mechanisms to be used for measuring, reporting, and controlling changes to the product requirements.

Software Requirement

Software requirements are documented to specify software capability that the user needs to solve a problem. Such a software capability is specified in the Software Requirement artifact.

Software Requirements Specification

The Software Requirements Specification focuses on the collection and organization of all requirements surrounding the project. It captures the software requirements for the complete system or a portion of that system.

Stakeholder Requests

It is important to capture all requests made on the project and how these have been addressed. Although the System Analyst is responsible for this artifact, many key stakeholders contribute. These stakeholders might include marketing people, users, customers, or sponsors. This artifact can contain references to any type of external sources—results of stakeholder interviews, requests for changes, statement of work, and others—to which the system must comply.

Storyboard

The main purpose of Storyboards is to understand the overall flow and interactions, not to prototype or test the look and feel of the user interface. This artifact is a logical and conceptual description of system functionality for a specific scenario, including the interaction required between the system users and the system. A Storyboard tells a specific story.

Supplementary Specifications

Many types of requirements do not fall within the scope of functional requirements. Therefore, these are not readily captured in the use cases. Supplementary Specifications capture such nonbehavioral system requirements. Such requirements include legal and regulatory requirements, quality attributes, and other nonfunctional requirements. We will discuss the concept of requirements later in this chapter.

Use-Case Model

The main purpose of use-case modeling is to get to the core of what a system must do to meet the stakeholders' needs. To achieve this, we must first focus on who (the Actors) will use it, or be used by it, and then on what functionality the system must provide to give value to the user. In relation to this, this artifact captures the model of the system's intended functions and its environment and serves as a contract between the customer and the developers. It is used as an essential input to activities in Analysis and Design, Implementation, and Test.

Requirements Attributes

This Requirement Attributes artifact provides a repository of the requirement text, attributes, and traceability for all requirements. This repository also aims to assist managing change from a requirements perspective. Therefore, everyone in the development organization should be able to access it.

Important Concepts

This section discusses the concepts that are important for the successful completion of this activity.

What Are Stakeholders?

A stakeholder is defined in the following way:

> An individual who is materially affected by the outcome of the system or the project(s) producing the system.

This definition is a combination of the definitions of stakeholder from the RUP—"the stakeholder role is defined as anyone who is materially affected by the outcome of the project"—and Leffingwell and Widrig (2000)—"a stakeholder is an individual who is materially affected by the outcome of the system." This new definition reflects the fact that the stakeholder community comprises both the individuals directly affected by the system and those who are indirectly affected by the system by their involvement in the project.

What Is a Requirement?

A requirement is defined as a condition or capability to which a system must conform.

There are many kinds of requirements. One way of categorizing them is described as the FURPS+ model (Grady, 1992), using the acronym FURPS to describe the major categories of requirements with subcategories as follows.

- **Functionality**—Functionality requirements may include feature sets, capabilities, or security.

- **Usability**—Usability requirements may include human factors, aesthetics, consistency in the user interface, online and context-sensitive help, wizards and agents, user documentation, and training materials.

- **Reliability**—Reliability requirements to be considered are frequency and severity of failure, recoverability, predictability, accuracy, or maintainability.

- **Performance**—A performance requirement imposes conditions on functional requirements. For example, for a given action, a performance requirement might specify parameters for speed, efficiency, availability, accuracy, throughput, response time, recovery time, or resource usage.

- **Supportability**—Supportability requirements might include testability, extensibility, adaptability, maintainability, compatibility, configurability, serviceability, installability, or localizability.

The + in FURPS+ reminds you to include such requirements as design constraints, implementation requirements, interface requirements, and physical requirements. For more details on these, please refer to the RUP product and Bass, Clements, and Kazman (2003).

Use Cases and the Other RUP Disciplines

Use cases play an important role in most RUP disciplines. They are at the heart of requirements; realization of these use cases is carried out within analysis and design, and the system is implemented and tests are planned and executed based on the use cases. Use cases actually drive the development process from understanding the requirements to implementing the system that meets those requirements. We will discuss these relationships in detail in covering their respective disciplines.

Requirements

The Use-Case Model is one of the key artifacts of the Requirements discipline. Requirements activities contribute toward maturing the use cases from being identified to agreed upon, which contributes to the evolution of the Glossary and Supplementary Specification artifacts.

Analysis and Design

Use cases identified during the Requirements discipline are now realized in the design model in terms of interacting objects in the Analysis and Design discipline. The design model describes the different parts of the implemented system and the way the parts should interact to perform the use cases to deliver the required functionality.

Implementation

Following the specification of interacting objects in the design model that realize the use cases, the next step involves implementing—coding and unit testing—these use cases in terms of the design classes. The code implements the functionality desired by the use case.

Testing

Use cases become the foundation for identifying the test cases and test procedures. In other words, the system is verified by performing each use case.

Project Management

Planning is the key element of project management and is done at several levels within a RUP project. For example, there are high-level project plan and detailed iteration plans. Use cases are at the heart of planning iterations and tracking the progress of a software development project. Constraints that impact the subset of use cases to be implemented during a given iteration might include the number of resources available, the results of previous iterations, and others.

Deployment

Use cases play the central role in developing user's manuals and in defining how to order units of the product.

Use-Case Model

The Use-Case Model, which determines what the system should do from the user's point of view, is one of the key artifacts produced by the Requirements discipline. A Use-Case Model drives the planning, design, development, and testing of the product.

A Use-Case Model consists of two key elements: actors and use cases (see Figure 6-3).

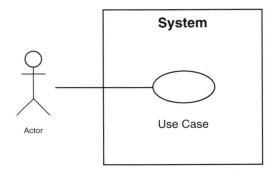

Figure 6-3   Use-Case Model

Actor

An actor represents a person or another system that interacts with the system. An actor is a role and not a particular system or person. The role can be played by multiple users of the system while they are interacting, or a single user can assume multiple roles. For instance, during a software development project, you might assume a role of Project Manager for some meetings the role of System Analyst for others. An actor is not part of the system and can receive information from or send information to the system.

Actors are crucial to gain a complete understanding of a system. By understanding who will use the system, you will be better able to understand the system's purpose.

Use Case

A use case defines a sequence of actions a system performs that yields a result of observable value to an actor. This is an important concept. While identifying the use cases, keep in mind that an actor should not be expected to perform several use cases to realize the value to be provided by the system. A use case specifies a dialogue between an actor and the system that must yield value. An actor initiates a use case, which invokes certain functionality in the system. The use cases must enable the system to deliver all the expected functionality.

Scenario

Scenarios are instances of use cases, and a use case can have many scenarios. A use case instance constitutes a specific sequence of actions that illustrate behavior of the system. Scenarios help us gain an in-depth understanding of what a system will do when a particular use case is invoked. Usually, a use case has a basic flow and several alternative flows of events. A single scenario presents one specific flow of events from initiation to end.

Requirements Traceability

Earlier in this chapter, we discussed the role of use cases in the RUP disciplines. We learned how use cases drive the entire development project from initiation to closure. One potential impact of this is the fact that change in a given use case needs to be carefully traced down to the actual functionality delivered by the system. Lack of traceability can result in a system that doesn't deliver the right functionality.

Requirements traceability enables tracing requirements to other requirements and other project artifacts. The main benefit of traceability, therefore, is the ability to determine with confidence whether every agreed-upon requirement is implemented by the system—the requirement specified by a use case, the use case realized in the design model and implemented in the code, the use case tested by associated test cases, and so on. As expected, another major advantage of traceability is in managing change—the ability to determine the impact of the change in terms of things that need to be updated as a result of change.

Requirements and Other Disciplines

You will learn throughout this book how the Requirements discipline integrates with other disciplines. The Requirements discipline is related to other process disciplines as follows.

- The Business Modeling discipline provides an organizational context for the system. This is represented as the Business Rules, Business Use-Case Model, and Business Analysis Model Artifacts.

- The Analysis and Design discipline gets its primary input from Requirements.

- The Test discipline validates the system against (among other things) the requirements.

- The Configuration and Change Management discipline provides the change control mechanism for requirements.

- The Project Management discipline plans the project and each iteration. The requirements work products are important inputs to the iteration planning activities.

- The Environment discipline develops and maintains the supporting artifacts that are used during requirements. Some of these artifacts include the Development Organization Assessment, which describes the current status of the software organization in terms of current processes, tools, peoples' competencies and attributes, customers, competitors, technical trends, problems, improvement areas, and the Development Process, which provides guidance and support for the members of the project.

Primary Role(s) and Responsibilities

The primary roles for the Requirements discipline are System Analyst and Requirements Specifier. It is their responsibility to establish and manage the system requirements, respectively.

System Analyst

This role leads and coordinates requirements elicitation by outlining the system's functionality and delimiting the system. The specific responsibilities of the System Analyst are presented in Figure 6-4.

Requirements Specifier

The Requirements Specifier specifies and maintains the detailed system requirements. Figure 6-5 shows the tasks that the Requirements Specifier performs and the artifacts for which the person(s) in that role are responsible. Please note that each of these tasks and artifacts was discussed earlier in this chapter.

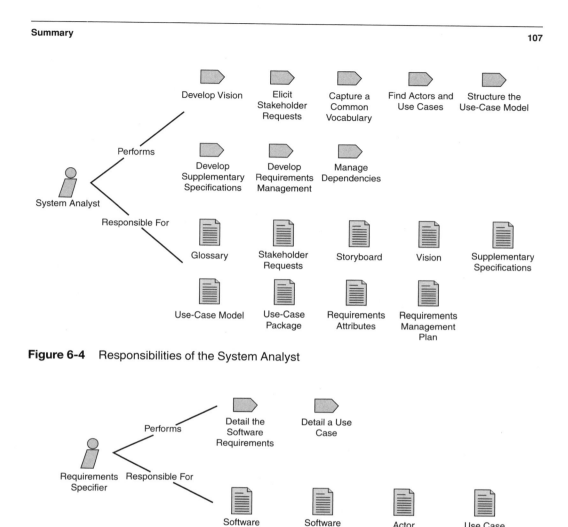

Figure 6-4   Responsibilities of the System Analyst

Figure 6-5   Responsibilities of the Requirements Specifier

Summary

This chapter discussed the Requirements discipline in detail. It covered the activities you perform to ensure that requirements are appropriately managed. These activities include eliciting, documenting, and maintaining requirements. It also discussed System Analyst and Requirement Specifier, which are the central roles for the Requirements discipline. The Requirements discipline plays an important role as it relates to other RUP disciplines and therefore is central to the project success.

Sample Questions

You can find the correct answers to these questions in the Appendix, "Answers to Sample Questions."

1. Requirements management describes the activities involved in which of the following? (Select all that apply.)
   a. Eliciting a set of requirements
   b. Documenting a set of requirements
   c. Maintaining a set of requirements
   d. Declaring a set of requirements

2. Which of the following is a primary requirements goal during the Inception phase of the project? (Select all that apply.)
   a. Analyzing the problem
   b. Understanding the stakeholder's needs
   c. Refining the system definition
   d. Managing the system scope
   e. Manage changing requirements

3. Which of the following is true for the Refine the System Definition activity? (Select all that apply.)
   a. Some actors are described.
   b. Some use cases are detailed.
   c. All actors and use cases are identified and outlined.
   d. Some actors and use cases are identified.

4. Which of the following activities gains agreement on the scope of the system and outlines the key requirements?
   a. Understand stakeholder needs.
   b. Define the system.
   c. Manage the scope of the system.
   d. Manage changing requirements.

5. Which of the following statements is true regarding scenarios? (Select all that apply.)
   a. Scenarios are instances of a use case.
   b. Scenarios are generalizations of many use cases.
   c. A use case can have many scenarios.
   d. A use case is an instance of a scenario.

6. Which of the following is essential to effectively develop the Requirements Management Plan? (Select all that apply.)
   a. Software Development Plan

    b. Risk Management Plan

    c. Iteration Plan

    d. Software Requirements

7. To fully understand the problem(s) that need to be addressed, you need to know who the stakeholders are in the conceptual vision for the project. These key stakeholders should be involved in gathering the set of features to be considered. How might they gather those features? (Select all that apply.)

    a. In a requirements workshop

    b. In the form of stakeholder surveys

    c. From requirements elicitation

    d. From stakeholder interviews

8. Which of the following is the purpose of the Define the System activity? (Select all that apply.)

    a. To begin converging on the scope of the high-level requirements by outlining the breadth of the detailed requirements of the system

    b. To analyze stakeholder requests and define the system use cases

    c. To establish traceability between stakeholder requests and use cases

    d. To identify use cases and actors and develop a Use-Case Model

9. The Requirements Specifier role is primarily responsible for which of the following? (Select all that apply.)

    a. Software Requirements

    b. Software Requirements Specification

    c. Actors and Use Cases

    d. Use-Case Model

10. The Requirements discipline consists of activities that ensure which of the following? (Select all that apply.)

    a. Effective requirements engineering

    b. Effective requirements management

    c. Creation of a vision

    d. Translation of the vision into a Use-Case Model

11. The purpose of the requirements tracing is to do which of the following? (Select all that apply.)

    a. Help identify use cases required to satisfy customer requirements

    b. Verify that all requirements of the system are fulfilled by the implementation

    c. Verify that the application does only what it was intended to do

    d. Help manage change

12. Which of the following is true for the Define the System activity? (Select all that apply.)
    a. The purpose is to begin converging on the scope of the high-level requirements.
    b. Use-Case Realization is achieved.
    c. It helps achieve alignment across the team in their understanding of the system.
    d. The Vision and the Use-Case Model are further refined.

13. The Use-Case Model consists of which of the following key elements? (Select all that apply.)
    a. System
    b. Use cases
    c. Use-case realizations
    d. Actors

14. The System Analyst is responsible for which of the following? (Select all that apply.)
    a. Glossary
    b. Storyboard
    c. Vision
    d. Use-Case Model

References

Bass, L., Clements, P., & Kazman, R. (2003). *Software architecture in practice*. Boston: Addison-Wesley.

Bittner, K., & Spence, I. (2003). *Use case modeling*. Boston: Addison-Wesley.

Grady, R. (1992). *Practical software metrics for project management and process improvement*. Englewood Cliffs, NJ: Prentice-Hall.

IBM Rational Unified Process v7.0.

Leffingwell, D., & Widrig, D. (2000). *Managing software requirements: A unified approach*. Boston: Addison-Wesley.

CHAPTER 7

Analysis and Design

By Ahmad K. Shuja

In the Rational Unified Process, analysis and design are combined into one discipline even though they are two separate techniques. The investigation and research of subjects (analysis) leads to new findings and better understanding of the domain, and it provides reasons and arguments to support an IT system as a solution to a problem (design). The boundaries are often not precisely drawn, and it is not uncommon for one person to fill the roles of both System Analyst and Designer. In RUP, however, the System Analyst role plays a more central role in the Requirements discipline than the Designer does. The Software Architect performs most of the analysis tasks, whereas the Designer is responsible for the design aspects.

Overview

Analysis and design play a key role throughout the software engineering process and from Inception through Construction in the RUP. Early in the lifecycle, the Analysis and Design discipline is concerned with establishing a feasible vision for the system and assessing appropriate techniques for building the solution. The extent of risk involved drives the level of analysis and design work performed during the Inception phase. Creating an initial architecture for the system is the aim early in the Elaboration phase, whereas later in the Elaboration phase, the aim turns to refining and baselining the architecture. The evaluation, validation, and design of architecture falls also into the scope of the Analysis and Design discipline, which emphasizes the role of this discipline and that RUP is an architecture-centric process framework. Such an approach enables teams to focus on the quality of the architecture and the solution to ensure that they meet the needs in an appropriate manner, which is one of RUP's key principles.

Models play a central role in the Analysis and Design discipline, as they do in the RUP overall. Models enable us to analyze system behavior and structure and provide effective ways to communicate the results to interested stakeholders. Model-Driven Development and Model-Driven Architecture emphasize the role of models as the foundational elements for implementation. This enables an increase in the level of abstraction at which the human development works. Analysis models evolve into design models and design models evolve throughout the life of the project. There are no hard and fast rules on when you can start producing implementation elements and integrate them into interesting builds of the system. RUP offers a number of ways to proceed from design to code, which include "Sketch and Code" and "Round-Trip Engineering (RTE) with Single Evolving Design Model."

In the Analysis and Design discipline, the Design Model constitutes the primary artifact created. We will discuss it later in this chapter.

Purpose

The purposes of the Analysis and Design discipline include the following:

- Transform the requirements into a design of the system-to-be
- Evolve a robust architecture for the system
- Adapt the design to match the implementation environment, designing it for performance

Analysis and Design Workflow

The activity diagram shown in Figure 7-1 presents the flow of analysis and design within a RUP project. Keep in mind that the architectural synthesis is executed during the Inception phase, whereas the candidate architecture is defined in the Elaboration phase. The other activities extend beyond the Elaboration phase and are performed repetitively during the Construction phase, iteration by iteration.

The Analysis and Design discipline within RUP is composed of a number of activities. Each of those activities is discussed in this section.

Perform Architectural Synthesis

This activity is performed early in the RUP lifecycle, and it constructs and assesses an architectural proof-of-concept to demonstrate that the system, as envisioned by the stakeholders, is actually feasible. It requires architectural analysis to be carried out, architectural proof-of-concept to be constructed, and evaluation of the architecture against the stakeholders' needs and risks. Let's discuss these in greater detail.

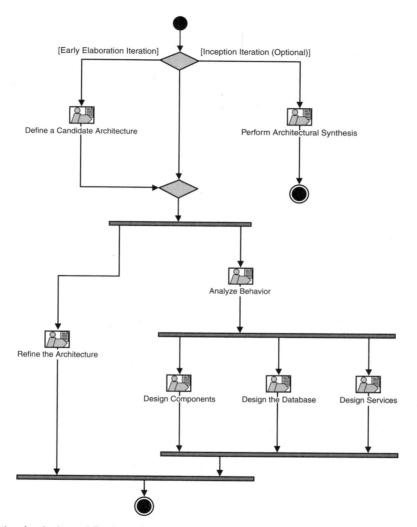

[Early Elaboration Iteration]

[Inception Iteration (Optional)]

Define a Candidate Architecture

Perform Architectural Synthesis

Analyze Behavior

Refine the Architecture

Design Components

Design the Database

Design Services

Figure 7-1 Analysis and Design workflow

One of the initial tasks to successfully perform architectural synthesis is analyzing the architecture. Accordingly, the **Software Architect** performs architectural analysis, defines a candidate architecture, and constrains the architectural techniques to be used in the system. Performing architectural synthesis requires performing architectural analysis and constructing and assessing the viability of the architectural proof-of-concept.

Successful architectural analysis involves the following:

- Facilitating system envisioning by exploring and evaluating available architectural options at a high level. An architecture overview is created during the earliest stages of a project. It shows early decisions and working assumptions on implementing the vision, and it contains decisions about the physical and logical architectures and nonfunctional requirements.

- Analyzing organizational and industry-wide assets for common frameworks, models, or classes.

- Defining the high-level organization of subsystems and introducing the contents of the layered architecture.

- Identifying key abstractions by finding entity analysis classes relevant to the system under design and utilizing artifacts such as the glossary, use cases, and domain models.

- Identifying associations between key abstractions that indicate significant activities of the system.

- Developing a deployment overview by producing a high-level overview of locations of the system and its users.

- Identifying analysis mechanisms and executing top-down or bottom-up analysis mechanisms to cope with such things as persistence, transaction management, fault management, messaging, or inference engines.

- Reviewing the architectural mechanism, subsystems, packages, entities, and classes and checking for inconsistencies. Scenarios and use cases should be used to validate the architectural choice.

Following the architectural analysis, we construct the architectural proof-of-concept. Constructing the architectural proof-of-concept involves the following:

- Deciding on a construction approach for the proof-of-concept and determining whether conceptual modeling, rapid prototyping, simulation, automatic code generation, executable models, or vertical prototypes is the most promising technique to achieve the desired results

- Selecting assets and technologies for the architectural proof-of-concept

- Using the selected technique and technologies, building the architectural proof-of-concept

After we have constructed the architectural proof-of-concept, we need to assess its viability against the stakeholders' needs and the risks. This assessment involves the following:

- First determining the evaluation criteria from architectural significant requirements

- Evaluating the architectural proof-of-concept by using techniques such as simulation, prototyping, or conceptual modeling

- Assessing the results and evaluating whether the architecturally significant requirements can be satisfied with the proposed architecture

Define a Candidate Architecture

This activity is executed early in the Elaboration phase and creates an initial sketch of the software architecture. Effectively defining the candidate architecture involves defining the following:

- An initial set of architecturally significant elements to be used as the basis for the analysis
- An initial set of analysis mechanisms
- The initial organization of the system and the use-case realizations to be addressed in the current iteration

This activity involves performing architectural analysis and use-case analysis. Architectural analysis is carried out during this activity (or repeated if already performed during the Inception phase in the Perform Architectural Synthesis activity) and is primarily beneficial when developing new and unprecedented systems.

During the Inception phase, you identify use cases that are required to meet the stakeholders' needs. To define the candidate architecture, identify which class(es) will realize the behavior of architecturally significant use cases. Note that not all use-case realizations are defined here. Accordingly, use-case analysis is carried out to ensure that use-case behavior is distributed across classes and clear responsibilities, required attributes, and appropriate associations of these classes have been identified. The Designer is responsible for analyzing the use cases and describing how to develop an **analysis-level use-case realization from a use-case**. A use-case realization is produced.

Activity: Analyze Behavior

This activity focuses on the analysis and design of behavioral requirements and is repeated in iterations across the project lifecycle. Analysis of behavioral requirements involves identifying analysis classes that satisfy the required behavior and determining how these classes fit into the logical system architecture. Therefore, this activity transforms the behavioral descriptions provided by the requirements into a set of elements upon which to base the design.

The **Software Architect** analyzes the behavior and identifies the design elements, which might include subsystems, classes, interfaces, events, and signals. Identifying design elements involves the following:

- Understanding the external and internal events and signals to which the system must respond
- Refining the analysis classes into appropriate design model elements
- Identifying subsystem interfaces to ensure smooth collaboration between subsystems

The Designer performs use case and operation analysis using the elements identified by the architect. Use-case analysis is carried out to develop an analysis-level use-case realization from a use-case, which involves identifying the classes that perform a use case's flow of events; distributing the use-case behavior to those classes (using analysis use-case realizations); identifying the responsibilities, attributes, and associations of the classes; and noting the usage of architectural mechanisms. During operation analysis, the Designer begins the transformation of a behavioral description at the system level into coarse-grained system structure (and associated interactions) and behavior at the subsystem level.

The **User Interface Designer** is responsible for designing the user interface. Because this is really about the end user, it is important to gain a thorough understanding of the characteristics of the users who will actually interact with this system to perform their job. Use cases and storyboards are harvested for the essential user interfaces in which users spend most of their time, and the primary user interface elements are identified. A navigation map[1] should be defined to ensure clarity.

In software, the user interface is the closest thing to a tangible product that the end user is going to get. It provides the interface for the end user to interact with the system and perform his job. Therefore, prototyping the user interface in most cases yields great value in terms of identifying the design aspects that need to be refined to enhance the user experience and making the user interface more usable. The User Interface Designer is responsible for developing the prototype. Creating the prototype involves designing the visual representation (paper or electronic) of the future system supporting a use-case scenario and implementing the User Interface Prototype to simulate the look and feel of the system by following a use-case scenario. This enables the users to gain a better understanding of how the solution / system will look. Users will provide the feedback on the User Interface Prototype , which will assist in uncovering any previously undiscovered requirements and further refine the requirements definition [Krebs, December, 2005].

It is important to review the design to ensure that it is appropriate and addresses the key stakeholder needs. The **Technical Reviewer** is responsible for reviewing the design. He is likely to uncover design defects that would have delayed project completion. He reviews the Design Model as a whole to ensure that the overall model structure is well formed, and he detects large-scale quality problems not visible by looking at lower-level elements. During the review, he confirms that all use cases and their scenarios are realized in the design model, that the internal implementation of the design elements performs the behavior required of them, and that the design guidelines were followed and that they're high quality. He concludes his review by preparing the **Review Record** and documenting identified defects.

Design Components

This activity refines the design of the system. In particular, it refines the definitions of design elements by working out the details of how the design elements realize the behavior required of them, refines and updates the use-case realizations based on new design elements identified (that is, keeping the use-case realizations updated), and enables the Technical Reviewer to review the design.

---

[1] A navigation map is a roadmap of the system's user interface visualized in a hierarchical tree diagram.

The Designer plays a key role during this activity and is responsible for the following.

- Designing use cases by creating use-case realizations. This happens by establishing a relationship between the use-case model and the design model through dependencies, by describing interactions between design objects through UML interaction diagrams (communication and sequence), and by describing the interaction between objects, capsules, or subsystems. (Subsystems are discussed in detail later in the chapter.) If it's beneficial, interaction diagrams can be simplified using subsystems.

- Describing persistence-related behavior to demonstrate how persistent objects are written, read, and deleted. Additional descriptions, as appropriate, are added to the interaction diagrams when the flow of events is not fully clear from the messages sent between the participating objects.

- Unifying design classes and subsystems to ensure homogeneity and consistency in the design model. As is true for all design-related activities, it is important that the design model is continually evaluated without going into too much detail.

- Documenting subsystem elements, their behavior, and subsystem dependencies.

- Designing the class structure of the subsystem or component, which involves creating initial design classes, identifying persistent classes, defining class visibility (public, private, or package), defining operations, and assigning responsibilities to the classes. In addition, it involves defining methods and describing the steps executed when a particular operation is called. The Designer also defines states, attributes, dependencies, associations, internal structure, and generalization. While designing class structures, the Designer also resolves use case collisions and handles nonfunctional requirements in general and evaluates your results.

- Designing testability elements and designing test-specific functionality. Successful designing of testability elements involves identifying test-specific classes and packages, designing an interface to the automated test tool, and designing test procedure behavior.

The **Capsule Designer** plays an important role in designing real-time systems and is responsible for describing the characteristics of capsule design for object-oriented software engineering. Designing a capsule involves creating ports and binding them to protocols, validating capsule interactions, defining a capsule state machine, defining requirements on passive classes, introducing capsule inheritance, and validating capsule behavior.

Design the Database

This optional activity identifies the design classes to be persisted in a database and designs the corresponding database structures. This activity involves designing classes, specifying data migration, designing databases, and reviewing the design.

The **Database Designer** is responsible for designing the database to implement persistence within an application. Designing the database involves developing the logical data model (optional), developing a physical database design that represents the detailed physical structure of the database, and reviewing the results to ensure the quality and integrity of the model.

The Database Designer is also responsible for describing how to migrate a legacy data source to a target database and for producing a Data Migration SPECIFICATION. Specifying data migration involves defining migration scope, analyzing the data source and establishing a profile, mapping the sources between physical models of the data source and the target database and describing the mapping of the data elements and the resolution of conflicts in the mapping, and identifying which parts of the data sources can be migrated automatically and which parts should be migrated manually.

Design Services

This activity is performed to provide detailed specification of service behavior and model the service portfolio in terms of service providers and partitions. The **Designer** is responsible for designing services, which involves defining and specifying the services and structure of a service-oriented solution in terms of collaborations of contained design elements and external sub-systems/interfaces. Designing services ensures that the capabilities from the portfolio of services are reused; that design patterns and mechanisms, as suited to the service being designed and in accordance with project design guidelines, are used; that the logical organization of the solution is described; that service elements (message design, service design, collaboration design, and policy identification and capture) are described; and that dependencies among services are captured.

Refine the Architecture

There is a fine line between finishing analysis and beginning design work, and this activity provides that natural transition. Appropriate design elements and design mechanisms are identified from respective analysis elements and analysis mechanisms. The system's runtime and deployment architectures are described and an implementation model is organized to ensure that the transition between design and implementation is seamless while ensuring that the consistency and integrity of the architecture is maintained.

The **Software Architect** plays a key role in this activity and is responsible for the following:

- Describing how to refine Analysis Mechanisms into Design Mechanisms. This involves categorizing clients of analysis mechanisms,[2] making an inventory of the implementation mechanisms, mapping design mechanisms to implementation mechanisms,[3] and documenting the architectural mechanisms.

---

[2]   Analysis mechanisms provide conceptual sets of services that analysis classes use. These services include the identification of the clients, the identification of a characteristic profile, and the grouping according to their profile.

[3]   Design mechanisms provide an abstraction of the implementation mechanisms, bridging the gap between analysis mechanisms and implementation mechanisms.

- Identifying the design elements of a service-oriented solution in terms of services and partitions and documenting the initial specification of those services and producing the Service Model. Identifying design elements can involve the identification of services,[4] aligning business models with IT services to track business goals (top-down, business process driven), applying the traditional component-based object-oriented software engineering, and transforming levels of abstraction from the business to the IT world (top-down, use-case driven). Design elements to be identified can also include

  - Services that are required to act as data-management services. This tends to focus more on the Data Model, Domain Model, or Business Analysis Model.

  - Business rules such that a traceable relationship between the service specifications can be derived from the business rules and between the message(s) derived from the business entity (rule driven).

  - Existing legacy applications that will be reused as part of the solution and identifying functionality (bottom-up, exposing existing assets).[5]

- Incorporating existing design elements while refining the architecture by identifying where existing subsystems or components may be reused based on their interfaces.

- Ensuring that the logical view stays up to date.

- Structuring the implementation model. This involves establishing the implementation model structure, adjusting implementation subsystems, defining imports for each implementation subsystem, deciding how to treat executable programs, deciding how to treat test assets, updating the implementation view, and evaluating the implementation model.

- Defining a process architecture for the system in terms of active classes and defining instances and relationships of the active classes to operating system threads and processes. Defining a process architecture involves analyzing concurrency requirements and defining the extent to which parallel execution is required for the system. The software architect also identifies and describes system processes and threads to optimize the use and activity of one or more CPUs controlling databases, transaction manager, and backup efforts. Defining a process architecture might also involve identifying the processes and threads that are created and destroyed throughout the system. In addition, the software architect might need to identify and define the means by which processes and threads will communicate. This involves allocating resources to process orchestration so that the system reacts consistently in bottleneck situations, mapping the flows of control onto the concepts supported by the implementation environment, and determining which threads of control classes and subsystems should execute within using the inside-out or outside-in strategy.

---

[4] It is most likely one of the first steps in the modeling of a service-oriented solution.

[5] This task helps comply with the Balancing Competing Stakeholder Priorities key principle and benefits from reducing custom development.

- Defining the deployment architecture for a distributed system in terms of physical nodes and their interconnections. This involves analyzing distribution requirements and defining the extent to which distribution is required for the system, defining the network configuration, and allocating system elements to nodes and distributing the workload of the system, either logical or physical.

Another role engaged in this activity is the **Technical Reviewer**, who is responsible for reviewing the architecture. The architecture review involves defining the scope and goals of the review, following the approaches used for specific scope/goal combination, reviewing the architecture according to the phase and iteration the project is in and providing general recommendations, and following the review, allocating responsibility for each defect identified.

Key Artifacts

Key artifacts for the Analysis and Design discipline include an Analysis Model, a Design Model, an Architectural Proof-of-Concept, a Data Model, a Reference Architecture, and a Software Architecture Document. Real-time systems have other artifacts as well.

Analysis Model

This artifact defines an object model describing the realization of use cases and serves as an abstraction of the Design Model. The Analysis Model is a generalization or abstraction of the design and does not provide details on how the system will deliver the needed functionality. To ensure consistency, you need to further refine and detail the Analysis Model, which is a rough sketch of the system, to create a Design Model. When you can justify a separate Analysis Model, it is crucial to keep the analysis and design models consistent. Weigh the extra effort required to maintain the Analysis Model against its perceived benefits.

Design Model

Most systems, even smaller systems, should be designed prior to implementation to ensure that they meet real business needs and avoid costly rework due to design errors. Visual models allow the design to be easily communicated. Tools are available that can ensure consistency with the implementation model and improve efficiencies. In RUP, the Design Model is the primary artifact of the Analysis and Design discipline. It is an object model describing the realization of use cases. The Design Model serves as an abstraction of the implementation model and its source code and is used as essential input to activities in implementation and testing. To help organize the model, you can aggregate the collaborating classes into packages and subsystems.

Architectural Proof-of-Concept

The purpose of this artifact is to determine whether there exists, or is likely to exist, a solution that satisfies the architecturally significant requirements. Architectural Proof-of-Concept is a solution—perhaps just conceptual—to the problem for which the architecturally significant requirements were identified to solve. These architecturally significant requirements were identified early in the inception phase.

Data Model

This artifact describes the logical and physical representations of persistent data that the application uses. When the application will utilize a relational database management system (RDBMS), the data model can also include model elements for stored procedures, triggers, constraints, and so on that define the interaction of the application components with the RDBMS.

Reference Architecture

This artifact is, in essence, a predefined architectural pattern, or set of patterns, possibly partially or completely instantiated, designed and proven for use in particular business and technical contexts, together with supporting artifacts to enable their use.

Software Architecture Document

The purpose of this document is to provide a comprehensive overview of the software system architecture. This artifact provides a comprehensive architectural overview of the system, using a number of different architectural views to depict different aspects of the system. (Architectural views are discussed briefly in Chapter 1, "Welcome to the IBM Rational Unified Process and Certification.") It provides a valuable communication medium between the Software Architect and other members of the project team and ensures that architecturally significant decisions made on the project are communicated effectively and efficiently.

Navigation Map

The purpose of the Navigation Map is to express the principal user interface paths through the system. Note that these are the main pathways through the screens of the system and not necessarily all of the possible paths. Therefore, the Navigation Map describes the structure of the user interface elements in the system, along with their potential navigation pathways.

Service Model

The Service Model is an abstraction of the IT services implemented within an enterprise. It supports the development of one or more service-oriented solutions and is used to conceive and document the design of the software services. The Service Model, therefore, is defined as a model of the core elements of a service-oriented architecture (SOA).

Other Artifacts for Real-Time Systems

Real-time systems are sometimes referred to as **safety-critical systems** because of hard response requirements and timeliness. The following additional artifacts are defined in the RUP for designing such real-time systems.

- **Capsule**—This represents a specific design pattern that has proven useful in modeling and designing systems that have a high degree of concurrency. The pattern represents an encapsulated thread of control in the system. A capsule can have ports through which it communicates with other capsules and can contain passive classes or subcapsules.

- **Event**—This artifact specifies an occurrence in time and space. Less formally, it represents an occurrence of something that the system must respond to. An event is used for both external occurrences to which the system must respond as well as internal occurrences such as exceptions.

- **Protocol**—This artifact specifies the communication pattern used between capsules. The protocol defines a set of incoming and outgoing message types (for example, operations, signals), and optionally a collaboration, which defines the required ordering of messages, and a state machine, which specifies the abstract behavior that the participants in a protocol must provide.

- **Signal**—This artifact specifies an asynchronous stimulus from one object or instance to another. It may cause a state transition in the state machine of an object.

Primary Roles and Responsibilities

The following roles participate in the Analysis and Design discipline. Before we dive into them, it is worth noting that within the IT industry, the role of an analyst is a bit of a loaded term. Some analysts are being asked to investigate the business processes of an organization and document business requirements. Other analysts play the role of a liaison between business and technology and focus on software requirements. RUP reserves multiple analyst roles for this purpose and divides the business and IT view into two different analyst roles: the business process analyst and the system analyst. The Analysis and Design discipline in RUP describes primarily the role of a system analyst, whereas the role of a business process analyst is described in detail in the business modeling discipline.

Software Architect

This role leads the development of the system's software architecture, which includes promoting and creating support for the key technical decisions that constrain the overall design and implementation for the project. Figure 7-2 shows the responsibilities of and the artifacts created by the Software Architect role. Note that some tasks and artifacts shown in Figure 7-2 do not belong to the Analysis and Design discipline, but this role is still responsible for them. Such tasks include Prioritize Use Cases, which is performed within the Requirements discipline, and Structure the Implementation Model, which is performed within the implementation discipline.

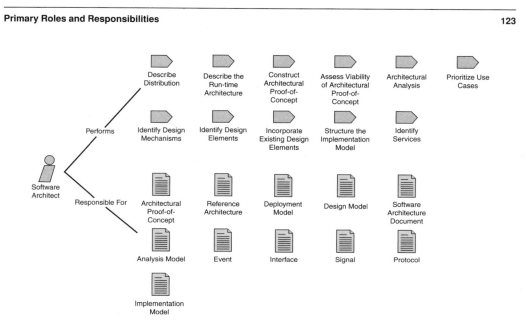

Figure 7-2 Responsibilities and artifacts created by the Software Architect role

System Analyst

This role leads and coordinates requirements elicitation by outlining the system's functionality and delimiting the system. Figure 7-3 shows the responsibilities of and the artifacts created by the Software Architect. Although most tasks that the person or persons in this role perform come from the Requirements discipline, this role is responsible for performing the Define System Context task within the Analysis and Design discipline. This role is also discussed in Chapter 6, "Requirements."

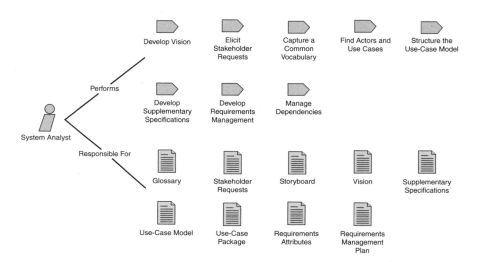

Figure 7-3 Responsibilities and artifacts created by the System Analyst role

Designer

This role leads the design of a part of the system, within the constraints of the requirements, architecture, and development process for the project. Figure 7-4 shows the responsibilities of and the artifacts created by the Designer role.

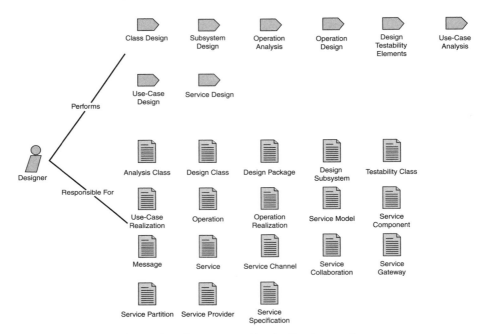

Figure 7-4   Responsibilities and artifacts created by the Designer role

User Interface Designer

This role coordinates the design of the user interface. This task includes gathering usability requirements and prototyping candidate user interface designs to meet those requirements. This role, however, is not responsible for implementing the user interface. Instead, this role ensures that the user interface is designed appropriately from a usability perspective by capturing user interface requirements and building the relevant prototypes, reviewing them with other stakeholders such as users, and finally reviewing and providing the appropriate feedback on the final implementation of the user interfaces. Figure 7-5 shows the responsibilities of and the artifacts created by the User Interface Designer role.

Database Designer

Most application development projects leverage relational databases for persisting data. This role leads the design of the persistent data storage structure to be used by the system. Figure 7-6 shows the responsibilities of and the artifacts created by the Database Designer role.

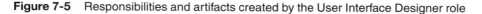

Figure 7-5   Responsibilities and artifacts created by the User Interface Designer role

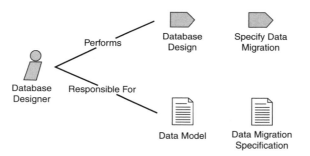

Figure 7-6   Responsibilities and artifacts created by the Database Designer role

Important Concepts

This section highlights a couple of the ways use cases relate to the Analysis and Design discipline. It also provides some further definition of the concepts of components and subsystems. Finally, it discusses some of the other important analysis and design concepts.

Use Cases and Analysis and Design

The Use-Case Model and Supplementary Specification comprise the two key inputs into the Analysis and Design discipline from the Requirements discipline. Analysis transforms the functional requirements, documented in the form of use cases, into a form that can be seamlessly mapped to a set of classes and subsystems. Although analysis does not account for nonfunctional requirements to maintain simplicity, the design activities evolve and detail the Analysis Model while keeping in view the constraints imposed by nonfunctional requirements, the implementation environment, performance and availability requirements, and others. Jointly, the Analysis and Design result is a Design Model that provides an abstraction of the source code and acts as a blueprint of how the source code is structured and written. As discussed earlier, the Design Model contains design classes, which can be structured into design packages, and demonstrates how the objects of these design classes collaborate to deliver a required functionality. This is also known as Use-Case Realizations.

During the early iterations of the Elaboration phase, the design activities focus on the creation of an Architectural Proof-of-Concept, which serves as an important foundation for developing a high-quality design model.

Use Case Realization in Analysis and Design

Use cases define system behavior, and objects implement the behavior. At runtime, objects collaborate to perform expected functions of the system. A use-case realization describes how a particular use case is realized within the design model in terms of collaborating objects. Classes need to be implemented for objects to exist, and objects can only collaborate if the rights and appropriate relationships have been implemented between classes. A use-case realization specifies what classes need to be implemented to realize each use case. Therefore, the complete behavior of a use case is allocated to collaborating classes. The use-case realization enables designers of participating classes to clearly understand the role of a particular class in realizing a use case and its relationship to other classes. This information enables further refinement of class responsibilities and interfaces. In terms of UML models, sequence, class, and communication, diagrams are built to design use-case realization.

Components and Subsystems

The term component refers to a range of different things, but often specifically to denote characteristics that enable replacement and assembly in larger systems. In the RUP, a component is defined as an encapsulated part of a system, ideally nontrivial, nearly independent, and replaceable. It is a part of a system that fulfils a clear function in the context of a well-defined architecture. Components implement clearly defined functionality that is made available through one or more interfaces.

Subsystem is a design model element that corresponds to the component. It has the semantics of a package, such that it can contain other model elements. The behavior of the subsystem is provided by classes or other subsystems it contains. A subsystem realizes one or more interfaces, which define the behavior it can perform.

Analysis Mechanism

An analysis mechanism represents a pattern that constitutes a common solution to a common problem. Analysis mechanisms can show patterns of structure, patterns of behavior, or both. They are used during analysis to reduce the complexity of analysis and to improve consistency by providing designers with a shorthand representation of complex behavior. Such mechanisms enable the analysis effort to focus on translating the functional requirements into software concepts without bogging down in the specification of relatively complex behavior needed to support the functionality but not central to it.

Use-Case Realization

A use-case realization represents how a use case will be implemented in terms of collaborating objects. Separating the use-case realization from its use case allows the use cases to be managed separately from their realizations. In other words, it enables us to separate requirements-related concerns from design-related ones. This is particularly important for larger projects or families of systems where the same use cases might be designed differently in different products within the product family. For each use case in the use-case model, there is a use-case realization in the analysis/design model with a realization relationship to the use case.

Summary

In this chapter, you learned the role that analysis and design plays in an architectural-centric process framework like RUP. The Analysis and Design discipline guides engineers from object-oriented analysis and design through architectural mechanisms to guidelines for user interface design. Analysis and design takes use cases as input artifacts and transforms them into a solution assuring that the stakeholder expectations are met. We have also discussed the role of the software architect, who plays a significant role in this discipline by deciding on the architectural approach—for example, service-oriented architecture (SOA) or component-based architecture.

Sample Questions

You can find the correct answers to these questions in the Appendix, "Answers to Sample Questions."

1. Which of the following artifacts are part of the Analysis and Design discipline? (Select all that apply.)
   a. Software Architecture Document
   b. Navigation Map
   c. Service Model
   d. Glossary

2. Which artifacts are used to identify analysis classes?
   a. User Interface Design
   b. Use Case
   c. Supplementary Requirements Specification
   d. Software Architecture Document

3. One of the purposes of the Analysis and Design discipline is to do which of the following?
   a. To transform the requirements into a design of the system to-be
   b. To implement and test the prototype of the system to ensure that the design works
   c. To ensure that there is an appropriate environment in place to carry out analysis and design activities
   d. To ensure that analysis and design activities are carried out as planned

4. Which role is responsible for leading the development of the system's software architecture?

   a. Software Architect

   b. System Architect

   c. Solution Architect

   d. Designer

5. Which of the following is accomplished during the Design Services activity? (Select all that apply.)

   a. Defining the services

   b. Specifying the services

   c. Structuring the service-oriented solution

   d. Designing service subcomponents

6. An Analysis Model is the abstraction of which of the following models?

   a. Logical Model

   b. Physical Model

   c. Design Model

   d. Use-Case Model

7. Which of the following activities is performed within the Analysis and Design discipline? (Select all that apply.)

   a. Define a Candidate Solution Architecture

   b. Design Services and Components

   c. Perform Architectural Synthesis

   d. Analyze Behavior

8. Use-case analysis is carried out to develop an Analysis-level Use-Case Realization from a Use-Case. This involves which of the following? (Select all that apply.)

   a. Identifying the classes that perform a use case's flow of events

   b. Distributing the use-case behavior to those classes (using analysis use case realizations)

   c. Identifying the responsibilities, attributes, and associations of the classes

   d. Noting the usage of architectural mechanisms

9. Which role is responsible for designing services?

   a. Software Architect

   b. Designer

   c. System Analyst

   d. Service Designer

10. The Software Architecture Document is used to do which of the following?
    a. Document the logical architecture of the software system
    b. Document and communicate architecturally significant decisions
    c. Document all the technical details established by the Software Architect(s)
    d. Plan the implementation of the product

11. Which of the following is true about the Analysis Mechanism ? (Select all that apply.)
    a. It represents a pattern that constitutes a common solution to a common problem.
    b. It is one of the artifacts produced during Analysis and Design.
    c. It may show patterns of collaboration between objects.
    d. It helps in reducing the complexity of analysis work.

12. Which of the following is true about use-case realizations? (Select all that apply.)
    a. It represents how a use case will be implemented in terms of collaborating objects.
    b. It is the same as the use-case model; it just has more details as they relate to implementing use cases.
    c. It enables the use cases to be managed separately from their realizations.
    d. For each use case in the use-case model, there is a use-case realization.

13. For each use case in a use-case model, what is the number of realizations?
    a. One
    b. Many
    c. Zero or one
    d. One or many

14. Which of the following is an artifact used in the real-time systems? (Select all that apply.)
    a. Capsule
    b. Event
    c. Protocol
    d. Signal

References

IBM Rational Unified Process v7.0.

Krebs, J. Form feeds function: The role of storyboards in requirements elicitation. *The Rational Edge*. Retrieved December 2005 from http://www-128.ibm.com/developerworks/rational/library/dec05/krebs/index.html.

Kruchten, P. (2000). *The Rational Unified Process: An introduction*. Boston: Addison-Wesley.

CHAPTER 8

Implementation

By Ahmad K. Shuja

In the Rational Unified Process, the Implementation discipline is where actual code is produced, subsystems are integrated, and the system is implemented. Unit tests are performed while implementing the system. In iterative and incremental development, implementation is initiated early in the project.

Overview

The Implementation discipline explains how to develop, organize, unit test, and integrate the components as they are incrementally developed in every iteration. Testing during implementation is limited to unit testing. Other tests, such as the system test and the integration test, are carried out within the Test discipline.

Purpose

The Implementation discipline has the following purposes:

- To define the organization of the code in terms of implementation subsystems organized in layers
- To implement the design elements in terms of implementation elements (source files, binaries, executable programs, and others)
- To test the developed components as units
- To integrate the results produced by individual implementers (or teams) into an executable system

Workflow

The activity diagram shown in Figure 8-1 presents the flow of implementation within a RUP project.

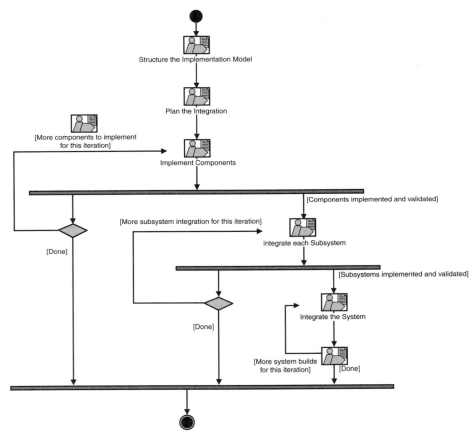

Figure 8-1   Implementation workflow

The Implementation discipline within RUP is composed of the following activities: Structure the Implementation Model, Plan the Integration, Implement Components, Integrate Each Subsystem, and Integrate the System.

Structure the Implementation Model

The Software Architect is responsible for structuring the Implementation Model. He produces a set of Implementation Subsystems that he can develop relatively independently. A well-organized Implementation Model prevents configuration management problems and allows the product to build up from successively larger integration builds. Structuring the Implementation Model involves establishing the Implementation Model structure, adjusting implementation subsystems, defining imports for each implementation subsystem, deciding how to treat executable programs and other derived objects, deciding how to treat test assets, updating the implementation view, and evaluating the Implementation Model.

Plan the Integration

This activity plans the integration of the system for the current iteration. Planning the integration is focused on which implementation subsystem should be implemented and in which order to integrate the implementation subsystems in the current iteration. You should plan the integration process early, at least in rough form, when the architecture is baselined. As the architecture and design evolve, examine and update the integration plan to ensure that the build plan is not made obsolete by changes in the architecture or the design. If you don't do this 100 percent just in time, iteration by iteration, you must examine and update it when the project plan changes because use cases can be moved from one iteration to another.

The **Integrator** is responsible for planning system integration and for developing the **Integration Build Plan**. Planning system integration involves identifying subsystems, defining build sets, defining a series of builds, and evaluating the Integration Build Plan. Note that the Iteration Plan artifact is a mandatory input that is required to prepare the Integration Build Plan.

Implement Components

This activity completes a part of the implementation so that it can be delivered for integration. In this activity, the following is carried out.

- **Implement design elements**—The Implementer implements the elements in the design model; that is, he writes source code, adapts existing source code, compiles, and links and performs unit tests. If he discovers defects in the design, he submits rework feedback on the design.

- **Fix code defects**—The Implementer also fixes code defects identified during the unit tests and performs further unit testing to ensure that no new defects have emerged and that the change is verified.

- **Evaluate quality**—Finally, the Implementer reviews the code to evaluate quality and compliance with the Programming Guidelines.

The Implementer is responsible for the following.

- **Implementing design elements**—This involves preparing for implementation, transforming the design to implementation, completing the implementation, evaluating the implementation, and providing feedback to design. In implementing the design elements, the Implementer produces an Implementation Element and Implementation Subsystem.

- **Analyzing runtime behavior**—This is done by determining the required execution scenario, preparing implementation components for runtime observation, preparing the environment for execution, executing the component and capturing behavioral observations, reviewing behavioral observations and isolating initial findings, analyzing findings to understand root causes, identifying and communicating follow-up activities, and evaluating the results.

- **Implementing testability elements and producing the Testability Element and the Test Stub**—This involves implementing and unit testing drives/stubs and implementing and unit testing the interface to the automated test tool.

- **Implementing and producing the Developer Test**—This is achieved by refining the scope and identifying the tests, selecting the appropriate implementation techniques, implementing the test, establishing external data sets, verifying the test implementation, and maintaining traceability relationships.

- **Executing developer tests and producing the Test Log**—This requires executing the unit tests, evaluating the execution of tests, verifying the test results, and recovering from halted tests.

The Technical Reviewer reviews the code and produces the **Review Record**. Reviewing code involves establishing checkpoints for the implementation, preparing review records, and documenting defects.

Integrate Each Subsystem

This activity integrates changes from multiple implementers to create a new consistent version of an Implementation Subsystem.

If several implementers work as a team on the same Implementation Subsystem, the changes from the individual implementers need to be integrated to create a new consistent version of the Implementation Subsystem. The integration results in a series of builds in a subsystem integration workspace. Each build is then integration tested by a tester or an implementer executing the developer tests. Following testing, the Implementation Subsystem is delivered into the system integration workspace.

The Implementer is responsible for implementing and executing the developer test. The Integrator integrates subsystems and produces the **Build** and the Implementation Subsystem. Integrating subsystems involves integrating implementation elements and delivering the implemented subsystem.

Integrate the System

This activity integrates implementation subsystems to create a new consistent version of the overall system. The Integrator is responsible for integrating the system and developing the Build. Integrating the system involves accepting subsystems and producing intermediate builds.

Key Artifacts

The key artifacts related to the Implementation discipline are the Build Plan, the Implementation Model, the Build, and the Developer Test.

Integration Build Plan

This artifact provides a detailed plan for integration within an iteration. The purpose of this artifact is to define the order in which to implement the components, determine which builds to create when integrating the system, and define how they are to be assessed. The Implementer uses this artifact to plan the order in which to implement design elements and what and when to deliver to system integration. The Integrator uses the integration build plan as a planning tool.

Implementation Model

The Implementation Model is a collection of components and the implementation subsystems that contain them. Note that the term **model** here is not meant to connote diagrams and other more abstract representations. Instead, an Implementation Model consists of Implementation Elements, Implementation Subsystems, and elements created to support developer testing.

Implementation Elements are parts of an implementation, specifically the lowest-level units of physical composition, replacement, version control, and configuration management. Therefore, these form physical parts that make up an implementation and include both files as well as directories. A piece of software code (source, binary, or executable) can be represented by an Implementation Element. A file containing information, such as a Read Me file, can also be represented by an Implementation Element.

A component can be an aggregate of other components. For example, an application might consist of several executables.

An Implementation Subsystem is a collection of Implementation Elements and other Implementation Subsystems. It is used to structure the Implementation Model by reducing the number of parts needed for consideration.

Build

The purpose of a Build, constructed from other elements in the implementation, is to deliver a testable subset of the runtime functions and capabilities of the system.

A Build is an operational version of a system or a part of the system that demonstrates a subset of the capabilities provided in the final product. The Build constitutes an integral part of the iterative development lifecycle and provides review points. Note that in the RUP, like in all iterative incremental development processes, progress is demonstrated via an executable, a (working) software deliverable rather than just documents or the like. The lifecycle "provides review points," but the Build is reviewable and objectively demonstrates progress toward completion. The Build is examined at the review points that the lifecycle provides.

Builds help uncover integration problems as soon as they are introduced. They represent ongoing attempts to demonstrate the functionality developed to date. In an iterative development, multiple Builds are produced throughout the lifecycle. One organization used to have an iteration Build that represented executable builds produced at the end of each iteration. Configuration Management is critical in such situations. Therefore, each Build is placed under configuration control in case there is a need to roll back to an earlier version when added functionality causes breakages or when there is otherwise compromised build integrity.

Numerous Builds occur during iterative software development. Each Build provides early review points and helps to uncover integration problems as soon as they are introduced.

Developer Test

The purpose of the Developer Test is to provide the implementation of a subset of required tests in an efficient and effective manner. Most of the Developer Tests are created in the same timeframes as the software components that need to be tested. Each Developer Test should consider the basic computer hardware; the basic underlying software environment; additional specialized input/output peripheral hardware; the required software of the specialized input/output peripheral hardware; the minimal set of software tools necessary to facilitate test, evaluation, and diagnostic activities; the required configuration settings of both software and hardware options; and any required preexisting consumables, such as populated data sets and receipt printer dockets.

Primary Roles and Responsibilities

The primary roles and responsibilities of the Implementation discipline include Software Architect, Implementer, and Integrator.

Software Architect

The Software Architect plays an important role in both the Analysis and Design and the Implementation disciplines. This role leads the development of the system's software architecture, which includes promoting and creating support for the key technical decisions that constrain the overall design and implementation of the project.

From an Analysis and Design perspective, the Software Architect has an overall responsibility for driving the major technical decisions, expressed as the software architecture. This typically includes identifying and documenting the architecturally significant aspects of the system, including requirements, design, implementation, and deployment views. Regarding the Implementation discipline, the Software Architect is responsible for structuring the implementation model.

Implementer

The Implementer is responsible for developing and testing components, in accordance with the project's adopted standards, for integration into larger subsystems (see Figure 8-2). When test components, such as drivers or stubs, must be created to support testing, the Implementer is also responsible for developing and testing the test components and corresponding subsystems.

This role develops software components and performs developer testing for integration into larger subsystems, in accordance with the project's adopted standards.

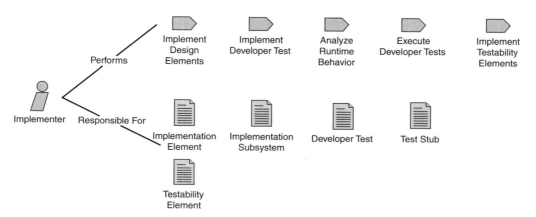

Figure 8-2   Responsibilities of Implementer

Integrator

This role leads the planning and execution of implementation element integration to produce builds (see Figure 8-3).

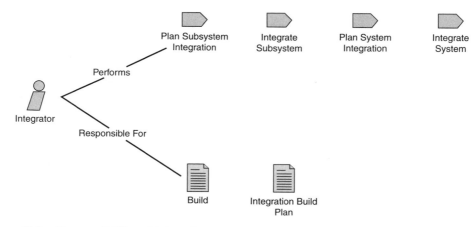

Figure 8-3   Responsibilities of Integrator

Important Concepts

The important concepts associated with the Implementation discipline include integration, prototypes, and runtime observation and analysis.

Integration

Large software systems require multiple software components, some off the shelf and others custom developed, to be integrated into a whole system. This is a specialized software development activity that combines separate software components to produce a software system.

Integration is done at several stages and levels during the implementation.

- Integrating the work of a team working in the same implementation subsystem before releasing the subsystem to system integrators
- Integrating subsystems into a complete system

The Rational Unified Process approach to integration is to incrementally integrate the software. Incremental integration means that code is written and tested in small pieces and then combined into a working whole by adding one piece at a time. The benefits include easy identification of faults, full testing of components, and early feedback on the execution of the system.

Prototypes

Prototypes are used to check business viability, to demonstrate key technology, to obtain project commitment or funding, to further understand requirements, and to check usability.

Runtime Observation and Analysis

This concept encompasses the observation of the software during runtime execution and analysis of the captured annotations where paths are traced through software components and then aggregated to understand global system behavior via statistical inference. Two key stages of such analysis are observing runtime behavior followed by analyzing those observations.

Because of the potential volume of the low-level information that can be captured from runtime behavior, the speed at which that information is generated, and the subsequent difficulty in understanding the potentially vast amount of information, automated tool support is a key factor in making this practice feasible.

Summary

The Implementation discipline provides guidance on the actual organization, development, unit testing, and integration of the system. It is related to other disciplines like the Requirements discipline, which describes how to capture requirements that the implementation should fulfill; the Analysis and Design discipline, which describes how to develop an architecture and design model that represent the intent of implementation; and the Test discipline, which describes how to integration test and system test each build during the integration of the system.

Sample Questions

You can find the correct answers to these questions in the Appendix, "Answers to Sample Questions."

1. In which activity are the changes integrated from multiple implementers to create a new consistent version of an implementation subsystem?
   a. Integrate each subsystem
   b. Integrate the system
   c. Integrate the components
   d. Implement new subsystem

2. Which activity evaluates the Integration Build Plan?
   a. Structure System Integration
   b. Plan System Integration
   c. Evaluate Integration Build Plan
   d. Evaluate System

3. Which of the following is a purpose of the Implementation discipline?
   a. Implement classes and objects in terms of components and source code
   b. Define the organization of the components in terms of implementation subsystems
   c. Test the developed components as units
   d. Create an executable system

4. Which role is responsible for integrating the system and developing builds?
   a. System Integrator
   b. Software Architect
   c. Integrator
   d. Developer

5. Which of the following is the primary artifact produced in the Implementation discipline?
   a. Implementation Model
   b. Build
   c. Develop Test
   d. Integration Build Plan

6. Which of the following is true about a Build? (Select all that apply.)
   a. A Build represents an operational version of a system or a part of the system that demonstrates a subset of the capabilities provided in the final product.
   b. A Build constitutes an integral part of the iterative development lifecycle and provides review points.
   c. A Build helps uncover integration problems as soon as they are introduced.
   d. Each Build is placed under configuration control in case there is a need to roll back to an earlier version when added functionality causes breakages or when there is otherwise some form of compromised Build integrity.

7. Which of the following applies to the Implement Components activity? (Select all that apply.)

   a. The Implementer implements the elements in the design model.
   b. The Implementer performs unit tests.
   c. Implementation Systems are produced.
   d. Code is reviewed to evaluate quality and compliance.

8. In which activity are the changes integrated from multiple implementers to create a new, consistent version of an Implementation Subsystem?

   a. Integrate each Subsystem
   b. Integrate the System
   c. Integrate the Components
   d. System Integration

9. How many Builds should be created during an iteration?

   a. One
   b. Two
   c. One or more depending on the iteration
   d. More than two

10. Which of the following is true for the Plan the Integration activity? (Select all that apply.)

    a. Planning the integration is focused on which implementation subsystem to implement.
    b. Planning the integration is focused on the order in which to integrate the implementation subsystems in the current iteration.
    c. The Implementer role is responsible for developing the Integration Build Plan.
    d. The Integration Build Plan serves as a mandatory input for Iteration Plan.

11. Which activity produces a set of implementation subsystems that can be developed relatively independently Plan the Integration?

    a. Plan the Integration
    b. Integrate Each Subsystem
    c. Produce Implementation Subsystems
    d. Structure the Implementation Model

References

IBM Rational Unified Process v7.0.

CHAPTER **9**

Test

By Ahmad K. Shuja

In the Rational Unified Process, the Test discipline provides guidance on evaluating the quality of the product. This evaluation is realized by finding and documenting defects in software quality, advising on the perceived software quality, validating and proving the assumptions made in the design and requirement specification through concrete demonstration, validating that the software product operates as expected and specified, and validating that requirements are implemented properly. This chapter discusses the activities that are performed when testing software that is built following the Rational Unified Process methodology and built in an iterative and incremental manner.

Overview

The Test discipline provides guidance on testing the system. The Rational Unified Process Test discipline focuses on testing systems that are developed in an iterative and incremental manner using the RUP guidelines. Therefore, it presents an iterative testing process that is scalable, customizable, designed for flexibility, and focused on efficiency. Iterative testing enables effective mitigation of risks early in the development lifecycle, enables the resources to focus their effort when and where they can have the most impact, and maximizes effectiveness by adapting the approach, process, or assets as you go. Therefore, the testing approach recommended by the Rational Unified Process focuses on maximizing the effectiveness of an organization's testing efforts.

Purpose

The purposes of the Test discipline are as follows:

- To find and document defects in software quality
- To generally advise on perceived software quality
- To prove the validity of the assumptions made in the design and requirement specification through concrete demonstration
- To validate that software product functions as designed
- To validate that the requirements have been implemented appropriately

Workflow

The activity diagram shown in Figure 9-1 presents the flow of testing within a RUP project.

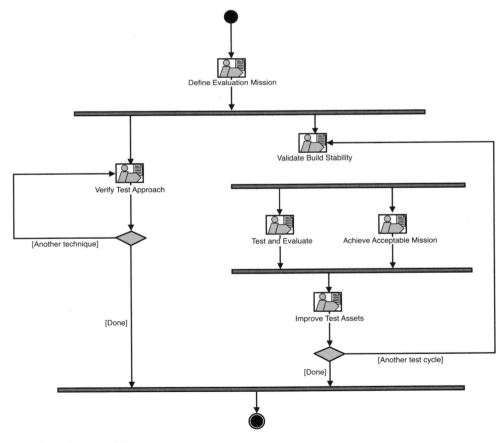

Figure 9-1   Test workflow

The Test discipline within RUP is composed of the activities covered in the following sections.

Define Evaluation Mission

This activity identifies the appropriate focus of the test effort for the iteration and gains agreement from stakeholders on the corresponding goals that will direct the test effort. For each iteration, this work is focused mainly on identifying the objectives for the testing effort and a good resource utilization strategy, defining the appropriate testing scope and how the progress will be monitored and assessed, and outlining the approach that will be used.

Successful definition of the Evaluation Mission requires the following:

- A **Test Manager** identifies test motivators and produces a **Test Plan**. Test motivators are identified by examining the iteration plan (Risk list, Change Request list, Use Cases, and so on) and identifying the key deliverables by which the execution of the plan will be measured. The Test Manager must also examine the details of the work to be done, identify potential sources of things that will motivate the test effort (work product, activity, event, and so on), and consider each test motivator in terms of the potential for quality risks. He must determine the relative importance of the motivators, update the traceability relationships, and evaluate and verify test results. In addition, he is responsible for understanding iteration objectives, investigating options for the scope of the assessment effort, presenting options to stakeholders, formulating the evaluation mission statement, identifying test deliverables, and gaining stakeholder agreement.

- The **Test Analyst** identifies targets of tests and produces a **Test Strategy**. He does this by determining what software will be implemented, identifying candidate system elements to be tested, refining the candidate list of target items, and defining the list of target items. The Test Analyst also defines assessment and traceability needs by identifying requirements, considering constraints and possible strategies, discussing those with the stakeholders, defining and agreeing on the assessment strategy, and defining tool requirements. This information is compiled as part of the Test Plan. The Test Analyst identifies test ideas and creates a **Test-Ideas List**.

- The **Test Designer** defines the test approach and produces the **Test Environment Configuration**. Defining a test approach involves examining the test motivators, test items, and software architecture. It requires considering the appropriate breadth and depth of the test approach, identifying existing test techniques for reuse and defining new techniques, outlining the test automation architecture, surveying the availability of reusable assets, and capturing the findings.

Validate Build Stability

This activity validates that the build is stable enough for a detailed test and evaluation effort to begin. The stability of each build is potentially validated once per build. However, it is not necessary to test every build. If build stability is validated, then it is further tested and evaluated during the **Test and Evaluate** activity. On the other hand, if the build is not stable enough to conduct further testing against, then testing and evaluation is carried out on the previous stable build. Therefore, for each build, the work performed during this activity might involve assessing the stability and testability of the build, achieving a clear understanding of the development work delivered in the build, and deciding on whether to accept the build for further testing as stated in the evaluation mission or to perform further testing on the previous build.

Validating build stability requires the following.

- The Test Analyst details the test ideas within a specific context driven by the target test items. This is achieved by examining the target test item and related Test-Ideas List; selecting a subset of the test ideas to detail; designing the test for each test idea; defining the required data sources, values, and ranges; sourcing sufficient consumable test data; and maintaining traceability relationships. The Test Analyst determines the test results and accurately records the test findings and the kind of follow-up that is needed.

- A Tester implements tests in the context of validating build stability. Typically, implementing tests involves selecting an appropriate implementation technique. In most cases, a mixture of techniques (which include manual test scripts, programmed test scripts, recorded or captured test scripts, or generated tests) is recommended to get more useful results. Implementing the test also involves setting up test environment preconditions, implementing the test, establishing external data sets, verifying the test implementation, restoring the test environment to a known state, and maintaining traceability relationships. The Tester also executes a set of related tests, records the results, and analyzes test failure. Test failures are analyzed by examining the test logs, capturing nontrivial incident data, identifying procedural errors in the test, locating and isolating failures, diagnosing failure symptoms and characteristics, identifying candidate solutions, and documenting the findings appropriately.

- The Test Manager assesses and advocates quality by focusing on supporting the overall effort of identifying the quality gaps, assessing their impact and risk, and finding effective solutions.

Test and Evaluate

This activity achieves appropriate breadth and depth of the test effort to enable a sufficient evaluation of the items being targeted by the tests, where sufficient evaluation is governed by the current test motivators and evaluation mission. This activity is typically performed once per test cycle and involves implementation, execution, and evaluation of specific tests, and corresponding reporting of incidents that are encountered. Successful execution of this activity requires the following.

- The Test Analyst identifies relevant test ideas for each combination of test motivators and targets test items, defines test details by detailing the test ideas within a specific context driven by the target test items, and determines test results by accurately recording the test findings and necessary follow-up.

- The Test Designer structures the test implementation by defining the overall structure for the test suite implementation.

- The Tester implements testing by developing standalone or collaborating tests identifying which tests should be executed together, executing a set of related tests and recording the results, analyzing test failures, and locating, isolating, and diagnosing failures and documenting them effectively.

Achieve Acceptable Mission

This activity delivers a useful evaluation result to the stakeholders of the test effort, where useful evaluation result is assessed in terms of the Evaluation Mission. This activity is performed once per test cycle. The activity revolves around keeping the Evaluation Mission in view, focusing on prioritizing tests, advocating the quality and the resolution of high-impact important issues, identifying regressions in quality introduced between test cycles, and where appropriate, revising the Evaluation Mission in light of the evaluation findings.

Successful execution of this activity involves the following:

- The Test Manager assesses and improves test effort by making timely changes to the test effort to increase its effectiveness, assesses and advocates quality by supporting the overall effort of identifying the quality gaps and assessing their impact and risk, and finds effective solutions.

- The Test Analyst determines test results by accurately recording the test findings and necessary follow-up.

Improve Test Assets

This activity maintains and improves the test assets and is significant if the intent is to reuse the assets in the subsequent test cycle. It involves the following.

- The **Test Guidelines** prepared earlier (as part of the activities performed within the Environment discipline) are now updated, revised, or refined based on the results toward the end of Test workflow. Note that the activity description states that the Process Engineer prepares test guidelines for the project. This is common across iterative development, where these tasks are performed at multiple points in time. Earlier in the project, artifacts are created, which are then refined and revised throughout the project.

- The Test Designer revisits and updates the Test Approach and revises the Test Strategy as appropriate. Note that the Test Approach was initially defined during the Define Evaluation Mission activity earlier in the Test workflow. The Test Designer also refines the techniques that will be employed, the testability elements, and the overall structure for the test suite implementation.

- The Test Analyst revisits and refines relevant test ideas for each combination of test motivators and target test items and refines the test details, the assessment and traceability needs, and the overall strategy that will be followed.

- The Tester updates the test implementation based on refinements made earlier—that is, revisiting the test suite and revising which tests should be executed together, and refining standalone or collaborative tests developed earlier.

Verify Test Approach

This activity is performed in parallel, following the definition of the Evaluation Mission, throughout the Test workflow. This is shown in Figure 9-1 as well. The Test Approach is verified early in each iteration as soon as there is some agreement on the mission of each iteration, and it continues as needed throughout the iteration. If, however, the Test Approach is well known and its applicability in the context is well established, this activity is considered optional.

The objective of this activity is to establish a clearer understanding of the constraints and limitations of each technique as it applies to a given project and to either find an appropriate implementation solution for each technique or find alternatives. This activity demonstrates that the various techniques outlined in the Test Approach will facilitate the planned test effort. The intent is to verify by demonstration that the approach will work, will produce accurate results, and is appropriate for the available resources. This activity involves the following:

- The Test Manager obtains testability commitment by defining, prioritizing, and promoting the testability needs and benefits.

- The Test Analyst defines test details by detailing the test ideas within a specific context driven by the target test items.

- The Test Designer defines test environment configurations to ensure that test effort can be supported appropriately, identifies testability mechanisms by identifying and outlining the mechanisms that will enable the test approach, and further defines testability elements by identifying the elements that will support and enable testing.

- The Tester implements the test suite by identifying which tests should be executed together and implements testing by developing standalone or collaborating tests.

Key Artifacts

Key Test artifacts are as follows:

- **Test Strategy**—This artifact defines the strategic plan for how the test effort will be conducted against one or more aspects of the target system. It includes an explanation of the general approach to be used and the specific types, techniques, and styles of testing that will be employed as part of the strategy.

- **Test Plan**—This artifact defines the goals and objectives of testing within the scope of the iteration (or project), the items being targeted, the approach to be taken, the resources required, and the deliverables to be produced.

- **Test-Ideas List**—This artifact enumerates ideas, often partially formed, that identify potentially useful tests to conduct. It is particularly useful earlier in the development cycle.

- **Test Environment Configuration**—Each Test Environment Configuration specifies an appropriate, controlled setting in which to conduct the required test and evaluation activities. This can be achieved by consolidating similar environments, typically where similar base-hardware and software profiles are used with only minor differences existing in the configuration settings. Therefore, this artifact specifies an arrangement of hardware, software, and associated environment settings that are required to enable accurate tests to be conducted that will evaluate one or more target test items.

- **Test Cases**—A Test Case specifies and communicates the specific conditions that need to be validated to enable an assessment of some particular aspects of the Target State Item and Test Case to define a set of test inputs, execution conditions, and expected results, identified for the purpose of making an evaluation of these aspects.

- **Test Data**—This artifact defines a collection of test input values that are consumed during the execution of a test. Expected results are referenced for comparative purposes during the execution of a test.

- **Test Script**—This artifact is a set of step-by-step instructions that realize a test, enabling its execution. These can take the form of either documented textual instructions that are executed manually or computer-readable instructions that enable automated test executions.

- **Test Suite**—This artifact defines a collection of related tests and provides a means of managing the complexity of the test implementation. Test Suites provide a hierarchy of encapsulating containers to help manage the test implementation. They provide a means of managing the strategic aspects of the test effort by collecting tests in related groups that can be planned, managed, and assessed in a meaningful way.

- **Test Log**—This artifact provides a detailed, typically time-based, record that provides verification that a set of tests was executed and some information relating to the success of those tests. This artifact contains raw output captured during a unique execution of one or more tests. It is unlikely to verify whether the test passes because the Test Log is typically too raw.

- **Workload Analysis Model**—This artifact is a model that identifies one or more workload profiles deemed to accurately define a system state of interest in which evaluation of the software or its operating environment can be undertaken.

- **Test Evaluation Summary**—This artifact organizes and presents a summary analysis of the Test Results and key measures of testing for review and assessment, typically by key quality stakeholders. In addition, the Test Evaluation Summary can contain a general statement of relative quality and provide recommendations for future test efforts.

- **Test Results**—This artifact summarizes the analysis of one or more Test Logs and Change Requests, providing a relatively detailed assessment of the quality of the Target Test Items and the status of the test effort.

- **Test Automation Architecture**—This artifact specifies various test automation design and implementation elements that embody the fundamental characteristics of the test automation system. It serves as a means of analyzing, managing, and communicating the fundamental characteristics and features of the test automation software system.

- **Test Interface Specification**—This artifact specifies the provision of a set of behaviors (operations) by a classifier (specifically, a Class, Subsystem, or Component) for the purposes of test access (testability). Each test interface should provide a unique and well-defined group of services.

Primary Roles and Responsibilities

The primary roles within the Test discipline and their respective responsibilities are covered in this section.

Test Manager

This role leads the overall test effort. It includes quality and test advocacy, resource planning and management, and resolution of issues that impede the test effort. Figure 9-2 shows the tasks and artifacts for which this role is responsible.

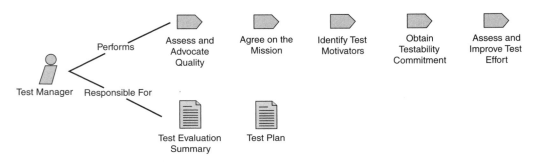

Figure 9-2   Test Manager role

Test Analyst

This role identifies and defines the required tests, monitors detailed testing progress and results in each test cycle, and evaluates overall quality. The role also represents stakeholders who do not have direct or regular representation on the project. Figure 9-3 shows the tasks and artifacts for which this role is responsible.

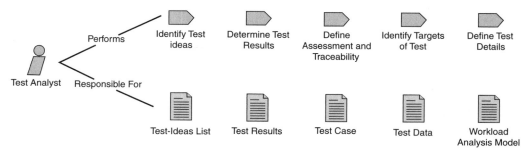

Figure 9-3   Test Analyst role

Test Designer

This role leads defining the test approach and ensuring its successful implementation. This includes identifying techniques, tools, and guidelines to implement the required tests and providing guidance to the test effort on corresponding resource requirements. Figure 9-4 shows the tasks and artifacts for which this role is responsible.

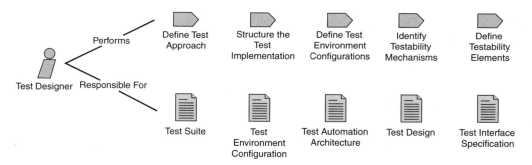

Figure 9-4   Test Designer role

Tester

This role conducts tests and logs the outcomes of his testing. Figure 9-5 shows the tasks and artifacts for which this role is responsible.

Reviewer

This role provides timely feedback to project team members on the work products they have submitted for review. Any member of the team can assume this role as long as he has appropriate prerequisite skills. Figure 9-6 shows the tasks and artifacts for which this role is responsible.

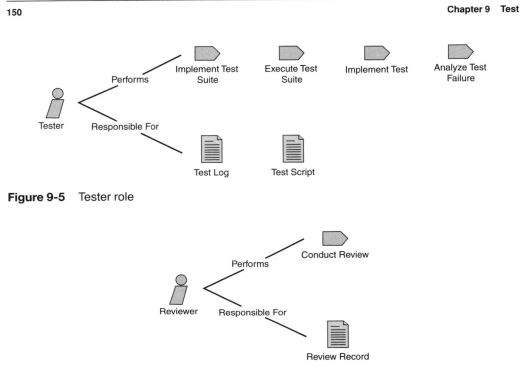

Figure 9-5   Tester role

Figure 9-6   Reviewer role

Important Concepts

The important Test concepts include integration with iterative development, dimensionality of the testing, and distinction between test cases and test scripts.

Testing and Iterative Development

In iterative development, testing is an integrated part of the complete development lifecycle and is used to provide a constant flow of information on evolving product quality. Testing occurs throughout the project lifecycle and provides timely feedback to the team. To achieve this, broad functionality—stability, coverage, and architecture performance—of the early prototypes can be tested. This testing is done early when there is still an opportunity to fix it. Testing in the later stages of the lifecycle focuses on ensuring that the final product is ready for delivery to the customers. If testing is carried out as it is designed in RUP, then the final testing really becomes very light.

Dimensions of Testing

According to Kruchten (2000), product quality can be assessed by performing different kinds of tests, each one with a different focus. These have been termed **test dimensions** and include quality, stage, and type of testing. Each one is explained in this section.

Quality Dimension

Quality refers to a range of things; principally, it means the absence of defects, but more importantly, it is fitness for a desired purpose. In other words, does the product do what we need it to do? A product might be free of defects, but if it does not perform what it is supposed to do, it will be useless. The quality dimension focuses on such aspects as reliability, functionality, and performance. Each aspect requires the execution of one or more types of tests during one or more test stages. Other subjective aspects of quality can include maintainability, extensibility, and flexibility.

Stage of Testing

In the RUP, testing is not a single time activity, as is the case in the traditional waterfall development lifecycle. In iterative development, different targets of test are tested in different stages of the software development. The test stages progress from unit testing the components through acceptance testing of the final product. The different stages are as follows:

- **Unit Test**—The smallest testable elements of the system are tested individually.
- **Integration Test**—Components, subsystems, or other integrated units are tested.
- **System Test**—The complete system or application is tested.
- **Acceptance Test**—The end users test the completed system or application to establish the readiness of the system for deployment.

Note that in iterative development, the testing stages in this list do not represent fixed phases that must rigidly occur in this sequence. Instead, testing begins early in the project lifecycle and happens often, and any test stage can be utilized in any iteration. For instance, a conceptual prototype can be subjected to acceptance testing to ensure that the product meets the vision.

Types of Tests

Tests can be organized around quality dimensions that align with the kinds of requirements described in the Requirements discipline as FURPS.

Functionality

Functionality tests involve the following:

- **Function Testing**—Function testing of the target of test should focus on any requirements for test that can be traced directly to use cases or business functions and business rules.
- **Security and Access Control Testing**—This testing focuses on application-level security, including access to the Data or Business Function and system-level security, including logging in to or remotely accessing the system.
- **Volume Testing**—This testing subjects the target of test to large amounts of data to determine if limits are reached that cause the software to fail. Volume testing also identifies the continuous maximum load or volume that the target of test can handle for a given period.

Usability

Usability testing is a method by which representative users of a product are asked to perform certain tasks in an effort to measure the user interface's ease of use.

Reliability

Reliability testing involves the following:

- **Integrity Testing**—The databases and the database processes should be tested as an independent subsystem. This testing should test the subsystems without the target of test's UI as the interface to the data.

- **Structure Testing**—The key to structure testing is that all decision outcomes must be exercised independently during testing, and the number of tests required for a software module is equal to the cyclomatic complexity of that module. The concept of structural testing is used in two main contexts: code internals and Web sites. Although different in nature, the root concept or idea behind structural testing is arguably the same in both cases. The older and perhaps more established use of the term structure testing relates to testing the internal structure of the software source code termed code internals. Structure testing of Web sites addresses the increasing demands of testing Web-based applications and is implemented and executed to verify that all links (static or active) are properly connected.

- **Stress Testing**—This is a type of performance test implemented and executed to understand how a system fails due to conditions at the boundary, or outside of, the expected tolerances. This typically involves low resources or competition for resources. Low-resource conditions reveal how the target of test fails in a way that is not apparent under normal conditions. Other defects might result from competition for shared resources, such as database locks or network bandwidth, although some of these tests are addressed under functional and load testing.

Performance

Performance testing involves the following:

- **Benchmark Testing**—Performance of a target of test is compared to known industry standards.

- **Contention Testing**—Tests focused on validating the target of test's ability to acceptably handle multiple actor demands on the same resource (data records, memory, and so on).

- **Load Testing**—This type of testing subjects the target of test to varying workloads to measure and evaluate the performance behaviors and capabilities of the target of test to continue to function properly under these different workloads. The goal of load testing is to determine and ensure that the system functions properly beyond the expected maximum load.

- **Performance Profiling**—Response times, transaction times, and other time-sensitive requirements are measured and evaluated.

Supportability
Supportability testing involves the following:

- **Configuration Test**—This testing verifies the operation of the target of test on different software and hardware configurations.
- **Installation Test**—Installation testing is performed to ensure that software can be installed under both normal and abnormal conditions (insufficient disk space, lack of privilege to create directories, and so on) and to verify that, once installed, the software operates correctly.

Regression Testing
The purpose of regression testing is to ensure that the defects identified in the earlier tests have been addressed and that the code changes have not introduced new defects. Regression testing ensures that the quality of a newer version of the target of test does not regress. To ensure this, previously executed tests are re-executed against the new version.

Test Ideas, Test Cases, and Test Scripts

Information used in designing tests is gathered from many places: design models, classifier interfaces, state charts, and code itself. At some point, this source document information must be transformed into executable tests:

- Specific inputs given to the software under test
- A particular hardware and software configuration
- Initialized to a known state
- Specific results expected

It is possible to go directly from source document information to executable tests, but it is often useful to add an intermediate step. In this step, test ideas are written into a Test-Ideas List, which is used to create executable tests. A **test idea**, sometimes referred to as a **test requirement**, is a brief statement about a test that could be performed. This less-specific intermediate form has two advantages.

- Test ideas are more reviewable and understandable than complete tests; it is easier to understand the reasoning behind them.
- Test ideas support more powerful tests.

A Test Case specifies and communicates the specific conditions that need to be validated to enable an assessment of some particular aspects of the target test items. A Test Case differs from a test idea in that the test case is a more fully formed specification of the test. Test Cases can be motivated by many things but usually include a subset of the Requirements, such as use cases, performance characteristics, and the risks that the project Is concerned with. As a general rule, test case specifications are most useful where the test implementation will be too complex to understand by itself without the support of a more abstract explanation provided by the test case.

A Test Script is a step-by-step instruction that realizes a test, enabling its execution. Test Scripts can take the form of either documented textual instructions that are executed manually or computer-readable instructions that enable automated test execution.

This distinction between Tests Cases and Test Scripts is especially valuable when doing test planning (via Test Cases before you have enough information to create Test Scripts).

Summary

An interesting difference exists between Test and the other disciplines in RUP: Test is tasked with finding and exposing weaknesses in the software product. It's interesting because, to get the biggest benefit, you need a different general philosophy than what's used in the Requirements, Analysis and Design, and Implementation disciplines. A somewhat subtle difference is that those three disciplines focus on completeness, whereas Test focuses on incompleteness. Therefore, testing forms an important part of the iterative development lifecycle, and the related activities are performed toward the end of each iteration. Note that early iterations might not result in an executable deliverable and therefore are possible exceptions.

Sample Questions

You can find the correct answers to these questions in the Appendix, "Answers to Sample Questions."

1. The purpose of regression testing is to ensure which of the following? (Select all that apply.)
   a. The target of test meets the end user needs and is ready for deployment.
   b. Any defects identified in the earlier tests have been addressed.
   c. The performance of the target of test meets industry standards.
   d. Code changes do not introduce new defects.

2. The purpose of the Test discipline is which of the following? (Select all that apply.)
   a. To find and document defects in software quality
   b. To generally advise on perceived software quality
   c. To validate that the software product functions as designed
   d. To validate that requirements were captured appropriately

3. Which activity identifies the appropriate focus of the test effort for the iteration and gains agreement from stakeholders on the corresponding goals that will direct the test effort?
   a. Define Evaluation Mission
   b. Define Evaluation Vision
   c. Plan Evaluation Mission
   d. Test and Evaluate

4. Which activity produces useful evaluation results?
   a. Verify Test Approach
   b. Achieve Acceptable Mission
   c. Test and Evaluate
   d. Improve Test Assets

5. Which of the following roles assesses and improves test effort by making timely changes to it to increase its effectiveness?
   a. Test Planner
   b. Test Manager
   c. Test Analyst
   d. Test Designer

6. The Verify Test Approach activity involves which of the following? (Select all that apply.)
   a. The Test Manager obtains testability commitment.
   b. The Test Analyst defines test environment configurations.
   c. The Tester implements the test suite.
   d. The Test Analyst defines test details.

7. Scope of testing within the Implementation discipline is limited to which of the following?
   a. Unit test of individual components
   b. System test
   c. Integration test
   d. Regression test

8. Which of the following roles is responsible for identifying Test Motivators?
   a. Test Manager
   b. Tester
   c. Test Analyst
   d. Test Coordinator

9. Test motivators are identified by examining which of the following? (Select all that apply.)
   a. The Iteration plan (Risk list, Change Request list, Use Cases, and so on)
   b. The details of the work to be done

  c. Potential sources of things that will motivate the test effort (work product, activity, event, and so on)

  d. Each test motivator in terms of the potential for quality risks

10. Which of the following is a technique used for implementing the test? (Select all that apply.)

  a. Manual Test Scripts

  b. Programmed Test Scripts

  c. Recorded or captured Test Scripts

  d. Generated Tests

References

IBM Rational Unified Process v7.0.

Kruchten, P. (2000). *The Rational Unified Process: An Introduction* (2nd Edition). Boston: Addison-Wesley.

CHAPTER 10

Deployment

By Ahmad K. Shuja

This chapter reviews the activities that are carried out in order to deploy the software products into the production environment. The activities are organized in a manner to ensure that deployed software products are available for users. Deployments mark the culmination of the software development effort.

Overview

The Deployment discipline describes three modes of product deployment:
- The custom install
- The shrink-wrapped product offering
- Access to software over the Internet

Purpose

The purpose of the Deployment discipline is to manage the activities associated with ensuring that the software product is available for its end users, including product deployment, testing at the installation and target sites, beta testing, creating end user support material, creating user training material, and releasing it to the customer (in the form of a shrink-wrapped package, download site, and so on).

Workflow

The activity diagram shown in Figure 10-1 presents the flow of deployment activities within a RUP project.

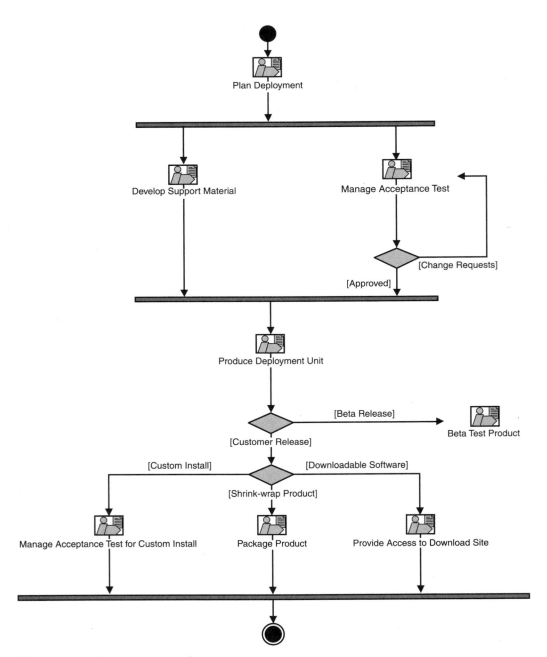

Figure 10-1   Deployment workflow

The Deployment discipline within RUP is composed of the activities discussed in the following sections.

Plan Deployment

Deployment planning starts early in the project lifecycle and addresses not only the production of the deliverable software but also the development of training material and system support material to ensure that the end user can successfully use the delivered software product. This activity plans the product deployment. Deployment planning needs to take into account how and when the product will be made available to the end user.

The Deployment Plan is the key artifact that the Deployment Manager produces while planning the deployment. Development of the Deployment Plan involves planning for producing, packaging, distributing, and installing of the software; migrating; and providing help and assistance to the user. The Deployment Manager also produces the **Bill of Materials**, which lists all deliverable items.

Develop Support Material

Support material covers the full range of information that will be required by the end user to install, operate, use, and maintain the delivered system. The Use-Case Model provides an easy way to get started in documenting how users work with the system. Note that the Supplementary Specification can also provide useful input into the development of supporting material. Supporting Material also includes training material for all the various positions that will be required to effectively use the new system.

This activity produces the collateral needed to effectively deploy the product to its users. The Course Developer develops Training Material, the Technical Writer develops End-User Support Material, the Graphic Artist produces Product Artwork, and the Implementer produces Installation Artifacts.

Manage Acceptance Test

The Deployment discipline places great emphasis on ensuring that the product is well tested prior to its release to the customer base. This activity ensures that the product is deemed acceptable to the customer prior to its general release.

The **Deployment Manager** ensures that the Test Environment is configured properly and manages the acceptance test, partners with other stakeholders to review the Test Results for anomalies, and produces any required Change Requests that require immediate attention and resolution and might delay or postpone subsequent plans for deployment to a wider user base. The Deployment Manager also organizes the installation of the product on one or more Test Environment Configurations that represent an environment acceptable to the customer as specified in the **Product Acceptance Plan**.

The **System Administrator** supports development and produces the **Development Infrastructure**.

In some cases, the installation process might be subject to an acceptance test, as might any preceding hardware upgrades and configurations. After the product is installed, the Tester typically runs through a preselected set of tests, usually based on a selected subset of the existing Test Suites, and determines the Test Results.

Produce Deployment Unit

After the Tester tests the product at the development site, he prepares it for delivery to the customer. The release can be created for the purposes of beta testing, a test deployment to the final users, or, depending on its level of maturity, for the final product. This activity describes the logistics of creating a product release that consists of the software and the necessary accompanying work products required to effectively install and use it.

This activity produces a deployment unit that enables the software product to be effectively installed and used. The Deployment Manager writes the **Release Notes**, and the **Configuration Manager** creates the **Deployment Unit**.

Beta Test Product

Beta testing involves implementing a beta program to solicit feedback on the product under development from the subset of the intended users. The feedback is used to augment the product. This activity describes the activities to enable iterative deployment of a product and systematic customer engagement in creating the final product. The Deployment Manager manages the beta test.

Manage Acceptance Test for Custom Install

As shown in Figure 10-1, for software installed at a customer's site, this activity ensures that the product is deemed acceptable to the customer prior to its release for use in his facility. This activity is a specialization of the **Manage Acceptance Test** activity to handle the special case of a custom install at the customer's site. Note that this activity includes all the same tasks as Manage Acceptance Test described earlier, but the context is that the tasks are performed at the customer's facility rather than in the development environment. Therefore, this activity is considered a specialization of the Manage Acceptance Test activity to handle the special case of a custom install at the customer's site.

Package Product

For shrink-wrapped software, this activity describes the tasks to take the software product, installation scripts, and user manuals and package them for mass production like any other consumer product. The Deployment Manager gathers artifacts in accordance with the Bill of Material and delivers them to the manufacturing organization to produce the Product. Following this, the Deployment Manager verifies the manufactured product by verifying the product against the Bill of Material, following product installation instructions, checking the product for usability, and shipping the product to customers.

Provide Access to Download Site

For software downloaded via the Internet as a software distribution channel, this activity describes the tasks to make the product available for purchase and download. The Deployment Manager adds product files to the server, enables client access to the product, enables customer feedback and support capabilities, and produces the Deployment Unit.

Key Artifacts

The key artifacts associated with the Deployment discipline include a styleguide, a deployment model, a deployment unit, the product, and user support material.

Manual Styleguide

The purpose of this artifact is to describe the stylistic conventions to be used to develop user support materials and document how to develop the end user support manuals. The Manual Styleguide gives advice on, and rules for, general and domain-specific spelling, sentence style, and technical writing issues.

Deployment Model

This artifact is used to capture and show the configurations of processing nodes at runtime (processing elements with at least one processor, memory, and possible other devices), devices (stereotyped nodes with no processing capability at the modeled level of abstraction), the communication links between them (connectors, between nodes, and between nodes and other devices), and the component instances and objects that reside on them.

The Deployment Model is leveraged and utilized by numerous roles, including these:

- The Software Architect uses it to gain a clearer understanding of the physical execution environment and build appreciation for issues related to distribution.
- The Database Designer uses it to understand the distribution of data in the system.
- The System Administrator leverages it to understand the physical environment in which the system will execute.
- The Deployment Manager uses it as a primary source in planning the product's transition to the user community.
- The Project Manager uses it to establish cost estimates and plan acquisition, installation, and maintenance as appropriate.

Deployment Unit

This artifact consists of a build (an executable collection of components), documents (user support material and release notes), and installation artifacts. A Deployment Unit is typically associated with a single node in the overall network of computer systems or peripherals and is sufficiently complete to be downloadable and run on a node.

As per the preceding definition, if the software product is available over the Internet, a user can download and install the Deployment Unit directly. In the case of shrink-wrapped software, the Deployment Unit is adorned with distinct packaging consisting of artwork and messaging and sold as a product. The contents of the Deployment Unit are noted in the Bill of Materials.

Product

This is the actual product or solution to be delivered to the customer. The entire project effort is geared toward creating a product that benefits the user community. The success of a product lies in its use.

The packaging of a product for market appeal distinguishes it from a Deployment Unit. A product can contain multiple Deployment Units and can be accessible as a downloadable commodity, in shrink-wrap, or on any digital storage media formats.

User Support Material

This artifact consists of materials that assist the end user in learning, using, operating, and maintaining the product.

End user support material is generated as part of the Deployment discipline and is typically required of any system that has an interface that users will interact with; systems that are principally embedded and have little or no user interface can omit this work product, although it might be applicable and useful even where APIs need to be documented. The Use-Case Model provides a useful foundation to document the way users will work with the system in an intuitive manner.

This work product often encloses one or more of the following documents and work products:

- User Guides
- Operational Guides
- Maintenance Guides
- Online demos
- Online help system
- Context-sensitive help
- Release notes

Primary Roles and Responsibilities

The primary roles in the Deployment discipline are those of Deployment Manager, Configuration Manager, Course Developer, Technical Writer, and Graphic Artist.

Deployment Manager

This role leads the planning of the product's transition to the user community. The Deployment Manager also ensures that those plans are enacted appropriately, manages any issues, and monitors progress (see Figure 10-2).

Configuration Manager

The Configuration Management function supports the product development activity so that Developers and Integrators have appropriate workspaces in which to build and test their work, and so that all artifacts are available for inclusion in the Deployment Unit as required.

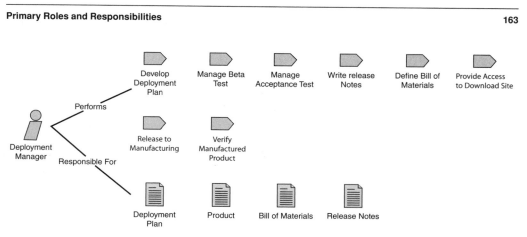

Figure 10-2   Deployment Manager role

The Configuration Manager is responsible for managing the overall Configuration Management infrastructure and the environment for the product development team (see Figure 10-3). In addition, the Configuration Manager has to ensure that the Configuration Management environment facilitates product review and change and defect tracking tasks.

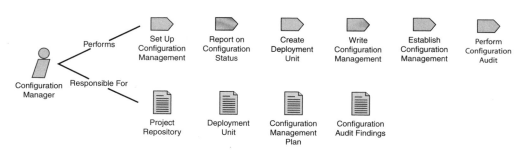

Figure 10-3   Configuration Manager role

Note that, as with few other RUP roles, the Configuration Manager also performs tasks and is responsible for associated artifacts from across multiple disciplines. In the case of Deployment, the Configuration Manager performs the **Create Deployment Unit** task and is responsible for producing the Deployment Unit.

Course Developer

This role develops training materials for training users on how to use the product (see Figure 10-4). A person playing this role requires an understanding of the product for which the training material is to be created, and, preferably, an understanding of that product from the perspective of the target users' needs.

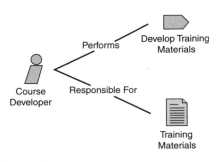

Figure 10-4   Course Developer role

Technical Writer

This role is responsible for producing end user support material such as user guides, help texts, release notes, and so on (see Figure 10-5). In doing so, the Technical Writer performs the **Develop Support Materials** and **Develop Manual Styleguide** tasks and is responsible for the User Support Material and Manual Styleguide artifacts.

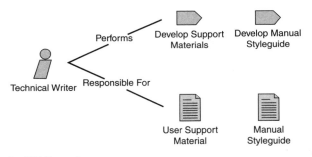

Figure 10-5   Technical Writer role

Graphic Artist

This role performs the **Create Product Artwork** task and is responsible for the **Product Artwork** artifact (see Figure 10-6). This is included as part of the product packaging.

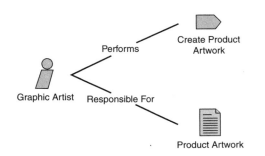

Figure 10-6   Graphic Artist role

Important Concepts

The important Deployment concepts include deployment modes and the relationship between the Deployment and Test disciplines.

Modes of Deployment

Various modes of deployment in the RUP include the following:

- Software in custom-built systems
- Shrink-wrapped software
- Software that is downloadable over the Internet

It is important to note that the major differences between the preceding modes of deployment are primarily based on the degree of involvement of the development organization in the way the software is packaged and distributed and how the end user will learn to use it. There is, however, a little difference in the development organization's involvement for the shrink-wrapped software versus the downloadable software. The key difference lies in the delivery mechanism and the development organization's involvement in either setting up the product Web site or in packaging or distributing the software.

Deployment Discipline Versus Test Discipline

Two types of tests performed within the Deployment discipline are acceptance and beta tests. These tests were discussed earlier in the chapter.

The Manage Acceptance Test activity consists of two tasks that are common across Test and Deployment disciplines. These are **Execute Test Suite** and **Determine Test Results**. Note that when performed within the Deployment discipline, the main focus is on acceptance testing. Test Log, Test Results, and Test Evaluation Summary artifacts are created.

Summary

Deployment enables the project team to finally deliver the desired solution to the customer. There are a number of different channels for delivering this solution. This discipline provides guidance on the best way to package the product and all related support material and documentation.

Sample Questions

You can find the correct answers to these questions in the Appendix, "Answers to Sample Questions."

1. Which of the following provides an easy way to get started in documenting the way the users work with the system? (Select all that apply.)

    a. Use-Case Model

    b. Deployment Plan

    c. End-User Support Material

    d. Supplementary Specification

2. The Deployment Unit is composed of which of the following? (Select all that apply.)

    a. Build

    b. Documents

    c. Installation of work products

    d. Release Notes

3. Which of the following roles is responsible for planning deployment?

    a. Deployment Manager

    b. Project Manager

    c. Implementer

    d. Configuration Manager

4. Which of the following roles is responsible for creating a deployment unit?

    a. Deployment Manager

    b. Project Manager

    c. Implementer

    d. Configuration Manager

5. The purpose of the Deployment discipline is to do which of the following?

    a. Manage the activities associated with ensuring that the software product is available for its end users

    b. Find and document defects in the product

    c. Validate software product functions

    d. Validate that the requirements have been implemented appropriately

6. Which of the following tests is performed within the Deployment discipline? (Select all that apply.)

    a. Acceptance Test

    b. Beta Test

    c. Deployment Test

    d. Installation Test

7. The Configuration Manager is responsible for which of the following tasks? (Select all that apply.)

    a. Create Deployment Unit

    b. Manage Configurations

    c. Create Configuration Management Plan

    d. Report on Configuration Status

8. Which of the following roles performs the Manage Acceptance Test task?
   a. Test Manager
   b. Project Manager
   c. Configuration Manager
   d. Deployment Manager

9. User Support Material includes which of the following documents? (Select all that apply.)
   a. User Guides
   b. Online Demos
   c. Release Notes
   d. Upgrades Information

10. Provide Access to Download Site involves which of the following? (Select all that apply.)
    a. Product files being added to the server
    b. Client access to the product being enabled
    c. Deployment Unit being finalized
    d. Deployment Unit being produced

References

IBM Rational Unified Process v7.0.

CHAPTER 11

Configuration and Change Management

By Ahmad K. Shuja

This chapter reviews the important concepts and activities performed to ensure that development methods are appropriately supported during the project lifecycle, product integrity is maintained, the product is developed and delivered as agreed upon, a stable environment is provided within which to develop the product, and changes are effectively managed. It also reviews the important Configuration and Change Management (CCM) concepts, the workflow, important roles, and their responsibilities.

Overview

The Rational Unified Process describes a comprehensive Configuration Management (CM) system that covers all CM aspects. CCM ensures that the controls required to guarantee the integrity of the numerous work products produced by different teams are intact. Many factors can contribute to compromising the integrity of the work products, such as simultaneous update, limited notification, and multiple versions. CCM helps implement controls that minimize the probability of costly confusions happening. Figure 11-1 shows the important components of CCM.

Change Request Management (CRM)

You need to carefully manage any changes submitted during and after the project lifecycle. Change mismanagement can lead to a product that was delivered on time but does not perform the expected functions or performs scope creep. The changes may be of the following two types:

- **Defects**—CRM supports defect-related activities, such as acquiring, assigning, correcting, and reporting. If you do not appropriately manage these, the probability of delivering a defective product increases.

- **Enhancement requests**—It is crucial to effectively manage enhancement requests to avoid scope creep. CRM supports the Change Control Board (CCB) in the administration of assessment and disposition of product change proposals.

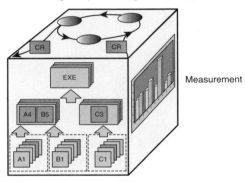

Change Request Management (CRM)

Measurement

Configuration Management (CM)

Figure 11-1   Configuration Management cube

You should formally submit changes via a Change Request, which you then use to track all stakeholder requests along with related status information throughout the project lifecycle. CRM addresses the organizational infrastructure required to assess the impact of a requested change on the cost and schedule of the existing product. CRM addresses the workings of a Change Review Team or Change Control Board (CCB). A CCB consists of representatives from all interested parties (stakeholders), including customers, developers, users, and any others who oversee the change process.

Measurement

Measurement is used to describe the state of the product based on the type, number, rate, and severity of defects found and fixed during the course of product development. Measurements, acquired either through audits or raw data, are useful in determining the overall completeness status of the project. Specifically, quality and progress are measured. These are defined as follows.

- **Quality** describes the state of the project based on type, number, rate, and severity of defects found and fixed during the course of product development.

- **Progress** helps in determining the overall completeness status of the project.

Measurement also enables change tracking, which describes what is done to components, why, and at what time. It serves as a history of and rationale for changes. It is quite separate from assessing the impact of proposed changes, as described previously under "Change Request Management (CRM)."

Configuration Management (CM)

CM describes the product structure and identifies its constituent configuration items that are treated as single versionable entities in the CM process. CM deals with defining configurations, building and labeling, and collecting versioned artifacts into constituent sets and maintaining traceability among these versions. Version selection ensures that the right versions of configuration items are selected for change or implementation. Version selection relies on a solid foundation of configuration identification.

Purpose

The purpose of the CCM discipline is to control changes to and maintain the integrity of a project's artifacts. In doing so, CCM allows for an effective CM process that

- Is built into the software development process
- Helps manage the evolution of the software development work products
- Allows developers to execute CM tasks with minimal intrusion into the development process

The Configuration and Change Management process encourages version control of work products (artifacts) in the development tools and de-emphasizes production of hardcopy documentation due to its inherent inefficiency. In addition, this process ensures that the level of control applied to each work product is based on the maturity level of that product. As work products mature, change authorization migrates from the implementer, to the subsystem or system integrator, to the project manager, and ultimately to the customer.

Workflow

The activity diagram shown in Figure 11-2 presents the flow of CCM activities within a RUP project. Each activity in this discipline represents a high-level goal that needs to be achieved to perform effective CCM. As shown in Figure 11-2, the activities **Plan Project Configuration and Change Control** and **Create Project Configuration Management (CM) Environments** are performed at the start of a project. The rest are performed on an ongoing basis throughout the project lifecycle.

The CCM discipline within RUP is composed of the activities in the sections that follow.

Plan Project Configuration and Change Control

This activity establishes an appropriate plan, called the Configuration Management Plan, which is used for managing and controlling change to the artifacts. These artifacts are developed throughout the software development process.

The **Configuration Manager** establishes CM policies by defining configuration identification, baselining, archiving practices, and defining configuration status reporting requirements. All this and more (discussed later in this chapter) are captured within the Configuration Management Plan.

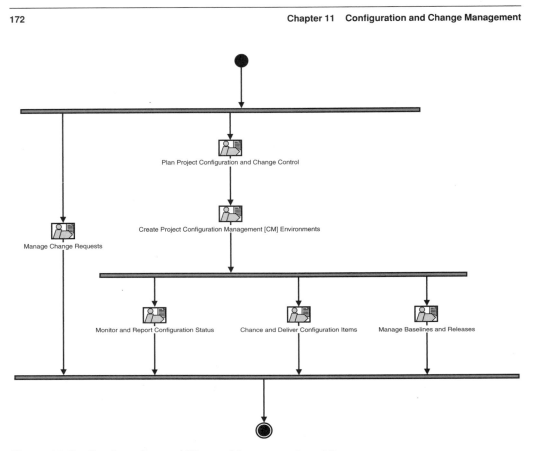

Figure 11-2   Configuration and Change Management workflow

The **Change Control Manager** establishes the change control process and the Change Control Board and defines the change review notification protocols. The change review notification protocols ensure that appropriate members of staff are notified when Change Requests are submitted.

Create Project Configuration Management (CM) Environment

This activity establishes an environment where the overall product can be developed, built, and made available for stakeholders. This environment provides private and shared workspaces and ensures that all project roles are able to access and work on the correct artifacts at the right time.

The Configuration Manager sets up the CM environment by setting up the CM hardware environment, mapping the architecture to the repository, creating an initial set of versioned elements, and defining baseline promotion levels.

The Integrator creates the integration workspace that is needed for the integration. When creating a new baseline, the Integrator needs to lock the integration workspace to ensure that there is a static set of files and that the developers deliver no new files.

Monitor and Report Configuration Status

This activity provides visibility to configuration change activity through ongoing monitoring and reporting.

The Configuration Manager reports on configuration status and defect trends and produces **Project Measurements**. In addition, the Configuration Manager performs physical and functional configuration audits and reports findings by producing **Configuration Audit Findings**.

Change and Deliver Configuration Items

This activity manages project artifacts and the work involved from their initial creation as private artifacts through to their delivery and general availability to the project team and other stakeholders.

Please note that **Any Role** (this role characterizes the tasks that any team member can perform) creates a development workspace, makes and delivers changes, and updates the workspace. In addition, the Integrator creates and promotes the baselines. As a result, the Workspace and Project Repository are updated.

Manage Baselines and Releases

This activity ensures that consistent sets of related or dependent artifacts can be identified as part of a "baseline" for various purposes, such as the identification of release candidates, product versions, artifact maturity, or completeness.

The Configuration Manager creates a copy of the deliverable items, baselined and under version control in the project repository, onto the necessary media for deployment in the target environment. The necessary media could be a CD-ROM, or in the case of a Web-downloadable product, a zipped copy available for download. The **Deployment Unit** is produced. As with the preceding activity, the Integrator creates and promotes the baselines here as well.

Manage Change Requests

This activity ensures that due consideration is given to the impact of a change on the project and that approved changes are made within a project in a consistent manner.

Note that Any Role can submit and update a **Change Request**. The Change Control Manager schedules a CCB Review Meeting, retrieves Change Requests for review, and reviews submitted Change Requests. In some cases, the Change Control Manager confirms duplicate or rejected Change Requests and updates the status as required.

The Project Manager schedules and assigns the work as per the Software Development Plan, Iteration Plan, and optionally a Change Request. In the case of a Change Request, which is optional, the work is scheduled and assigned within the Manage Change Requests activity.

The Test Analyst resolves the Change Request, verifies changes in the test build and in the release build, and evaluates and verifies the results.

Key Artifacts

Key artifacts for the CCM discipline include change requests, the CM plan, configuration audit findings, the project repository, and the workspace.

Change Request

This artifact is used to document and track requests for a change to the product. It provides a record of decisions and, with an appropriate assessment process, ensures that the change impact of the request is considered. A change request might represent either a defect or an enhancement request.

CM Plan

This artifact describes all Configuration and Change Control Management activities you will perform during the course of the product or project lifecycle. This plan details the policies and procedures applied to identify, protect, and report on all project artifacts. In addition, it contains the schedule of activities; the assigned responsibilities; the required resources, including staff, tools, and computer facilities; and the project change control process. This change control process ensures that all changes are managed effectively, appropriate stakeholders are informed, and the exact nature and impact of change is appropriately assessed and understood prior to applying the change.

Configuration Audit Findings

This artifact identifies a baseline, any missing required artifacts, and incompletely tested or failed requirements.

Project Repository

This artifact stores all versions of project files and directories. It also stores all the derived data and metadata associated with the files and directories. Depending on the size of a project, there could be multiple project repositories.

Workspace

This artifact enables controlled access to the artifacts and other resources required to develop the consumable product. Workspaces provide secure and exclusive access to versioned project artifacts. Two kinds of workspace can be identified: the development workspace and the integration workspace. On a project, there is one shared integration workspace and possibly multiple development workspaces.

Primary Roles and Responsibilities

The primary roles and responsibilities of the Configuration and Change Management discipline include the Configuration Manager, the Change Control Manager, the Integrator, and a concept referred to as the Any Role.

Configuration Manager

This role manages the overall CM infrastructure and environment for the product development team. The CM function supports the product development activity so that developers and integrators have appropriate workspaces in which to build and test their work and so that all work products are available for inclusion in the Deployment Unit as required. The Configuration Manager role also has to ensure that the CM environment facilitates product review and change and defect tracking tasks. Finally, this role is responsible for writing the CM Plan and reporting progress statistics based on change requests.

Figure 11-3 shows the tasks that this role performs and the artifacts for which he is responsible.

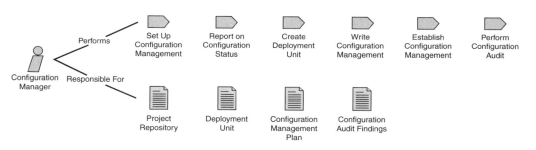

Figure 11-3 Configuration Manager role

Change Control Manager

This role defines and oversees the change control process. The role is often shared with a Configuration (or Change) Control Board (CCB) and consists of representatives from all interested parties, including customers, developers, and users.

Figure 11-4 shows the tasks that this role performs and the artifacts for which he is responsible.

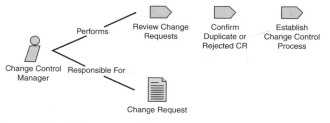

Figure 11-4 Change Control Manager role

Integrator

This role leads the planning and execution of implementation element integration to produce builds. Figure 11-5 shows the tasks that this role performs and the artifacts for which he is responsible.

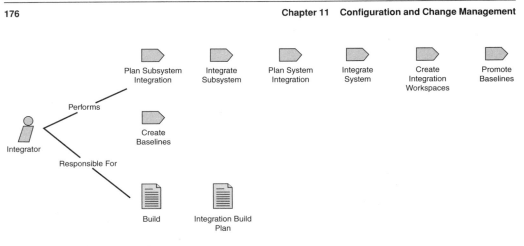

Figure 11-5   Integrator role

Any Role

This role characterizes the tasks that any team member can perform. In the case of CCM, Any Role performs the tasks shown in Figure 11-7 and produces the Workspace.

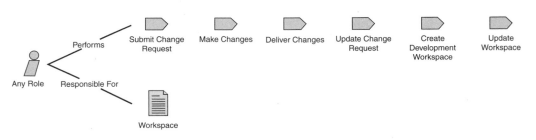

Figure 11-6   Any Role

Important Concepts

Some of the important CCM concepts include CM tools, the scope of CCM, the product directory structure, the promotion method, and the benefits of a CM system.

CM Tools

Configuration Management tools support members of the project team (especially those involved in the development) by enabling the following:

- Baselining of versions and concurrent development
- Configuration identification and management
- Configuration status accounting and change tracking

- Version selection
- Software manufacturing
- Measurement accounting by element

Product Directory Structure

The product directory structure contains elements of the product under development. As illustrated in Figure 11-7, it serves as a logically nested placeholder for all versionable product-related work products.

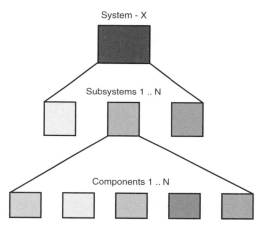

Figure 11-7   The product directory structure

Promotion Method

As the project progresses through the lifecycle and baselines become more complete and stable, "promotion levels" are used to characterize the baseline in terms of its completeness and stability. Promotion levels become especially critical in an iterative development lifecycle like the RUP because products of the project is continually refined and incremental builds are produced. Promotion levels, however, need to be defined as appropriate to address the individual project needs. Having said this, a common set of definitions can be reused in many different projects. Examples of promotions levels are as follows:

- Integration Tested
- System Tested
- Acceptance Tested

Benefits of CM System

Some of the key benefits achieved from the CM system are as follows:

- Supports development methods
- Maintains product integrity
- Ensures completeness and correctness of the configured product
- Provides a stable environment within which to develop the product
- Restricts changes to work products based on project policies
- Provides an audit trail on why, when, and by whom any work product was changed

Summary

Configuration and change management plays a crucial role in ensuring the development and the delivery of the agreed-upon product. Changes will happen during the life of a project, and some features need to be added and others need to be compromised to manage the scope and ensure delivery of the right product. This chapter reviewed the key elements for ensuring that CCM is implemented appropriately.

Sample Questions

You can find the correct answers to these questions in the Appendix, "Answers to Sample Questions."

1. Which of the following activities belongs to the Configuration and Change Management discipline? (Select all that apply.)
   a. Manage Change Requests
   b. Monitor and Report Change Status
   c. Manage Baselines and Releases
   d. Create Configuration Management Plan

2. Which of the following roles are responsible for creating the Deployment Unit? (Select all that apply.)
   a. Configuration Manager
   b. Integrator
   c. Developer
   d. Test Analyst

3. Which of the following is an element of the CM cube? (Select all that apply.)
   a. Change Request Management (CRM)
   b. Measurement
   c. Configuration Management
   d. Analysis and Reporting

4. Which of the following artifact(s) belongs to the Configuration and Change Management discipline? (Select all that apply.)
   a. Configuration Management Plan
   b. Change Management Plan
   c. Integration Management Plan
   d. Change Request

5. Which of the following role(s) can submit a Change Request?
   a. Configuration Manager
   b. Change Manager
   c. Any Role
   d. Project Manager

6. The purpose of the Configuration and Change Management discipline is to do which of the following?
   a. Control change to, and maintain integrity of, a project's artifacts
   b. Ensure proper configuration
   c. Validate software product functions
   d. Validate that the requirements have been implemented appropriately

7. Which of the following is a valid type of change? (Select all that apply.)
   a. New Features
   b. Defects
   c. Scope
   d. Enhancement Requests

8. The Change Control Board can consist of which of the following members? (Select all that apply.)
   a. Customers
   b. Developers
   c. Users
   d. Others overseeing the change process

9. Measurement is used to describe the state of the product based on which of the following attributes of defects found and fixed during the course of product development? (Select all that apply.)
   a. Number
   b. Rate
   c. Category
   d. Severity

10. Which of the following is true about the product directory structure?

    a. It contains the elements of the product in production

    b. It contains the elements of the product under development

    c. It is a directory tool used to structure components of a product

    d. None of the above

11. Which of the following is a valid example of promotion levels? (Select all that apply.)

    a. Unit Tested

    b. Subsystem Tested

    c. Integration Tested

    d. Acceptance Tested

12. Which of the following activities provides visibility to the configuration change activity?

    a. Monitor and Report Configuration Status

    b. Monitor Configuration Status

    c. Manage Configuration Changes

    d. Change and Deliver Configuration Items

13. Which of the following artifacts describes all the Configuration and Change Control Management activities that will be performed during the course of the project lifecycle?

    a. Change Management Plan

    b. Configuration Management Plan

    c. Software Development Plan

    d. Project Plan

14. Which of the following roles is responsible for creating and promoting baselines?

    a. Change Manager

    b. Configuration Manager

    c. Integrator

    d. Any Role

References

IBM Rational Unified Process v7.0.

CHAPTER 12

Project Management

By Ahmad K. Shuja

Project Management is one of the supporting disciplines in the Rational Unified Process. The Rational Unified Process does not cover all the knowledge areas that come within the scope of project management standards, such as the *Project Management Body of Knowledge (PMBOK)* by the Project Management Institute. Instead, the Rational Unified Process focuses primarily on the crucial aspects of an iterative development process. These include managing risk, planning an iterative project, and monitoring the progress of an iterative project. For those interested in project management standards, we recommend that project managers utilize sources like the *PMBOK® Guide* or *PRINCE2*. This chapter, however, focuses on the material required to prepare for the RUP certification examination.

Overview

According to the Project Management Institute *Project Management Body of Knowledge®*, **project management** is the application of knowledge, skills, tools, and techniques to project activities to meet project requirements. It is accomplished through the application and integration of the project management processes of initiating, planning, executing, monitoring and controlling, and closing. In the Rational Unified Process, the Project Management discipline provides the framework whereby a project is created and managed. In doing so, all other core disciplines—Requirements, Analysis and Design, Implementation, Test, and Deployment—are utilized as part of managing the project. The RUP Project Management discipline utilizes the project management principles—balancing competing objectives, managing risk, and overcoming obstacles to deliver the "right" product—and enables RUP project managers to manage software projects in a way that will significantly increase the probability of delivering successful software.

Purpose

The Project Management discipline has three purposes:

- To provide a framework for managing software-intensive projects
- To provide practical guidelines for planning, staffing, executing, and monitoring projects
- To provide a framework for managing risk

Project Management Discipline Workflow

The Project Management discipline workflow is shown in Figure 12-1.

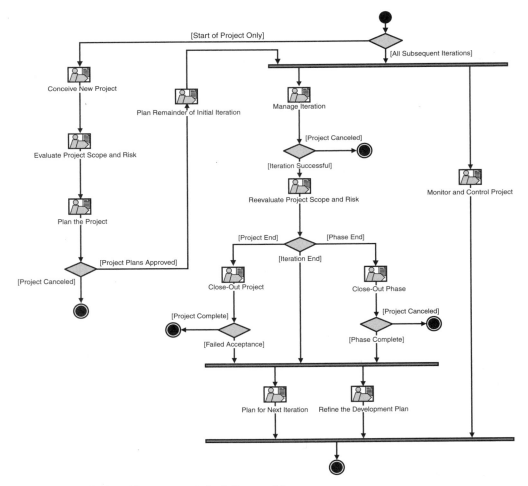

Figure 12-1   Project Management discipline workflow

This workflow enables us to see various activities performed within the Project Management discipline and the sequence in which these should be performed. Note that this sequence *does not* imply that one activity must be completely finished before moving on to the next one. In fact, the Project Manager performs each of these activities multiple times throughout the project lifecycle. Every time he repeats an activity, the associated artifacts are further detailed or refined based on increased knowledge. This sequence is significant from the perspective that certain goals need to be achieved at some level prior to initiation of the following activities. For instance, a Project Manager cannot just scope the project and evaluate risks if he does not know what vision he is trying to accomplish. Similarly, before he can manage, monitor, and control the project, he needs to plan and initiate the project at a reasonable level, and before he can close the project, he needs to initiate it. The key Project Management activities are covered in the following sections.

Conceive New Project

The key objective of this activity is to obtain enough funding to proceed with the scoping and planning effort. In the initial iteration of the Inception phase, the Project Manager performs this activity to conceive a new idea. He identifies risks and creates a **Risk List**. Then he analyzes and prioritizes these risks, and determines the appropriate risk management strategies. One of the other key artifacts created is the **Business Case**. Developing a Business Case involves describing the product that all stakeholders agree upon, defining the business context to help the project stakeholders understand and agree upon the intended market for the product. Agreeing upon the intended market might also involve defining the intended market for the product, stating the objectives for developing the product, developing the financial forecast, describing the project constraints, and describing options. The executive or senior management then reviews the Business Case and performs an investment appraisal. Executive or senior management will determine if it makes business sense to undertake the project. Following the approval, they initiate a project and create a first draft of the **Software Development Plan (SDP)**. Initiating the project involves assigning the Project Review Authority (PRA—an organizational entity responsible for overseeing the project), the Project Manager, and the Project Planning Team. These roles define the high-level project plan and approve the product acceptance criteria.

Evaluate Project Scope and Risk

As the software development progresses through iterations, the Project Manager needs to evaluate project scope and relevant risks. This activity reappraises the project's scope and risk and updates the Business Case accordingly. Key artifacts that are refined at the end of this activity include the Risk List and the Business Case.

Plan the Project

This is one of the most important activities within the Project Management discipline. It involves developing the components and enclosures of the Software Development Plan. The SDP contains the enclosure artifacts that will be discussed in detail later in this chapter. In addition to the creation of these artifacts, the Project Manager defines the project organization and staffing required to ensure project success. He also defines the following:

- Monitoring and control processes required to establish project indicators.
- Status reporting procedures and correction action mechanisms.
- Phases and iterations to estimate the total scope.
- Effort to develop a coarse-grained plan for the project. This coarse-grained plan focuses on major milestones and key deliverables in the product lifecycle and encompasses a set of iterations within the project phases. Objectives for each of these iterations are defined.
- Effort to develop the schedule and budget for the project and to develop a resource plan for the project.
- Effort to define the tasks for the orderly completion of the project.

The Project Manager compiles the SDP, which requires ensuring that its content sections have been appropriately completed (fairly high level and coarse grained early in the Inception phase and very detailed by the end of the Elaboration phase). The SDP also involves developing project management plans, discussed later, which cover metrics, requirements, risk, change/problem management, and so on, coordinating development of supporting plans with the responsible roles, and integrating these plans into the SDP when they are completed. Initial Project Planning Review is held near the end of the Inception phase, when the SDP is fully developed and includes a high-level phase plan that the project team has a high degree of confidence in. The Project Manager holds subsequent Project Planning Reviews at scheduled points, where he executes the SDP to be revised (for example, at the end of each iteration). He also holds these reviews at unscheduled points if he needs to change the plan as a result of problems in the project. Note that at the conclusion of this activity, he should know enough about the risks and possible business returns of the project to make an informed decision.

Plan Remainder of Initial Iteration

As the name suggests, the primary purpose of this activity is to create an Iteration Plan for the remainder of the initial iteration. This activity, therefore, creates a fine-grained Iteration Plan that guides and controls the remainder of the initial iteration in the Inception Phase. This activity is essentially the same as **Plan for Next Iteration**. The significance of explicitly showing this as a separate activity is to communicate the importance of planning for the remainder of the initial iteration. The emphasis is on the discovery and refinement of requirements; in later iterations, as we will see, the main focus is on the construction of software to realize those requirements.

The Project Manager needs to determine the Iteration Scope, which is driven by the top risks to the project, the functionality required of the system, the time allocated to the iteration in the Project Plan, and the phase and its specific objectives. In addition, the Project Manager must define Iteration Evaluation Criteria, which are oriented toward user acceptance and qualitative measures.

For Elaboration, the focus is on assessing the stability of the architecture and interface, the rate of change in the architecture, and performance of key functionality. For Construction and Transition iterations, the focus is on finding errors so that they can be fixed. Last, the Project Manager must define iteration activities based on the goals of the iteration and assign the activities to individual project team members.

The Project Manager reviews the Iteration Plan to ensure that it will satisfy the objectives set out for the iteration as documented in the Software Development Plan.

Manage Iteration

This activity contains the tasks that begin, end, and review an iteration. It ensures that necessary resources required to perform the work of an iteration are acquired, the work to be done is allocated, and the results of an iteration are assessed. The activities identified in the Iteration Plan are executed during this activity, which is concluded by an iteration assessment and evaluation to determine if the objectives of the iteration have been met.

As part of managing an iteration, the Project Manager determines the staffing needs for the iteration and consults with human resources to provide resources with the needed competencies, to map staff skills to roles, to form appropriate teams, and to ensure that appropriate training and mentoring are provided to staff members who lack skills required to perform their roles. In addition, the Project Manager initiates the iteration and allocates the staff and nonpersonnel resources of the project to each of the activities that will be completed in this iteration, as defined in the current Iteration Plan. The **Management Reviewer** reviews the Iteration Evaluation Criteria. This is a formal review of the tests and reviews that will be used to demonstrate to the customer that the objectives for an iteration have been met. It is an important review because it ensures that the project team and customer have consistent expectations for how success in the work of the iteration will be measured.

Note that the Project Manager identifies and assesses risks once again during this activity.

In assessing the iteration, the Project Manager produces an **Iteration Assessment** artifact. This involves collecting metrics (more discussion on metrics can be found in Kruchten, 2000), assessing the results of the iteration relative to the evaluation criteria that were established for the iteration plan, considering external change, examining the evaluation criteria to determine whether they are realistic, and creating the change requests based on the results of the assessment. Note that, unlike other waterfall-type development methodologies in which the key focus during most of the project lifecycle is on nonexecutable artifacts (mostly documents), in the RUP, executable code is the most important measurement that the project is moving ahead and that planned progress is being made.

Finally, the Project Manager carries out a formal review between the project team and a customer representative to reach agreement that each of the iteration evaluation criteria has been satisfied, and that the project is ready to proceed with the next iteration. The Project Review Authority is defined by the Project Manager and plays a critical role during this review.

Reevaluate Project Scope and Risk

This activity reappraises the project's scope and risk and updates the Business Case. It involves identifying and assessing risk and, if required, further refining the Business Case. If risks have changed, the Project Manager updates the **Risk List**.

Close-Out Phase

In this activity, the Project Manager brings the phase to closure by ensuring that the phase objectives have been achieved. When the final iteration of the phase completes, he holds a major milestone review as part of **Close-Out Phase** activity. He plans for the next phase, assuming the project is to continue.

In preparing for closing out the phase, the Project Manager ensures that the phase has concluded smoothly. He conducts a Lifecycle Milestone Review at each phase end. These reviews are intended to achieve concurrence among all stakeholders on the current state of the project. They are usually formal and are conducted with some ceremony, to demonstrate to all stakeholders that the aims of the phase were achieved. Phases and the respective objectives are discussed in greater detail in Chapter 14, "Phases, Activities, and Milestones." The Project Manager will have planned, going into the final iteration of the phase, to have all required work products ready for the Lifecycle Milestone Review. It marks a point at which management and technical expectations should be resynchronized, but the issues to be considered should relate mainly to the management of the project; major technical issues should have been resolved with the final iteration of the phase.

Plan for Next Iteration

This activity creates an Iteration Plan, which is a fine-grained plan to guide the next iteration. The Project Manager and Software Architect decide which requirements to explore, refine, or realize. They carry out detailed planning during this activity, which then leads into the next iteration.

Refine the Development Plan

This activity refines the SDP, as needed. As shown in the Project Management workflow, in parallel with the Plan for Next Iteration activity, changes to the SDP are made during this activity. This involves capturing lessons learned and updating the overall Project Plan in the SDP for later iterations.

Monitor and Control Project

The Project Manager performs this activity in parallel with most Project Management activities, as shown in the Project Management workflow. The routine daily, weekly, and monthly tasks of the project management are performed in this activity, with the idea that exceptions might need to be made based on the experience of the previous iteration. To complete this activity, the Project Manager performs the following tasks:

- Monitor project status to capture the current status of the project and to evaluate the status against plans.

- Report project status for review by the PRA.

- Give any issues that are beyond the Project Manager's authority to the PRA for resolution.

- Handle exceptions and problems as they become known.

- Carry out PRA review, where the project progress, issues, and risks are reviewed with the PRA. This PRA review is a status meeting that is held on a regular basis. As expected, this meeting is also used as a forum for raising issues that are beyond the scope of the Project Manager's authority to resolve. As with most status meetings, this meeting is scheduled and conducted, and meeting minutes are recorded and distributed.

Close-Out Project

In this activity, the Project Manager readies the project for termination. At the conclusion of the project, a PRA is held as part of Close-Out Project activity. At this point, the project terminates, unless the review determines that the delivered product is not acceptable, in which case a further iteration is scheduled. To complete this activity, the Project Manager prepares to close out the project and carries out a final acceptance review.

The Project Manager prepares for project close-out after the final delivery of software in the Transition Phase. The expectation is that there are no remaining problems that might impact formal acceptance, and that any issues that do remain are documented and handed over for resolution to the customer or other maintenance organization. The project team and a customer representative conduct the final acceptance review. At this review, the customer verifies that the product and supporting documentation delivered by the project meet the requirements and objectives as agreed upon in the SDP.

Key Artifacts

Earlier sections of this chapter showed the different artifacts that are produced, used, or modified as a result of a certain task. This section briefly reviews each of those artifacts, which form part of the Project Management Artifacts Set. The Project Management discipline contains the following key artifacts.

Business Case

This artifact provides the necessary information from a business standpoint to determine whether this project is worth investing in. For a commercial software product, the Business Case should include a set of assumptions about the project and the order of magnitude return on investment (ROI) if those assumptions are true. The Project Manager checks these assumptions again at the end of the Elaboration phase, when the scope and plan are defined with more accuracy.

Noncommercial software has a range of other aspects that need to be captured, including but not limited to the following:

- Alignment of the product of this project (software product or service) with business goals and project vision
- Improvements or efficiencies expected to be realized as a result of this software
- Role played by the product of this project in enabling the core business
- Other areas that will rationalize the investment

Software Development Plan

The purpose of this artifact is to gather all the information necessary to control the project. This artifact describes the software development approach and is the top-level plan generated and used by the managers to direct the development effort. This artifact provides a project overview, describes the project team and a project plan (by phases), and serves as a reference to iteration plans for each iteration (within a phase). This artifact, therefore, is comprehensive and includes a number of artifacts developed during the Inception phase. SDP is maintained throughout the project lifecycle. The main enclosures include these:

- **Measurement Plan**—This plan requires the Project Manager to do the following:
  - Decide which of the project's requirements and constraints are important enough to require monitoring and accordingly will define the primary management goals.
  - Validate the goals by reviewing them with relevant stakeholders to ensure that their focus is correct, that there is adequate coverage of all areas of interest and risk, that it is possible to reduce the goals to collectible metrics, and that adequate resources can be committed to the measurement program.
  - Decompose complex goals and define the subgoals and the metrics required to satisfy these subgoals.
  - Identify the primitive metrics needed to compute the metrics.
  - Write and evaluate the Measurement Plan, which will capture goals, subgoals, associated metrics, and required resources.
  - Ensure that instructions, procedures, tools, and repositories for metrics collection, computation, display, and reporting are in place.
- **Risk Management Plan**—This plan is developed to plan the identification, analysis, and prioritization of risks and to identify the risk management strategies for the most significant project risks.
- **Product Acceptance Plan**—The final acceptance of a project's deliverables by the customer is often the source of some friction between the customer and the software project teams. This is usually the result of a mismatch between the customer's view of how the product is supposed to function and the methods used to assess the product's

compliance with the stated requirements. By jointly writing a Product Acceptance Plan during the Inception Phase, the customer and the project team can avoid this situation. This collaboration helps the project team build a product the customer can accept and helps set the customer's expectations for how the product should perform. The Product Acceptance Plan also specifies how problems identified by the customer during product acceptance will be addressed.

- **Problem Resolution Plan**—This describes how to develop a system to handle problems that occur during the course of a project. Often, the procedure for managing each category of problem varies, such as by using different Change Control Boards or following different procedures for implementing solutions. When this is the case, the Problem Resolution Plan should describe the process for managing each category of problem separately.

- **Quality Assurance Plan**—The Project Manager defines or reviews the Quality Assurance program for appropriateness and acceptability and coordinates with the developers of the referenced plans. Successful development of the Quality Assurance Plan involves ensuring the creation of quality goals for the project, agreement by the customer, and inclusion in the Software Requirements Specification; defining the quality assurance roles and responsibilities; coordinating with the developers of the plans referenced within the Quality Assurance Plan; and defining the quality assurance tasks (including audits and reviews) and schedules.

Iteration Plan

This artifact is a time-sequenced set of activities and tasks, with assigned resources and task dependencies for the iteration; it is a fine-grained plan. As discussed earlier, SDP contains references to the Iteration Plan. Iteration objectives, evaluation criteria, and target dates are normally included in the SDP.

Review Record

This is created to capture the results of a review activity in which one or more project artifacts are reviewed.

Risk List

This artifact is a sorted list of known and open risks to the project, sorted in decreasing order of importance and associated with specific mitigation or contingency actions. Impact and probability are considered in calculating risk.

Issues List

This artifact gives the Project Manager a way to record and track problems, exceptions, anomalies, or other incomplete tasks requiring attention that relate to the management of the project. In general, these are items that are not being tracked through Change Management or as tasks in the Project or Iteration Plans, although they can derive from these.

Status Assessment

One of the objectives of the process is to ensure that the expectations of all parties are synchronized and consistent. The periodic Status Assessment provides a mechanism for managing everyone's expectations throughout the project lifecycle.

Work Order

This artifact is the Project Manager's means of communicating to the responsible staff what is to be done and when. It becomes an internal contract between the Project Manager and those assigned responsibility for completion.

Deployment Plan

To ensure that the system successfully reaches its users, the Deployment Plan includes a description of the set of tasks necessary to install and test the developed product, a schedule of events, persons responsible, and event dependencies such that the new system can be effectively transitioned to the user community. Note that a smooth transition is a key factor in satisfying the client, and this plan aims to minimize the impact of the cutover on the client's staff, production system, and overall business routine.

Primary Roles and Responsibilities

The primary roles and responsibilities of the Project Management discipline include the Project Manager, the Management Reviewer, and the Review Coordinator.

Project Manager

This role plans, manages, and allocates resources; shapes priorities; coordinates interactions with customers and users; and keeps the project team focused. The Project Manager also establishes a set of practices that ensure the integrity and quality of project work products. Figure 12-2 shows the tasks that the Project Manager performs and the artifacts for which he responsible. Note that only the most important tasks and key artifacts are discussed in this chapter.

Management Reviewer

This role evaluates project planning and project assessment work products at major review points in the project's lifecycle. Figure 12-3 shows the tasks that the Management Reviewer performs and the artifacts for which he is responsible. Please note that only the most important tasks and artifacts are discussed in this chapter.

Review Coordinator

This role facilitates formal reviews and inspections, ensures that they occur when required, and verifies that they are conducted to a satisfactory standard. Figure 12-4 shows the tasks that the Review Coordinator performs.

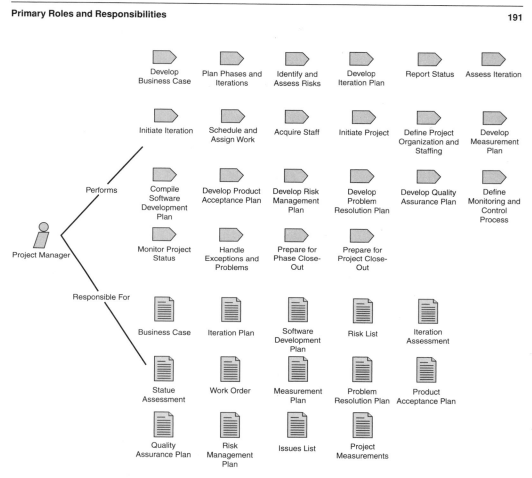

Figure 12-2　Responsibilities of the Project Manager

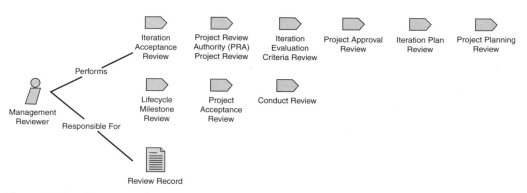

Figure 12-3　Responsibilities of the Management Reviewer

Figure 12-4   Responsibilities of the Review Coordinator

Important Concepts

The important Project Management concepts include the role of project management in the iterative development projects, risk management, and risk management strategies.

Project Management in Iterative Development Projects

Project management plays an important role in orchestrating an iterative development project. Without proper project management, the progress will be made in a random and haphazard manner, and you will have very little idea when the project will be finished. Rough estimates will be established on the resources needed for the project and when they will be needed. This especially becomes complex in iterative development projects, where members from across customer, user, development, management, and other teams need to collaborate to deliver an executable iteration build. In a traditional waterfall project, the software development lifecycle typically starts with Requirements, followed by Analysis and Design, Implementation, Test, and Deployment. However, looking at the famous RUP hump chart in Figure 12-5, it is clear that in iterative development projects, activities from across each of these and other disciplines are executed at any given point in the project lifecycle. Such execution requires well-disciplined and highly coordinated project management. Project management at the core of a project is represented in Figure 12-6 to ensure effective execution of the iterative and incremental development lifecycle.

Disciplines	Phases			
	Inception	Elaboration	Construction	Transition
■ Business Modeling				
■ Requirements				
■ Analysis and Design				
▣ Implementation				
▢ Test				
▢ Deployment				
▢ Configuration and Change Mgmt				
▢ Project Management				
▢ Environment				
Iterations	Initial	E2	C1 C2 CN	T1 T2

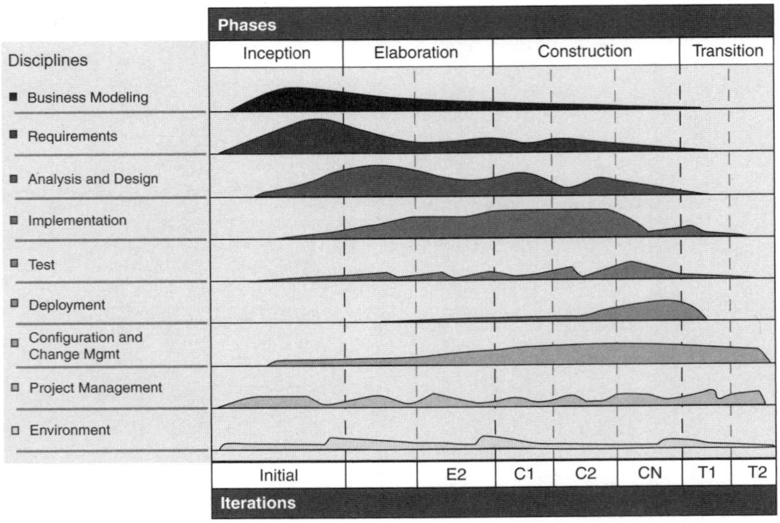

Figure 12-5   Hump chart

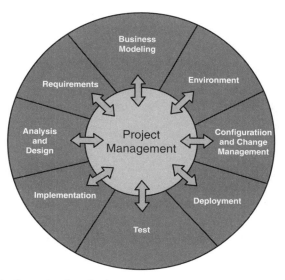

Figure 12-6 Orchestration role of project management

For a Project Manager, each iteration appears to be a small, self-contained project during which all the disciplines of software development are applied to produce a release of the product that meets a specific shared set of objectives (Bittner and Spence, 2006).

Looking across multiple iterations, Project Managers provide the direction to the project as a whole, organizing each iteration and associated deliverables in a way that ensures smooth delivery of the complete solution. As shown in Figure 12-7, to achieve this objective, the Project Managers must organize and manage the project as a whole and the constituent iterations at the same time.

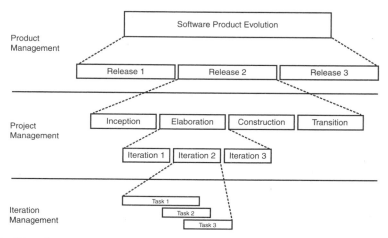

Figure 12-7 Planning at different levels

Note that each iteration requires careful planning, as iteration objectives must be met before an iteration is concluded and the deliverables delivered.

Risk Management

Risks keep evolving over the life of the project; unanticipated risks will be exposed, others that were identified will retire, serious ones will be easily mitigated, and so on. The Inception and Elaboration phases of RUP focus on confronting the top risks prior to entering the Construction phase. That is where RUP differs from traditional software development; it advocates managing top risks early in the project lifecycle. According to Bittner and Spence (2006), the goal of risk management is to identify and address those risks to which the project has the highest exposure and for which it does not have a strategy in place to control. In the RUP, the entirety of the project planning and management is driven by the risks. One of the most commonly used approaches is to keep an active list of the top ten risks that can affect the project and that are within the project team's ability to control. Ten risks are usually enough to manage during an iteration. Toward the end of each iteration, project risks are reassessed and the following iteration planned accordingly. Each subsequent iteration is likely to include additional risks in the top ten ones to replace those that have been successfully addressed.

Risk Management Strategies

RUP is all about proactively managing risks and not waiting passively for risks to materialize and then reacting to those problems. For each perceived risk identified in the Risk List, the Project Manager needs to decide on a risk management strategy. Possible strategies are as follows:

- **Risk avoidance**—This strategy requires the project to be reorganized such that it cannot be impacted by the risk in question.

- **Risk transfer**—This strategy requires the project to be reorganized such that someone or something else (for example, insurance) bears the risk.

- **Risk acceptance**—This strategy states that nothing will be changed and the decision will be made to live with risk as a contingency. When accepting the risk, risk mitigation becomes critical. Risk mitigation requires that some immediate proactive steps are taken to reduce the probability or the impact of the risk. In addition, a contingency plan is defined to decide on the course of action to be taken if the risk becomes a real problem.

Summary

Project management plays the central role in orchestrating the entire project from initiation to deployment and closing. The responsibility of project management in an iterative development environment becomes significantly complex and therefore requires expert project management as well as iterative development lifecycle skills. This chapter discussed the recommended project management activities performed as part of a RUP project. More knowledge and reference material can be found in the RUP product.

Sample Questions

You can find the correct answers to these questions in the Appendix, "Answers to Sample Questions."

1. Which of the following phrases reflects the purpose of the Project Management discipline? (Select all that apply.)

    a. To provide a framework for managing software-intensive projects

    b. To provide practical guidelines for planning, staffing, executing, and monitoring projects

    c. To provide a framework for managing risk

    d. To provide a framework for accurately estimating cost and time for building the required system

2. Which of the following is the Project Manager role responsible for? (Select all that apply.)

    a. Risk Management Plan

    b. Product Acceptance Plan

    c. Quality Assurance Plan

    d. Requirements Management Plan

3. Which of the following is true for an Iteration Assessment? (Select all that apply.)

    a. Compare the iteration actual cost, schedule, and content with the iteration plan

    b. Determine rework (if any) to be done

    c. Determine what risks have been eliminated, reduced, or newly identified in this iteration

    d. Prepared a detailed plan for the next iteration

4. Which of the following plays a central role in the Project Management discipline? (Select all that apply.)

    a. Project Manager

    b. Management Reviewer

    c. Team Lead

    d. Review Coordinator

5. The Close-Out Phase activity brings the phase to closure by ensuring which of the following? (Select all that apply.)

    a. All major issues from the previous iteration are resolved.

    b. The state of all artifacts is known (through configuration audit).

    c. The required artifacts have been distributed to stakeholders.

    d. The initial plan for implementing features of the next release are outlined.

6. Which of the following is a risk management strategy? (Select all that apply.)

   a. Risk acceptance

   b. Risk avoidance

   c. Risk ignorance

   d. Risk transfer

7. How many iteration plans are in a project?

   a. One per project

   b. One per phase

   c. One per iteration

   d. Four per project

8. The Software Development Plan contains which of the following? (Select all that apply.)

   a. Measurement Plan

   b. Risk Management Plan

   c. Product Acceptance Plan

   d. Change Management Plan

9. Which of the following is an activity in the Project Management discipline? (Select all that apply.)

   a. Monitor Project

   b. Manage Iteration

   c. Plan Remainder of Initial Iteration

   d. Refine the Development Plan

10. Which of the following roles can be combined with the Project Manager role when assigning team responsibilities? (Select all that apply.)

   a. Development Manager

   b. Test Manager

   c. Service Manager

   d. Process Specialist

11. Which of the following is carried out during the Close-Out Project activity? (Select all that apply.)

   a. The Project Manager readies the project for termination.

   b. Requirements are reviewed and are refined for the second release.

   c. A formal review takes place between the project team and a customer representative.

   d. The customer verifies that the product and the supporting documentation delivered by the project meet the requirements and objectives as agreed in the Software Development Plan.

12. The Software Development Plan contains which of the following artifacts? (Select all that apply.)
    a. Problem Resolution Plan
    b. Product Acceptance Plan
    c. Iteration Plan
    d. Use Cases to be implemented

13. Which of the following is important in calculating risk? (Select all that apply.)
    a. Impact
    b. Probability
    c. Urgency
    d. Magnitude

14. Which of the following artifacts lists the things that can potentially lead to loss or damaging results?
    a. Issue list
    b. Risk Management Plan
    c. Risk list
    d. Software Development Plan

15. How often is an iteration assessment carried out?
    a. Once per iteration
    b. Once per phase
    c. Once per project
    d. At the Project Manager's discretion

16. For a successful iteration assessment, which of the following is the most important part of an iteration plan?
    a. Evaluation Criteria
    b. Plan
    c. Uses Cases
    d. Iteration Goal and Artifacts

References

Bittner, K., & Spence, I. (2006). *Managing iterative software development projects*. Indianapolis: Addison-Wesley.

IBM Rational Unified Process v7.0.

[PMBOK] (2004). *A guide to the project management body of knowledge (PMBOK Guide)*, 3rd Edition. Newtone Square, PA: The Project Management Institute.

[PRINCE2] http://www.ogc.gov.uk/methods_prince_2.asp

Environment

By Ahmad K. Shuja

Chapter 2, "Key Principles for Business-Driven Development," discussed the principles that underlie successful business-driven development (BDD). One of them is Adapt the Process. The Environment discipline requires the Process Engineer and Project Manager to tailor a process framework to a project's needs. The result is a roadmap for the extended project team that defines the rules with which the project will comply. This chapter focuses on the roles, activities, and artifacts involved in adapting a process, in this case the RUP.

Overview

In the past, many organizations built their homegrown process models, which were often tied to a specific organizational structure. Over time, templates for artifacts appeared and turned from a pseudo-standard to official project documentation within each organization. A common misunderstanding is that applying RUP to a project means that the existing structures and communication channels did not work. Before you apply RUP, you need to adapt it to specific organizational needs. Adapting RUP involves identifying and incorporating existing organizational best practices with practices and processes recommended by RUP, thereby tailoring RUP. If the organization does not have a common process in place, the RUP process framework can potentially jump-start this discussion by providing common workflows, activities, and templates. After you define the process, you can link software and hardware requirements to the activities and artifacts, enabling an automation of the process and integrated data exchange. This chapter is dedicated to helping with the adaptation of the process, also known as **tailorization** of the process. The Environment discipline provides the supporting environment for a project. In doing so, it supports all other disciplines. The Environment discipline focuses on the activities that are necessary to configure the process to meet its specific needs. It defines what improvements are realistic under the project's given circumstances, which includes current process, current tools, current staff skills and their capabilities for change, and current problems and possible improvement objectives.

The following discussion briefly looks at some of the components of the Environment discipline that support the key enablers for adapting the process.

Purpose

The purpose of the Environment discipline is to provide the software development organization with the software development environment—both processes and tools—that will support the development team. Regarding the tools, the Environment discipline also aims to support tool selection, acquisition, setup, and configuration.

Environment Workflow

The Environment workflow shown in Figure 13-1 presents the activities carried out to configure the environment for the project. It is important to decide what artifacts are to be used and how they are to be used. To gain desired effectiveness, tailor each identified artifact to fit the project needs. Note that you only carry out the Prepare Environment for Project during the Inception phase. This chapter discusses in detail what is included in preparing the development environment for the project.

The Environment discipline within RUP is composed of the activities discussed in the following sections.

Prepare Environment for Project

You only carry out this activity during the Inception phase. It ensures that an appropriate development environment, including both process and tools, is prepared for the project. Preparing the development environment involves tailoring the development process, developing the **Development Case**, preparing templates and guidelines for the project, and selecting and acquiring required tools. A small team best performs the tasks within this activity. The members of this team possess good general knowledge of the Development Process. If the organization has a dedicated process group focusing on the process and development environment, the Process Engineer role is often staffed from this group.

Prepare Environment for an Iteration

Based on the lessons learned following initial iterations, further refinements are made to the Development Case leading to the actual refinement of the development environment. This activity involves refining the Development Case, ensuring that guidelines and templates meet iteration needs, developing necessary Manual Styleguides, and confirming that appropriate tools are in place. Different roles engaged in performing the tasks within this activity are Process Engineer, Technical Writer, and Tool Specialist. We will discuss these later in the chapter.

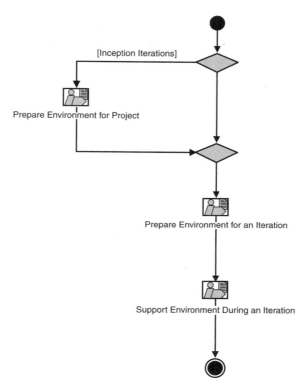

Figure 13-1   Environment workflow

Support Environment During an Iteration

Supporting the development environment continues with the project to ensure that an appropriate environment is in place that enables project members to do their jobs efficiently and effectively. Supporting the development environment might involve installing required software, ensuring that hardware is functioning properly, and making sure that potential network issues are resolved without delays. The System Administrator is the main role responsible for supporting the environment during an iteration.

Key Artifacts

The key artifacts for the Environment discipline include the development process, the development case, project-specific guidelines, project-specific templates, the development infrastructure, the development organization assessment, and the Manual Styleguide.

Development Process

A Development Process is recommended for all projects. It is a configuration of the underlying RUP framework that meets the specific needs of the project. It is meant to provide process support and guidance for the project team members. In other words, the Development Process describes the process (what artifacts will be produced for each discipline, who will produce them, and in what timeframe they will be produced) that a project must follow to produce the project's desired results. The Development Process is also referred to as the Software Development Process and contains the project-specific guidelines, the project-specific templates, and the Development Case.

Development Case

The Development Case is optional for small projects but recommended for medium to large ones. This artifact describes the development process that you have tailored for your organization or for a specific project. It is recommended that you develop the Development Case in increments, covering more and more of the disciplines in each iteration. You create the Development Case early in the project and refine it following the lessons learned at the end of each iteration. The Development Case normally includes phases and milestones, which artifacts to use, how to use them, who will produce them, when they will be produced, to what level of detail, which activities to perform, additional activities, how to work in each discipline, and iteration plan descriptions.

Project-Specific Guidelines

This artifact provides prescriptive guidance on how to perform a certain task or a set of tasks in the context of the project. Note that these guidelines are also appropriate whenever certain project-specific standards must be followed or best practices need to be communicated. This artifact is recommended as appropriate for project tasks because many projects choose to re-use guidelines rather than create their own. On the other hand, small teams with experienced members and a shared philosophy might decide not to formally document some guidelines. Note that if a team decides not to produce guidelines, there is a risk that standards and quality might drift over time.

Project-Specific Templates

These are the templates required for artifacts used in the project. These templates are useful in providing a base template that should be tailored to fit the needs of the project. Project-Specific Templates are recommended as applicable to project artifacts.

Development Infrastructure

The Development Infrastructure includes the hardware and software, such as the computers and operating systems, on which the tools run. The Development Infrastructure also includes the hardware and software used to interconnect computers and users. Note that all projects will have a Development Infrastructure. Many projects will re-use an existing development infrastructure rather than create their own.

Development Organization Assessment

This artifact describes the current status of the software organization in terms of current process, tools, team members' competencies and attitudes, customers, competitors, technical trends, problems, and improvement areas. This artifact is used to guide the Process Engineer in tailoring the process for an organization or for a particular project. Development Organization Assessment is an optional artifact. However, in the case of larger organizations, this assessment is often critical to making good process-related decisions.

Manual Styleguide

This artifact helps to ensure consistency across the style and quality of user support material. A Manual Styleguide is recommended for most projects with user support material. Note that many projects will re-use an existing style guide rather than create their own.

Primary Roles and Responsibilities

The primary roles and responsibilities associated with the Environment discipline include Process Engineer, System Administrator, Tool Specialist, and Technical Writer.

Process Engineer

This is a support role in the RUP. Although a support role, the Process Engineer provides valuable services to ensure project success. The main goal of the Process Engineer role is to equip the project team with an appropriate development process and to make sure that the team members are not hindered in doing their jobs. To achieve this goal, the Process Engineer tailors the process to meet specific project needs, educates and mentors project members on process-related issues, ensures that lessons learned are captured and incorporated into future process refinements, and assists the Project Manager in planning the project. The specific responsibilities of the Process Engineer are illustrated in Figure 13-2.

Figure 13-2 Responsibilities of the Process Engineer

System Administrator

This role maintains the development infrastructure, both hardware and software. This includes installation, configuration, backup, and more. Figure 13-3 shows the tasks that the System Administrator performs and the artifacts for which he is responsible.

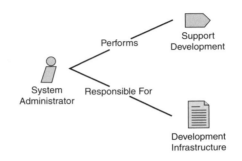

Figure 13-3   Responsibilities of the System Administrator

Tool Specialist

This role supports the tools used by the project. This includes selecting and acquiring tools, configuring and setting them up, and verifying that they work. Figure 13-4 shows the tasks that the Tool Specialist performs and the artifacts for which he is responsible.

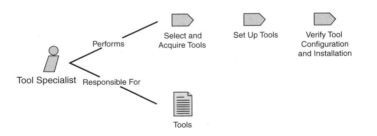

Figure 13-4   Responsibilities of the Tool Specialist

Technical Writer

This role produces end user support material such as user guides, help texts, release notes, and so on. Figure 13-5 shows the tasks that the Technical Writer performs and the artifacts for which s/he is responsible. Note that the Technical Writer role has responsibilities that span the Environment and Deployment disciplines. The Technical Writer is also responsible for developing a Manual Styleguide within the Environment discipline.

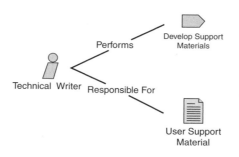

Figure 13-5   Responsibilities of the Technical Writer

Important Concepts

Important concepts for the Environment discipline include tailored process and tool support for process tailoring,

Tailored Process

For RUP to be adopted in an organization, it needs to be adapted to address the specific needs of that organization. The RUP constitutes guidance on a rich set of software engineering practices. It is not expected that the organization will take RUP out-of-the-box and try to adopt it as is. The message is not new—one size does not fit all. No single project will benefit from using all of RUP. To the contrary, projects that try to use all of RUP might suffer from significant inefficiencies. There is no one right process for all circumstances. The RUP framework is built as a configurable process product so that it can be tailored to meet an organization's or project's specific needs. In general, you can tailor RUP at two levels.

- **Organizational level**—At an organizational level, a standard set of processes is defined. Process Engineers modify, improve, or configure a common process or processes to be used organization-wide. This considers issues such as the application domain, re-use practices, and core technologies mastered by the company. As a result, there may arise a need to introduce new disciplines or additional phases. In addition, some activities might need to be removed and others might need to be tailored. An organization might end up with a standard set of processes instead of a single process. Each process can be adapted to a different type of development or a different type of business. For example, in some organizations, the predefined classic RUP configuration can serve as a single organization-wide process that is tailored for each project. In other more complex organizations building a variety of different software products, there may be a greater need to have a standard set of processes. The level of tailoring required really depends on the organization's specific needs as to what standard process or processes are defined.
- **Project Level**—At the project level, the Process Engineer takes a standard process defined for the organization and further refines it for a given project. At this level, the

Process Engineer considers the size of the project, the re-use of company assets, the initial cycle ("green-field development") versus the evolution cycle, COTS-based development, and so on. Therefore, a standard process is tailored to meet project-specific needs. Keep in mind that a standard process might have been defined already for one type of development project, such as green-field, which is then further refined for a *specific* green-field project.

Other categories of process customization work include these.

- Extend the RUP framework by creating RUP plug-ins.
- Configure the process by selecting the relevant method content and plug-ins in the RUP framework.
- Instantiate the process by fine-tuning the configuration to fit the exact needs of a project.

A detailed discussion on tailoring RUP is provided in Chapter 15, "Tailoring."

Tool Support for Process Tailoring

Tailoring is made more efficient and more easily enabled through **Rational Method Composer (RMC)**. For those projects that are only concerned with project-specific tailoring (or where an organizational-level process does not exist), tailoring the RUP typically starts with one of the predefined configurations within RMC. The configuration that may fit closest to a given type of the project (one is defined for medium-sized projects and the other is a classic one) can be tailored by using RMC; the delivery process is instantiated for the project.

Detailed discussion of tool support for process tailoring is provided in Chapter 16, "Tools."

Summary

The setup of a project's environment is crucial for the project team's success. The purpose of a process is to guide team members through the software engineering process and prevent or avoid obstacles and pitfalls. During the environment discipline, a RUP process instance is aligned with existing and successful processes of the target organization. The tool specialists and process engineers automate the process by linking software engineering tools to the process elements and integrating them with each other.

Sample Questions

You can find the correct answers to these questions in the Appendix, "Answers to Sample Questions."

1. Which role in a RUP project is in charge of developing the project-specific process content? (Select all that apply.)
   a. Process Engineer
   b. Stakeholder
   c. Project Manager
   d. Tool Mentor

2. In which of the following tasks is the Tool Specialist involved? (Select all that apply.)
   a. Select and Acquire Staff
   b. Set Up Tools
   c. Verify Tool Configuration and Installation
   d. Develop Development Case

3. The Development Case drives the content of which of the following?
   a. The development process
   b. The development infrastructure
   c. The development environment
   d. The development tools

4. Which of the following statements is true about the Development Cases? (Select all that apply.)
   a. The Development Cases are created on a program-level and apply to all projects within that initiative.
   b. The Development Case describes the development process that is chosen for the project.
   c. The Development Case includes phases and milestones.
   d. The Development Case includes artifacts that are to be used and who will produce them.

5. Which of the following is contained in the Development Infrastructure? (Select all that apply.)
   a. Software
   b. Hardware
   c. Operating systems
   d. Style guidelines

6. Which of the following artifacts is contained in the development process? (Select all that apply.)
   a. Project-specific guidelines
   b. Project-specific templates
   c. Development Case
   d. Whitepapers

7. Which of the following activities is performed within the Environment discipline? (Select all that apply.)
   a. Assess Environment
   b. Prepare Environment for Project
   c. Support Environment During an Iteration
   d. Support Environment During Project

8. Which of the other eight disciplines does the Environment discipline serve?

   a. Configuration and Change Management

   b. Implementation

   c. Project Management

   d. All other disciplines

9. What artifacts is the Process Engineer responsible for? (Select all that apply.)

   a. Development Process

   b. Development Organization Assessment

   c. Software Development Plan

   d. Development Infrastructure

10. Which of the following artifacts is optional within the Environment discipline? (Select all that apply.)

   a. Development Organization Assessment

   b. Project-Specific Guidelines

   c. Manual Styleguide

   d. Development Case

References

IBM Rational Unified Process v7.0.

CHAPTER 14

Phases, Activities, and Milestones

By Jochen Krebs

The RUP process elements covered in this chapter use the UMA process architecture introduced in Chapter 4, "Basic Process Elements," and align it with the RUP method content elements from Chapter 3, "Basic Content Elements," to form a start-to-end lifecycle. This chapter takes a closer look at the delivery processes, capability patterns, activities, and milestones in the context of RUP. By the end of this chapter, you will have answers not only to questions such as, "What happens in RUP?" but also to the question, "When do things happen in RUP?"

Overview

A **lifecycle** is a complete (start-to-end) description of a process; in UMA terms, it is called a **Delivery Process**. As the name suggests, lifecycles are meant to be released to a project or organization. Classic RUP (for large projects) is a lifecycle that aligns the content elements introduced in Chapters 5 through 13 with process elements. The arrangement and grouping of these activities is proto-typically in a time-based sequence, but also quite often they are performed in parallel, which is typical for iterative-incremental software engineering. It is important to understand that method content elements can be arranged in any number of ways across a wide possibility of scenarios. The lifecycle we are focusing on in the context of the entire book is the basis for the RUP certification and represents only one possible scenario; however, it is a popular and successful one. Many RUP customers adjust RUP to their own environment, which results in a different lifecycle that is based on the original RUP but is a variation on it. Part IV, "Tailoring and Tooling," discusses techniques and tools that are available for RUP customization.

This chapter introduces how the method content elements are grouped and arranged, resulting in Classic RUP (for large projects) and the Business Modeling Lifecycle. Both lifecycles are subjects of the certification. These lifecycles provide the content for iterative projects, separating a project into four major sequential phases: Inception, Elaboration, Construction, and Transition. **Phases** are UMA activities that conclude with a milestone. Each phase, however, consists of iterations that are expressed as **Capability Patterns**. The advantage of this process engineering approach is that processes can be assembled faster by sharing the same tasks across phases. For example, the Plan for Next Iteration activity can be re-used throughout the entire lifecycle as it is. Frequently repeating process patterns, which are often seen in iterative-incremental software processes (like RUP), are therefore much easier to build using Capability Patterns.

Each Capability Pattern can contain activities, including phases and iterations (stereotyped activities in RUP). Furthermore, a Capability Pattern can include milestones and task descriptors. The structure of a Capability Pattern is the Work Breakdown Structure (WBS), which you can use to configure and align the elements in a hierarchy and order. By default, RUP provides three views on the breakdown structure and its activities:

- Work Breakdown Structure listing all the activities and task descriptors
- Team Allocation, which bundles work and artifacts to the responsible party or performer
- Work Product Usage, which lists all the artifacts associated with the process element

The completion of a phase is evaluated at a milestone, and each milestone has completion criteria that verifies the end of a phase. Only if the criteria are fulfilled can a true transition to another phase occur. Milestones monitor the completion of work and the achievement of set goals. They also serve as estimation and financial feasibility checkpoints.

Due to the emphasis on different types of tasks during each phase of the project, the phases vary by length and resource intensity. Figure 14-1 provides a general recommendation for a RUP project.

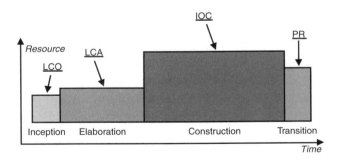

Figure 14-1   Effort/schedule of the RUP phases including their milestones

Every phase has specific goals and objectives, which are measured at the milestones at the end of each phase. To illustrate the objectives for these phases, we will compare and map an oil drilling project to a RUP project.

Inception

Let's assume we want to harvest oil and we initiate a new project to build a plant. First we need to locate possible oil sources. For example, in the U.S., oil has been found in Texas and Alaska, so the surrounding areas are promising but not necessarily the only source with which to start. During Inception, you investigate maps, take soil samples, and investigate reports from other organizations. The overall goal of this relatively short phase (compared to the other phases) is to provide recommendations for possible oil locations and to get funding for the next phase, a sample drilling. At this point, the project team has located oil but does not necessarily know the overall potential of the find or the amount of equipment it will require to bring it in. This phase is characterized as less plan driven but more creative and innovative.

Objectives

The RUP Inception phase is brief and aims at gaining concurrence among the stakeholders as to the business objectives of the system. As a result of such concurrence, it should be deemed worth proceeding with the project to the next step. For enhancement projects or maintenance projects, Inception is often even shorter but still performed to achieve common agreements among the stakeholders. If our project would cost only 1 USD, we would spend approximately 5 cents of the dollar during Inception.

The primary objectives include these:

- Establishing the project's software scope and boundary conditions, including an operational vision, acceptance criteria, and what is intended to be in the product and what is not

- Discriminating the critical use cases of the system, the primary scenarios of operation that will drive the major design trade-offs

- Exhibiting, and maybe demonstrating, at least one candidate architecture against some of the primary scenarios

- Estimating the overall cost and schedule for the entire project (and more detailed estimates for the Elaboration phase)

- Estimating potential risks (the sources of unpredictability)

- Preparing the supporting environment for the project

Workflows

Figures 14-2 and 14-3 lay out the activities in the Inception phase of a RUP project. Notice the focus on establishing the project environment, deriving a vision, and executing common project planning activities.

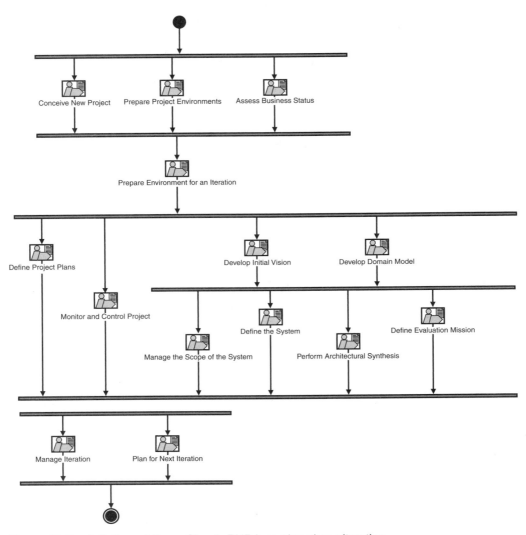

Figure 14-2   Activity workflow—Classic RUP Inception phase iteration

Figure 14-3   Activity workflow—Business modeling Inception phase iteration

Lifecycle Objective Milestone

The milestone for the Inception phase is referred to as the Lifecycle Objective (LCO). During the Inception phase, the project team focuses primarily on producing work products that will help the project get the necessary funding for the next phase. The team also gathers and defines information to successfully explore during the Elaboration phase, which follows the Inception phase.

Therefore, none of the artifacts are necessarily expected to be completed; rather, the expectation is that they will be complete enough to demonstrate sufficient breadth to move on in the project. These work products include the following:

- Vision (core requirements, features, and constraints)
- Business Case (assessment of the situation and projects)
- Risk List (initial draft)
- Software Development Plan (high-level initial estimate, phase plan)
- Iteration Plan (plan for the first iteration of Elaboration)
- Development Process (agreement on chosen software engineering process)
- Development Infrastructure (the tools for Elaboration are in place)
- Glossary (initial Glossary capturing important terms)
- Use-Case Model (most critical use cases and actors are defined, and some of them are briefly outlined)

The evaluation criteria for the LCO milestone include the following:

- Stakeholder concurrence on scope definition and cost/schedule estimates
- Agreement that the right set of requirements has been captured and that there is a shared understanding of those requirements
- Agreement that the cost/schedule estimates, priorities, risks, and development process are appropriate
- Identification of all risks and a mitigation strategy for each

Elaboration

During Elaboration, the members of the team working on our oil project example want to prove that there is oil but also want to establish an estimate of how much oil will be available. Sample drilling will be executed, facts about the depth and location of the oil will be gathered, the necessary equipment to reach the oil will be obtained and put in place, and the architecture necessary to collect the oil will be established. Lessons will be learned from unsuccessful drillings, and estimates and forecasts will be derived from the successful ones. It is not the objective of the Elaboration phase to harvest the oil and establish a productive environment, but rather estimate the funding necessary for doing so and build a case to implement the plan and architecture on a large-scale plan. At the end of Elaboration, the oil project team should feel confident about the feasibility of the project, have a good grasp of the risks, and have put an architecture for the plant in place. Even though all milestones are considered go-kill decision points for a project, the milestone following Elaboration is crucial for the final success of the project.

Objectives

With a relatively small but skilled staff, the Elaboration phase is characterized by strong focus on the architecture of the system. Usually Elaboration is one or two iterations long, and the length of these iterations could be longer than during the Construction phase. The team creates architectural prototypes and compares them based on architecturally significant scenarios. They mitigate some high-priority technical risks associated with important functionality. Besides the architectural work during Elaboration, the project team continues to evolve the requirements. Going back to the 1 USD project, we would spend roughly 20 cents during Elaboration.

The primary objectives include these:

- Ensuring that the architecture, requirements, and plans are stable enough and the risks sufficiently mitigated to be able to predictably determine the cost and schedule for the completion of the development. For most projects, passing this milestone also corresponds to the transition from a light-and-fast, low-risk operation to a high-cost, high-risk operation with substantial organizational inertia.

- Addressing all architecturally significant risks of the project.

- Establishing a baselined architecture derived from addressing the architecturally significant scenarios that typically expose the top technical risks of the project.

- Producing an evolutionary prototype of production-quality components, as well as possibly one or more exploratory, throw-away prototypes to mitigate specific risks such as the following:

  - Design/requirements trade-offs

  - Component reuse

  - Product feasibility or demonstrations to investors, customers, and end users

- Demonstrating that the baselined architecture will support the requirements of the system at a reasonable cost and in a reasonable amount of time.

- Establishing the supporting environment. To achieve these primary objectives, it is equally important to set up the supporting environment for the project. This includes tailoring the process for the project, preparing templates and guidelines, and setting up tools.

Workflows

The activities executed during the Elaboration phase reflect the overall goals and objective of the phase, proving and recommending an architecture based on the list of candidate architectures. New risks and requirements will appear and be integrated into the set of work products initiated during the Inception phase. The workflows shown in Figure 14-4 and Figure 14-5 illustrate the activities performed during Elaboration.

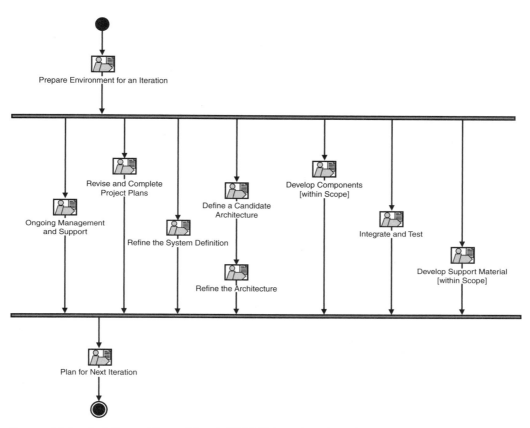

Figure 14-4 Activity workflow—Classic RUP Elaboration phase iteration

Lifecycle Architecture Milestone

The milestone for the Elaboration phase is establishment of the Lifecycle Architecture (LCA). During the Elaboration phase, the Software Architect works especially closely with the Project Manager and the System Analyst. This core team is usually smaller than the project team necessary during the Construction phase. The set of requirements (for example, use-case scenarios) drive the architectural prototype(s) and are used to validate important features and requirements. Based on the findings and the progress of the requirements specification, the Project Manager will be able to present to senior management at this point an improved estimate and schedule. At the LCA milestone, high-priority risks should be removed and the requirements more stable. The emphasis on work products during Elaboration includes the following:

- Prototypes (executables that validate different architectural approaches)
- Risk List (revised)

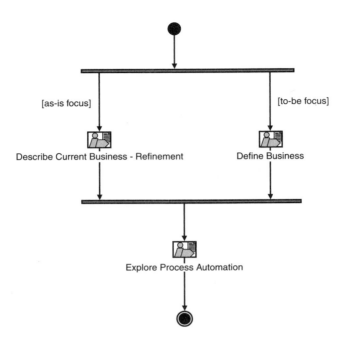

Figure 14-5   Activity workflow—Business modeling Elaboration phase iteration

- Development Process (the process as well as guidelines and templates have been refined, tailored, and streamlined for Construction)
- Development Infrastructure (tools and process automation support for Construction are in place)
- Software Architecture Document (created and updated with architectural findings)
- Demonstration that the baselined architecture will support the requirements
- Design Model (defined and architecturally important components assessed against scenarios)
- Data Model (created and entities, relationships and tables listed)
- Implementation Model (major components prototyped)
- Vision (revised based on the architectural findings)
- Software Development Plan (updated for Construction and Transition phases, including improved cost and schedule estimates)
- Iteration Plan (plan for the first iteration of Construction)
- Use-Case Model (the vast majority of use cases are specified)
- Supplementary Specifications (nonfunctional are documented)

- Test Suite (tests for the architectural scenarios are implemented)
- Test Automation Architecture (creates and defines the various test automation techniques for Construction)
- Business Case (revised based on the exploratory work during Elaboration)

The evaluation criteria for the LCA milestone include these:

- The product vision and requirements are stable.
- The architecture is stable.
- The key approaches to be used in test and evaluation are proven.
- Testing and evaluation of executable prototypes have demonstrated that the major risk elements have been addressed and have been credibly resolved.
- The iteration plans for the Construction phase are of sufficient detail and fidelity to allow the work to proceed.
- The iteration plans for the Construction phase are supported by credible estimates.
- All stakeholders agree that the current vision can be met if the current plan is executed to develop the complete system, in the context of the current architecture.
- Actual resource expenditure versus planned expenditure is acceptable.

Construction

Construction is usually the most resource-intensive phase, which affects the financial and timely success of the project. That means for our oil project that many workers will build the plant and implement the drills. The project will build the overall plant step-wise to its completion. After a certain amount of progress, it is not uncommon for a project to open some drills for production to increase productivity and gain early return on investment (ROI).

Objectives

The change from Elaboration to Construction in a RUP project is very visible. First, the resources are usually increased, which makes the project continue on a faster pace (measured in delivered functionality). Second, the iterations are commonly shortened to encourage more frequent user feedback, providing more opportunity to find out if the feedback is validating the stated requirements. Therefore, project-external stakeholders are more frequently involved due to the length of the iterations (2 to 4 weeks) and the nature of the phase.

Inside the project, the Project Manager steers the project and balances the resources and schedule with the desired functionality. During the Construction phase, the Software Architect focuses on ensuring that the developers use and follow the defined architecture. The testing strategy is executed by running the test and producing daily builds with executables as output at the end of each iteration. As a general rule of thumb, the 1 USD project would spend about 65 cents in this phase.

These are the primary objectives:

- Minimizing development costs by optimizing use of resources and avoiding unnecessary scrap and rework.

- Achieving adequate quality as rapidly as practical.

- Achieving useful versions (alpha, beta, and other test releases) as rapidly as practical.

- Completing the analysis, design, development, and testing of all required functionality.

- Iteratively and incrementally developing a complete product that is ready to transition to its user community. This implies describing the remaining use cases and other requirements, fleshing out the design, completing the implementation, and testing the software.

- Deciding if the software, the sites, and the users are ready for the application to be deployed.

- Achieving some degree of parallelism in the work of development teams. Typically, even on smaller projects, some components can be developed independently of one another, allowing for natural parallelism between teams (resources permitting). This parallelism can accelerate the development activities significantly; but it also increases the complexity of resource management and workflow synchronization. A robust architecture is essential if any significant parallelism is to be achieved.

Workflows

RUP newcomers often mistake the Construction phase for the Implementation phase. The workflows shown in Figures 14-6 and 14-7 help clarify the idea that construction consists of all RUP aspects and all RUP disciplines (see Chapter 3, "Basic Content Elements"). Each iteration provides context for requirements management, iteration management of the current iteration, planning of the subsequent iteration(s), and component design. It is true that there is a bigger emphasis on programming during construction than in the Inception or Elaboration phases, but that does not diminish the need for ongoing, proper planning and management in the other disciplines. For example, the Ongoing Management and Support activity in Figure 14-6 is composed of requirements and change management.

Initial Operational Capability Milestone

The milestone for the Construction phase is termed Initial Operational Capability (IOC). During the Construction phase, the project team focuses on building the system. At the end of each iteration, the project team has to demonstrate the increased functionality in an executable. Parallel to that, other team members continue to work on work products targeting the deployment of the system into its environment. At the IOC milestone, the project work products have steadily moved toward completion and the system is ready for transition.

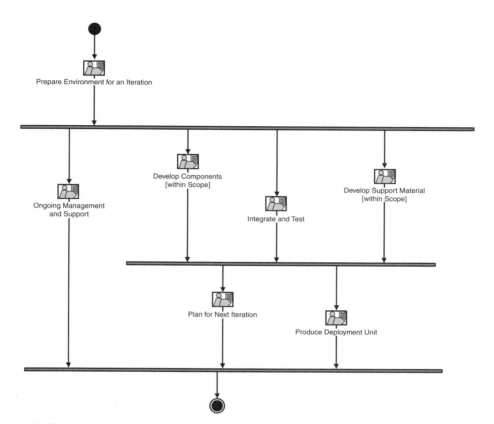

Figure 14-6   Activity workflow—Classic RUP Construction phase iteration

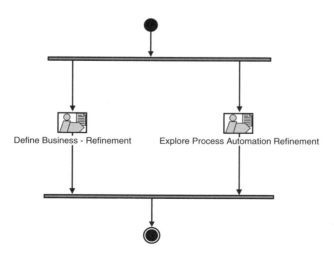

Figure 14-7   Activity workflow—Business modeling Construction phase iteration

Many of the following artifacts have come to completion:

- The System (the build, ready for beta testing)
- Deployment Plan (initial version, containing the deployment strategy)
- Implementation Model (iteratively expanded model from the Elaboration phase)
- Test Suite (proven tests that validate the stability of the system)
- User Support Material (preliminary drafts of training and user manuals based on use cases)
- Iteration Plan (a plan for the next iteration in Transition or the remainder of the project)
- Design Model (evolved to near completion)
- Development Process (revised and constantly improved throughout the project, ready for Transition)
- Development Infrastructure (process automation and tool support for the Transition phase is in place)
- Data Model (updated with all remaining details throughout Construction; mirrors the actual executable)
- Review of the business modeling work products

The evaluation criteria for IOC include the following:

- The product release is stable and mature enough to be deployed in the user community.
- All the stakeholders are ready for the transition into the user community.
- The resource expenditures are still acceptable.

Transition

During Transition, a project is rolled out into its planned environment. The training plan for the staff is executed, final acceptance tests are executed, and paperwork is submitted. The oil project would transition to operation and monitoring, and the operational aspects of the system would take over from the engineering aspects.

Objectives

During Transition, the project team drives two major initiatives. The first is to receive official acceptance from the customer, and the second is to prepare the user environment to work effectively with the system according to the specification.

The available features and requirements can drive marketing efforts, and training can be executed for end users and maintenance staff. Acceptance testing peaks with minor defect fixing and fine-tuning. Production databases are activated and replace testing databases.

Besides engineering skills, the Transition phase requires soft skills for education, user enablement, and marketing messages. In terms of spending, a 1 USD project would spend its last 10 cents of the budget.

The primary objectives of the Transition phase include the following:

- Beta testing to validate the new system against user expectations
- Beta testing and parallel operation relative to a legacy system that it's replacing
- Converting operational databases
- Training of users and maintainers
- Rolling out to the marketing, distribution, and sales forces
- Deployment-specific engineering such as cutover, commercial packaging and production, sales rollout, and field personnel training
- Tuning activities such as bug fixing, enhancement for performance, and usability
- Assessing the deployment baselines against the complete vision and acceptance criteria for the product
- Achieving user self-supportability
- Achieving stakeholder concurrence that deployment baselines are complete
- Achieving stakeholder concurrence that deployment baselines are consistent with the evaluation criteria of the vision

Workflows

The emphasis of the Transition phase is reflected in the workflows shown in Figures 14-8 and 14-9. They demonstrate how the user and maintenance material is completed and how final testing steps drive the systems toward its release into the final user environment.

Product Release Milestone

The milestone for the Transition phase is simply the Product Release (PR). After multiple iterations with customer feedback in the Construction phase, the PR milestone at the end of the Transition phase should not be a big surprise for either party. The customer receives the final version of the product and documentation. Final beta testing is completed, and the user and customer community are satisfied with the release. After the PR milestone is passed, the system moves from the engineering mode into operational mode.

Many of the following artifacts are now complete:

- The Product Build (in-line with the requirements stated throughout the project)
- User Support Material (completed material important for the external system experience by end users and operations)
- Implementation Elements (the documentation and the finalized product are in synch)

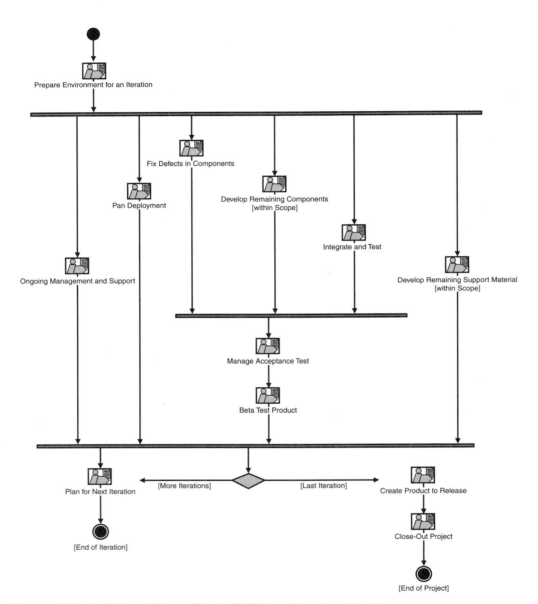

Figure 14-8   Activity workflow—Classic RUP Transition phase iteration

The evaluation criteria for the Transition phase involve the answers to these questions:

- Is the user satisfied?
- Did the resource expenditures turn out to be acceptable?

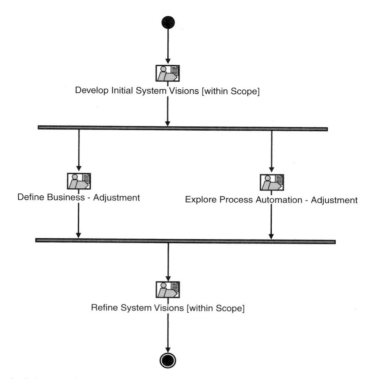

Figure 14-9   Activity workflow—Business modeling Transition phase iteration

Summary

The RUP lifecycle consists of four phases: Inception, Elaboration, Construction and Transition. Although each phase exhibits a certain perspective on the project, the phases include *n*-iterations. Each iteration is bound to the goal of the phase but will also consist of activities reflecting the various aspects of the content elements or disciplines. The end of the phase is determined by evaluating the exit criteria of the milestone.

The flow in time, expressed by the alignment of phases and iterations, is supported by activities and subactivities with either sequential order or parallel execution of activities and the tasks that compose them. The RUP process elements (Delivery processes, Capability patterns, Activities or Sub-Activities) can be modeled using workflow diagrams or through work breakdown structures.

Sample Questions

You can find the correct answers to these questions in the Appendix, "Answers to Sample Questions."

1. Which of the following is a milestone in RUP? (Select all that apply.)
   a. Product Release
   b. Lifecycle Release
   c. Lifecycle Objective
   d. Product Objective

2. Which of the following RUP process elements is *not* an activity in UMA? (Select all that apply.)
   a. Delivery Process
   b. Iteration
   c. Phase
   d. Capability Pattern

3. Which of the following reflects the correct order of RUP phases?
   a. Transition, Elaboration, Construction, Inception
   b. Elaboration, Inception, Construction, Transition
   c. Inception, Elaboration, Construction, Transition
   d. Inception, Construction, Elaboration, Transition

4. Which milestone follows the Inception phase?
   a. Product Release
   b. Lifecycle Architecture
   c. Initial Operability Lifecycle
   d. Lifecycle Objective

5. In which phase is the Vision created?
   a. Inception
   b. Elaboration
   c. Construction
   d. Transition

6. Which of the following phases focuses on architectural prototypes?
   a. Transition
   b. Construction
   c. Elaboration
   d. Inception

7. Which of the following statements is true about the RUP development process? (Select all that apply.)

   a. Every project is given a fixed development process to follow. It does not change.

   b. In every project, there is a decision made upon a development process during Inception.

   c. In every project, there is constant review of the effectiveness of the development process, and changes are made as needed.

   d. Review of the development process comes after the Transition phase is completed.

8. Which of the following elements is most effective in building a process element that repeats throughout the entire lifecycle?

   a. Delivery Process

   b. Roadmap

   c. Example

   d. Capability Pattern

9. Which of the following statements is true about RUP iterations? (Select all that apply.)

   a. They usually last 2 to 6 weeks.

   b. Each phase contains only one iteration.

   c. Each iteration results in an executable

   d. They last 2 to 6 months.

10. Every two weeks, a project produces an executable that is used to demonstrate progress to the customer in the form of implemented functionality. Which RUP phase is the project in?

    a. Inception

    b. Elaboration

    c. Construction

    d. Transition

References

Boehm, B. (1995). Anchoring the software process. http://sunset.usc.edu/publications/TECHRPTS/1995/usccse95-507/ASP.pdf.

IBM Rational Unified Process v7.0.

PART IV

Tailoring and Tooling

CHAPTER 15

Tailoring

By Jochen Krebs

Every project is different, and so are the organizations in which the projects are executed. Besides their uniquenesses, these organizations share many commonalities and similarities for which a general process framework like RUP can be used. The differences must then be detailed and refined to make the process work in the particular situation. The framework gives an organization a disciplined and repetitive approach, leading to more efficiency in execution. Process engineers, on the other hand, need to refine the framework to meet the situational needs. They can tie RUP to an individual project or to the organization. This chapter discusses some techniques and strategies for adapting RUP to its environment. We then take a look at the available tools in Chapter 16, "Tools."

Overview

As the name RUP for Large Projects indicates, the content of RUP introduced in this book targets larger-scale projects usually 8 to 12 months long (often longer) and a project team size of more than 10 members. Even though RUP for Large Projects is a standardized template for a typical IT application development project, it won't fit your particular project situation. Especially if your project is smaller in scope or requires less focus on one area of concern, the need for adjusting RUP becomes important.

Adjusting RUP to a certain project or organization usually involves the following four steps:

1. **Develop the Method Elements**—This includes the creation of new elements as well as the changes to existing RUP content. For example, an IT organization typically has well-proven project templates and accepted project terminology. In that case, a project team wants to use its mission document template and use the word *mission* instead of the term

vision (used in RUP). These areas for improvement have to be identified prior to the start of the project, which greatly increases the acceptance of the final process. In a similar fashion, organizations would capture their home-grown techniques as guidance elements and attach them to other RUP process elements. This can, of course, also include the removal of standard RUP content; in a nutshell, it means adjusting and personalizing the process to an organization's needs.

2. **Configure the Method Elements**—After the content is developed, the Project Manager and Process Engineer need to decide which elements are used in the constraints in the particular project. For example, an organization has a series of tool mentors written for a variety of projects. The Process Engineer would configure the process toward the project, selecting tool mentors for the tools that the project team chooses.

3. **Develop the Process for the Configuration**—The RUP process comes as an out-of-the-box solution or as an end-to-end process that can also be customized similar to the content elements. Rather than focusing on the content elements, the Process Engineer might align the content elements in the flow of time. For example, the Process Engineer could move an activity to a point earlier or later in the process and modify the dynamics of the process.

4. **Make the Process Available**—This new process (a variation of RUP) needs to be rolled out to the project(s) so that the team members will see when they will need to work on the mission document and use the correct predefined template.

The previous steps introduce a typical tailoring scenario, such as creating content, structuring content, aligning the process with content, and making it available. The following approaches are examples of how to bring RUP into an organization or project. These approaches are in order from the easiest, least integrated model to the most sophisticated but integrated process model.

- Using RUP as an "as-is" Web site and documenting the changes for a project in an external document, such as the development process artifact in RUP.

- Using a combination of an external reference document with the personalization feature of RUP, called *MyRUP* (introduced in Chapter 16).

- Using the IBM Rational Method Composer (RMC) to configure and assemble processes from a library of existing method content and process elements. RMC is also introduced in Chapter 16.

- Authoring additional guidance elements, which are then added to existing content using RMC.

- Developing a new delivery process using RMC by selecting and deselecting content and process elements.

- Managing and extending the existing method framework with new method content elements and process elements. Configuring and releasing the content as a specific variant of the RUP using RMC.

The environment discipline in RUP (see Chapter 13) not only provides content for setting up the tool environment of a project but also the process environment of a project. The Development Process Artifact with its contained artifacts **Development Case**, **Project-Specific Guidelines**, and **Project-Specific Templates** will capture the results of making the RUP concrete and applicable for a specific project situation. The **Development Process Artifact**, however, takes an external view to the process. The consumer of RUP needs this artifact to filter the off-the-shelf RUP content, whereas the IBM RMC modifies the process directly, leaving behind one tailored process.

Tailoring Approaches

The actual implementation of RUP in a project can take many different forms, depending on the adoption style. Some organizations favor a step-wise RUP implementation, whereas others take the so-called big bang approach in which the entire RUP is rolled out in one piece. Each of the adoption approaches discussed later in this section requires a different lifecycle planning process. Therefore, this section begins by examining different lifecycles.

Lifecycles

The incremental lifecycle (see Figure 15-1), for example, is characterized by one short Inception iteration, followed by one Elaboration iteration and then multiple Construction iterations.

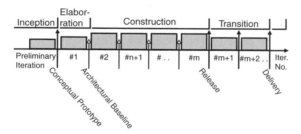

Figure 15-1 Incremental lifecycle

In the same way that you apply RUP in application development, you can tailor the RUP rollout. For example, in an incremental scenario, you apply RUP in one project before a second- and then a third-use RUP. Subsequently, in this step-wise approach, the organization is transformed.

In contrast to the Incremental lifecycle, you use the Evolutionary lifecycle (see Figure 15-2) when the requirements are not well established or are unknown, which would require multiple Elaboration iterations to specify the requirements and establish an architecture.

A Process Engineer can map the Evolutionary model for an IT system to process engineering. For example, he might start identifying the process requirements for iterations, phases, or techniques. Then he can develop and publish the process (fragments) back to the team and learn from the feedback. The process adapts to the situation and gets closer to reality with each step.

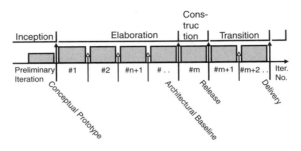

Figure 15-2   Evolutionary lifecycle

The main difference between the Evolutionary lifecycle and the Incremental Delivery lifecycle (see Figure 15-3) is the fact that the project team actually deploys, iteratively, versions of the IT system while going through the development process. The main advantage of this approach is that the team can make the implemented functionality available to the user community much earlier than the complete system. This allows the user community to utilize early pieces of the system early on, providing a great source of return of investment (ROI).

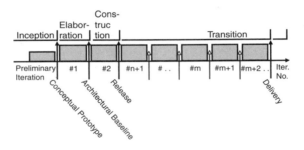

Figure 15-3   Incremental Delivery lifecycle

A project using the Grand Design lifecycle (see Figure 15-4) is separated into four phases, with each phase having only one iteration in it. That approach works if the requested functionality is well understood and the desired architecture is familiar among the project team members. It is also a common strategy for short projects. A RUP deployment following the Incremental Delivery approach is characterized by packaging of these process fragments in cohesive units and deploying them into different projects. If, for example, a Process Engineer develops the content for use cases and receives positive feedback, the package is published and deployed to the projects. Other pieces will follow in future increments, but the organization can benefit from the earlier work.

Adoption Styles

The approaches presented in this section discuss the RUP adoption alternatives and possible pros and cons. In reality, a hybrid approach between two or more approaches is most common. These styles also include a hybrid lifecycle approach combined with the RUP adoption approach.

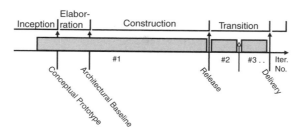

Figure 15-4   Grand Design lifecycle

Big Bang

In the so-called big bang approach (see Figure 15-5), the process engineering team tailors the entire RUP to its needs. That means all disciplines and all phases are adopted in one piece (gray boxes represent scope of adoption). In the big bang approach, a project team usually assesses the project needs and maps them to RUP. Similar to other projects that are wide in scope, the big bang approach introduces a few challenges to the development organization.

Foremost of those challenges is that the big bang adoption is the most time-consuming approach. The assumption behind the big bang approach is that you need to "get it right!", which is almost impossible because processes are moving targets. Even though RUP presents a well-proven set of software engineering process patterns, Process Engineers need to tweak the process to make the project its most efficient.

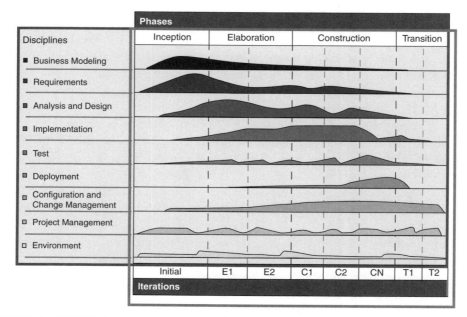

Figure 15-5   RUP big bang adoption approach

The time spent in adoption of the big bang approach often causes a problem for the IT project waiting for the process. It is not atypical that the moment an organization accepts the process as a new software engineering process, projects are already lined up. The long time-frame that the big bang adoption style consumes commonly does not scale to the project waiting to use it.

Another issue with the big bang approach is that there is a chance that the process is over-engineered from the beginning to accommodate various but often unnecessary situations, and some projects end up with unneeded guidance. In that case, the project team using the process feels overwhelmed by the content and complexity.

However, the big bang approach does offer large organizations a chance to roll out a process on a large scale in one single step, which is cost effective in terms of training and mentoring. This approach, of course, includes lots of compromises because individual project concerns might not be heard and included, but it provides a consistent communication platform for large enterprises.

This adoption approach is recommended on an organizational level, after a few projects have successfully implemented and used RUP. Based on these experiences, the most common and successful pieces of RUP are then collected and rolled out as a big bang on an organizational level.

To address the concerns and issues of the big bang approach, RUP is often implemented piece-wise in a vertical, horizontal, vertical-horizontal, or content-filter approach on projects before an organizational big bang is applied.

Phases (Vertical)

In the vertical approach (see Figure 15-6), the entire RUP is "sliced up" into the four phases—Inception, Elaboration, Construction, and Transition—including their associated milestones. With this approach, a project can quickly benefit from the advantages these four perspectives take on a project. For example, the Elaboration phase enforces architectural prototyping and validation, high-risk mitigation, and requirements refinement monitored by the Lifecycle-Architecture Milestone (LCA). The four phases would also introduce the notion of iterative-incremental software engineering without compromising the existing project artifacts, tasks, and roles.

A possible challenge with this approach is that the milestones require completion of certain artifacts that might not exist in the current process of the project. Therefore, consistency checks between the milestones and the existing artifacts in the project need to be made prior to the start of the project. Because work products are continuously improved and refined throughout all four phases, the vertical adoption approach does not work with a waterfall software engineering process.

Starting with the phases first, however, allows you to focus on certain issues and problems with an existing software engineering process without reinventing the entire process. The benefits include an early emphasis on architecture, iterative development, early risk mitigation, and the notion of go/no-go decision points.

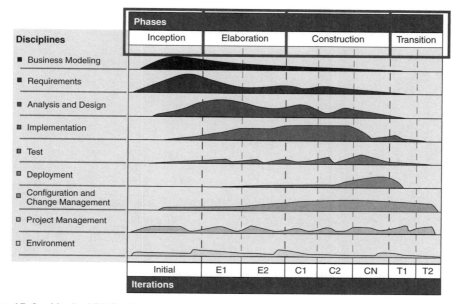

Figure 15-6   Vertical RUP adoption approach

Disciplines (Horizontal)

In a horizontal adoption approach (see Figure 15-7), the emphasis of the implementation is put on the disciplines, most commonly the biggest pain points of an organization first. For example, a project might struggle with requirements management or test (scope indicated using gray rectangles in Figure 15-7). This horizontal approach would give the project immediate support. In this case, the RUP content is used to deliver the project work products without the phases and milestones. One advantage is that project team members can familiarize themselves with the underlying content of RUP and its vocabulary and terminology. Other benefits, such as the emphasis on architecture, can be introduced in subsequent projects. Consistent templates and work products will ease the transition to a later complete deployment of RUP.

The horizontal approach allows projects to roll out a consistent way of producing project work products without a major shift to the entire RUP model in one big piece. It is also not uncommon that early horizontal adoption includes only a few of the nine RUP disciplines to make the adoption even "lighter."

Horizontal is also often the easiest to transition to as an organization, because the disciplines often represent job responsibilities and organizational structures.

One downside of this approach is that the four phases provide significant benefits to "challenged" processes, such as the waterfall model. These benefits, which are implemented through iterations and phases, would not be addressed with this horizontal approach.

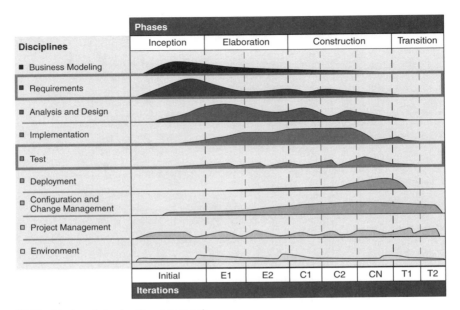

Figure 15-7   Horizontal adoption approach

Discipline-Phase Matrix (Vertical-Horizontal)

The mix of both the vertical and the horizontal approaches combines the benefits of both approaches and makes this a popular RUP adoption approach in the industry. For example, a project with an error-prone process based on the waterfall approach isolates the most critical issues in their existing process (for example, requirements management). Based on that exercise, the areas of most concern in the process are fixed prior to the less important ones. In this case, the project fixes one RUP discipline before solving the issues of the others, while achieving the depth of all four phases and their milestones.

In the example illustrated in Figure 15-8, the project only implements the Requirements discipline including the four phases, which roughly represents one-ninth of a big bang approach. The project also fixes their major challenges first and benefits instantly from the implementation. With this approach, Process Engineers can iteratively deploy RUP in a project and step-wise refine the disciplines and phases as they are being adopted. This approach works well because each RUP discipline usually addresses a cohesive and isolated set of roles that does not interfere with roles from other disciplines.

As a variant on the previous example, the Process Engineer could also only focus on one discipline and one or two phases (Inception and Elaboration). That would further reduce the time-to-project for the process, and projects could start applying RUP with little turnaround time.

Content Filter

With a filter over the entire RUP content, you can separate relevant content from irrelevant content for a particular project. For example, as a basic but not uncommon approach, project use the RUP work product templates exclusively. Then RUP itself would serve as a template repository with guidance information. Even though the work habits and workflow of the project would not change, the project would appear as a RUP project due to the consistent template style. The project team would also adopt the future project vocabulary.

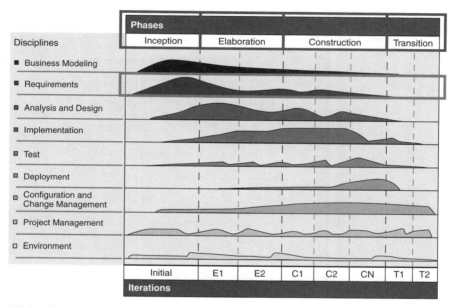

Figure 15-8   Vertical-horizontal adoption process

In a different filter, techniques could be made available out of the techniques available in RUP. For example, use cases are selected as a technique for requirements engineering. Later, the project might decide to also use use cases for analysis and design and testing. A filter could facilitate this transition, growing from a single technique to an integral part interfacing with other disciplines.

The advantage of this approach is that the techniques and RUP-wide content filters cross-cut the entire software engineering team. Everyone on the team will feel and experience RUP, whereas other approaches focus solely on one or two roles. Techniques are also a good approach to focus on one subject area and benefit from the interdiscipline touchpoints.

Extension

Adopting and instantiating RUP in a project most likely also means that you need to extend RUP in certain areas. These areas are commonly the areas that have worked successfully in the past. No project member wants to see his "way of work" going away, especially if it has proven successful. Therefore, organizations can change the existing content or add to the disciplines.

It is not uncommon for some organizations to need to add entire disciplines to the RUP process framework, such as Marketing, Product Management, or Operations and Support.

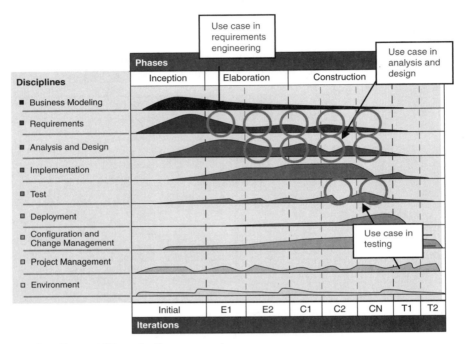

Figure 15-9   Content filter adoption approach

Recommended Practices for Process Adoption

Every project has a process, even though sometimes the process is not really obvious or visible. Especially for larger or distributed projects, the ground rules of the project need to be employed consistently. Adopting RUP on a project level or an organizational level is a project in itself, especially developing the first draft of the process.

Applying RUP out-of-the-box does not commonly fit the situation. Highlighting the differences between a project's as-is and to-be situations and mapping the to-be scenarios toward RUP are always a recommended first step in the process adoption. It has also been proven that an incremental adoption process is more successful than a big bang approach.

Like IT projects, a process adoption project needs to be planned and managed, with the best effect coming about if process mentors are utilized to guide or review the project.

Changing a person's or project's habit is the most challenging part of the adoption project. With continuous training and onsite mentoring, the project team must be involved and informed to increase the overall acceptance of the process.

Summary

In reality, RUP comes in many forms and flavors, which often requires variety in adoption techniques. Even though the big bang approach seems to be the best approach in terms of coverage of the underlying key principles, it is often too time consuming and over-engineered. The stepwise approach addresses this concern and focuses either on the relevance of the RUP content or the problems and errors experienced with the existing process applied in the project. The combination of content filters used with a vertical-horizontal deployment approach is a very useful technique to implement a stepwise process deployment.

References

Bergstrom, S., & Raberg, L. (2004). *Adopting the Rational Unified Process: Success with the RUP*. Boston: Addison-Wesley.

IBM Rational Unified Process v7.0.

CHAPTER 16

Tools

By Jochen Krebs

The previous chapter presented tailoring approaches and techniques that you can apply to make RUP fit to a project situation or to a rollout on an organizational level. This chapter introduces the tooling used to implement and automate these approaches. The two tooling options for RUP customization are called MyRUP and the IBM Rational Method Composer, both of which are discussed in the context of applicability and usage. Tailoring RUP—especially knowing the benefits and effectiveness of each tool—is an important concept in the certification exam.

Overview

The entire RUP process framework is delivered as a set of HTML pages, and the size of the process is determined by its so-called configuration. For example, the only configuration relevant for the RUP certification, and therefore the context of this book, is called Classic RUP (for large projects). There are, however, other available configurations. For example, there is RUP for small projects, RUP for COTS (Commercial off the Shelf), or RUP for service-oriented architectures (SOA), to name a few. The chosen configuration is shown in the title of the browser page.

The advantage of having the RUP content released as HTML pages is the easy availability of the product. Everyone equipped with a web browser can launch the pages and navigate throughout the product similarly to the way someone would navigate through the Internet. By simply copying RUP on a company-wide web server, project teams can use the product within seconds. However, the challenge with the generated HTML pages is that the HTML pages are static. This is great for organizations in the sense that they want to roll out a consistent process. Individuals, on the other hand, might like to take this process and filter or adapt it to their own needs without changing the company-wide process. This need leads to the two tooling options we will discuss in more detail.

First we will look at MyRUP, which serves as a tool *after* the process has been published. The second tooling option, IBM Rational Method Composer/RMC, influences and manages the content *before* the content is published.

MyRUP

MyRUP (aka MyView) is used for personalizing RUP content. As the name indicates, MyRUP helps project team members fine-tune RUP to their own personal work environment. But that does not mean that MyRUP couldn't be used to tailor RUP to a specific project or organization. For example, a business analyst on a project can reduce the entire RUP content (see Figure 16-1) so that only content relevant to his role is presented (see Figure 16-2).

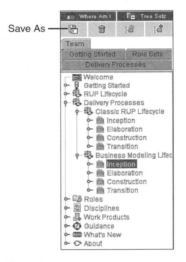

Figure 16-1   Original RUP tree hierarchy

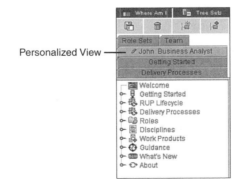

Figure 16-2   New RUP view

The Save As option allows the user to create his own view, which is then used as a filter on the existing content.

The business analysis can now use the new view to reduce the relevant content through the MyRUP menu (see Figure 16-3). He can remove entire element groups, such as the Test domain, with one command, or remove a single element within a group.

Figure 16-3   MyRUP commands

The result is a lighter version of the RUP process content, which is now targeted toward a project, a project team member, or a group of people. For example, Figure 16-4 shows only the relevant work products, roles, and disciplines relevant for John. In this case, the project team member would play the roles of a Business Architect, Business Designer, Business-Process Analyst, Requirements Specifier, Stakeholder, and System Analyst.

Without getting bogged down in the details of the entire RUP, a personalized view offers a quick access point for all relevant content. If desired, the user can navigate to the entire RUP by simply selecting another tab (for example, the team) in the tree hierarchy.

Besides reducing content, MyRUP can be used to add new content. In the example shown in Figure 16-5, the Business Analyst likes to add a document to his process view where he captures personal tips and tricks for domain modeling. This powerful feature allows process engineers to harvest these personal additions and make them available on a broader level.

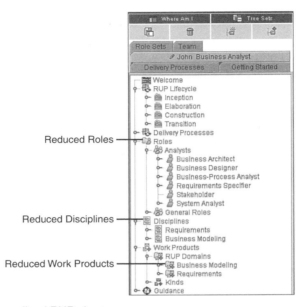

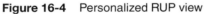

Reduced Roles ──────

Reduced Disciplines ──────

Reduced Work Products ──────

Figure 16-4   Personalized RUP view

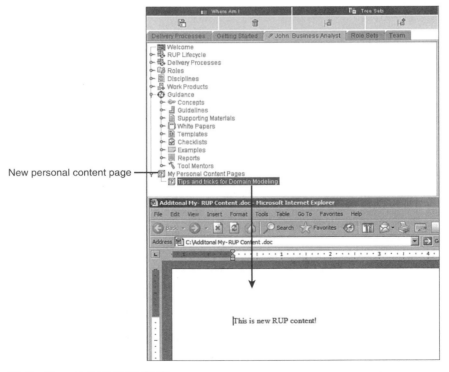

New personal content page ──────

Figure 16-5   New content in MyRUP

The advantage of MyRUP is the simplicity of personalizing content without programming or authoring skills. There is also a capability to actively influence the process rather than "being given" a process top-down. That has a big positive psychological impact. Process engineers can use the various MyRUPs to see which content seems relevant and should be added for a broader audience. One disadvantage of the MyRUP approach is the limited capability to easily modify existing content. MyRUP only allows adding unstructured content and removing elements from the tree view.

MyRUP can serve, to some extent, to support the content filter, horizontal, vertical, and horizontal-vertical approach, introduced in Chapter 15. In a limited fashion, it can serve to support process extension.

IBM Rational Method Composer (RMC)

The Rational Method Composer (RMC) is a comprehensive process authoring tool. RMC is built on top of Eclipse (www.eclipse.org), which provides extensive method authoring and publishing capabilities and uses the same UMA architecture introduced in Part II, "Rational Unified Process: Content and Process Elements."

Compared to MyRUP, RMC is meant to manipulate existing RUP content or add new content prior to the release of the HTML site. Therefore, RMC can tailor RUP to potentially every possible situation. Even though the features of RMC could fill an entire book, we will highlight the most significant features for method authoring following a simplified scenario.

RMC offers two important perspectives: browsing and authoring (see Figure 16-6). Through these perspectives, the process engineer can either author (authoring) or test (browsing) the process prior to the actual publication.

Each window within the authoring view provides a different level of detail to the process engineer. For example, the Library window shown in Figure 16-7 lists all the plug-ins in a single repository. The repository is a collection of so-called plug-ins, which you can load and unload from the library. The library shown in Figure 16-7 contains, in addition to RUP, content for COTS and J2EE development, among others. These plug-ins bundle certain content and process elements under one umbrella. You can then use the plug-ins to share content by importing them into other libraries.

The notion of plug-ins allows process engineers to create their own method plug-ins and add them to an existing library. Instead of changing the content of RUP directly in the original RUP plug-in, the process engineer can use an elegant approach to keep the tailored elements separate from the original RUP elements. This is a huge advantage considering that IBM Rational plans to release updated RUP versions in the future. Let me give you two examples to clarify this point. First, if a process engineer would decide to make changes directly in the official RUP plug-ins (which is possible), future IBM Rational software updates would overwrite the content, creating a huge maintenance problem. Second, content from specialized plug-ins might refer to content from the original RUP base. This would leave behind inconsistencies. As a rule of thumb, it is strongly recommended that you create separate plug-ins that refer only to other content. Let's take a look at the technique behind it.

Library window   Perspectives

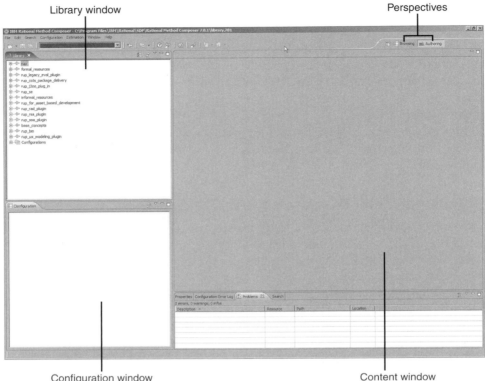

Configuration window   Content window

Figure 16-6   RMC overview

Plug-ins

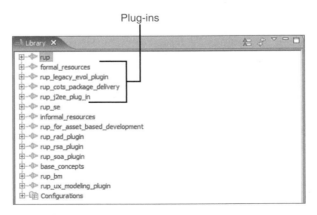

Figure 16-7   The Library window

For example, Figure 16-8 illustrates a new method plug-in with the name RUP Certification.

New plug-in ——————

Default and
automatically created ——————
Standard Categories

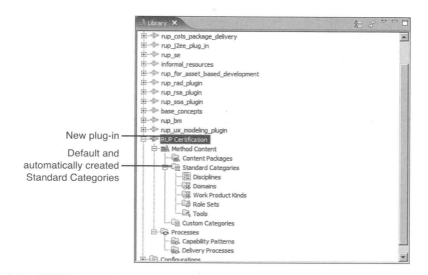

Figure 16-8   RMC library with new method plug-in called RUP Certification

After you've created the plug-in, you can place all new content related to the RUP certification there, keeping the official RUP content untouched. As a process engineer, you repeat the same steps for your own relevant content elements.

Let's assume that you would like to create a plug-in that covers specialized content about how to acquire RUP certification. But more importantly, you would like to connect the new content with the existing RUP content, so that in future releases, the certification content is always at the fingertips of the RUP user. As shown in Figure 16-9, you would begin by creating a new Guidance.

After we create the type of Guidance (in this case, a roadmap), RMC opens a content page for this element. This form-based page allows the process engineer to enter the textual or graphical information for the element. Figure 16-10 presents such a content page. Different element types will have different fields available to describe it.

Under the content packages folder, the process engineer organizes the content elements using the default folders Roles, Tasks, Work Products, and Guidance. Standard categories group elements of the same kind. Custom Categories, on the other hand, do not follow the same mechanism and can be used by process engineers to develop and organize elements to be published in the tree hierarchy.

We could repeat the same steps for other work products, tasks, roles, and guidance elements following the same authoring method pattern. Due to its characteristics, each element provides a different content page, which collects the information in the form and allows the process engineer to interconnect elements.

Default structure under every content package

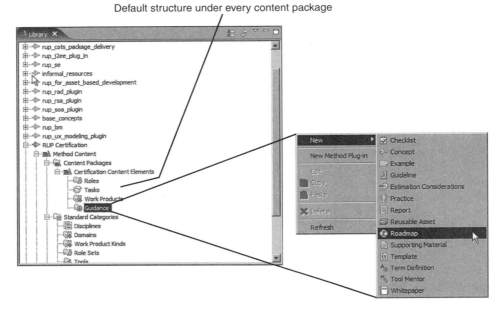

Figure 16-9   Creating a new guidance element

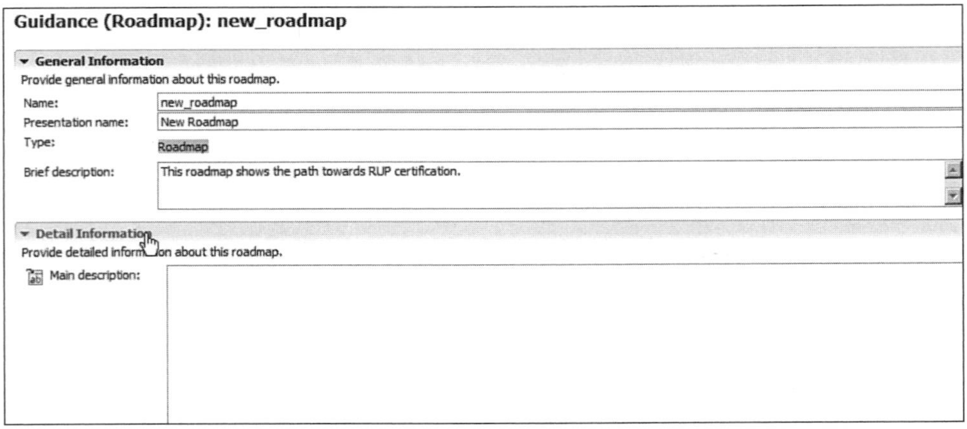

Guidance (Roadmap): new_roadmap

▼ **General Information**
Provide general information about this roadmap.

Name: new_roadmap
Presentation name: New Roadmap
Type: Roadmap
Brief description: This roadmap shows the path towards RUP certification.

▼ **Detail Information**
Provide detailed information about this roadmap.
🔲 Main description:

Figure 16-10   Sample content page for roadmap guidance

It is important to understand that RMC internally uses unique references for each element. Through this reference mechanism, you can attach to or remove elements from each other, creating an interlinked network of content you browse through the published websites. This presents a big advantage for process engineers; for example, if elements are entirely deleted, RMC will automatically remove these references.

To drive this example to completion, let's say that you would like to publish your newly created roadmap for certification and connect it to the original RUP content. In this scenario, the newly created certification content might primarily extend existing RUP content. In other cases, it might change or replace existing RUP content that is no longer applicable in the context of certification. For our certification purpose, we will need to create a configuration. In RMC, a **configuration** is a mechanism to filter and group information persistent in the library and make it accessible to end users. Configurations are used to publish content and are something the end user will later see and browse. This concept presents a huge advantage for the process engineer, who needs to roll out many slightly different versions of a process to a variety of projects. For example, one project using .NET technology and another project using Java technology would share similar processes even though the technology guidance is different. The library would capture the RUP content only once, whereas the configuration would create two different views on that same library content.

For example, Figure 16-11 shows that after a configuration has been selected, the Configuration window shows all content elements associated with it. This example also demonstrates that Classic RUP (for large projects) is a configuration in RMC that takes a specific view on the RUP content captured in the library.

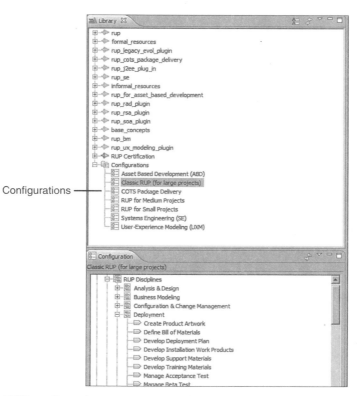

Figure 16-11   RMC configurations

To be able to release a different flavor of RUP in an organization, we need to create a new configuration and select the plug-ins from which to extract the content.

We can easily verify this step by switching to the browsing perspective and selecting the newly created configuration (see Figure 16-12).

Figure 16-12   Browsing perspective with new configuration

The browsing perspective allows the process engineer to preview and verify that the content is appropriately interlinked, correct, and ready for release. The release of the newly assembled process (a configuration) is then released through the publication feature of RMC, which generates the HTML files that can then be consumed by the project team as their customized version of RUP. Do you remember the Development Case artifact from the Environment discipline in Chapter 13, "Environment"? A configuration presents an automated version of this work product.

The goal of this scenario was by no means to give a complete introduction to RMC, but to provide a view on a simple authoring scenario. We created a new plug-in, which holds one content element (roadmap), created a configuration that points to RUP and the newly created plug-in (certification), and validated the inclusion of the new guidance element in the newly created configuration.

To alter existing RUP content, RMC provides three variability types (beside the default of "no variability") for each content element:

- Extends
- Replace
- Contributes

If one element extends another, the extended element will coexist in its original version while the extending element carries the content of the original and the extended one. This variability is useful if a process engineer likes to use original content but would like to have the new content coexist with the original content. This variability type is the least chosen one in practice because of redundancies.

The replace variability type differs from the extends variability type in that you are actually leaving only one content element behind—the replacing one. The replaced element will not be visible after publication. This variability is useful if a process engineer is not interested in the RUP element and wants to replace the entire element with a newly created content element.

The contributes variability type allows the process engineer to add content to existing (original) content, keeping the original content untouched and keeping the contributing additions in a separate element. This is useful, for example, if a process engineer wants to add a sentence or paragraph to an existing RUP element.

In terms of process elements, RMC offers process engineers the capability to assemble activities, capability patterns, and delivery processes in work breakdown structures (WBS). For example, Figure 16-13 shows the activities and task descriptors for the capability pattern Develop Initial Vision.

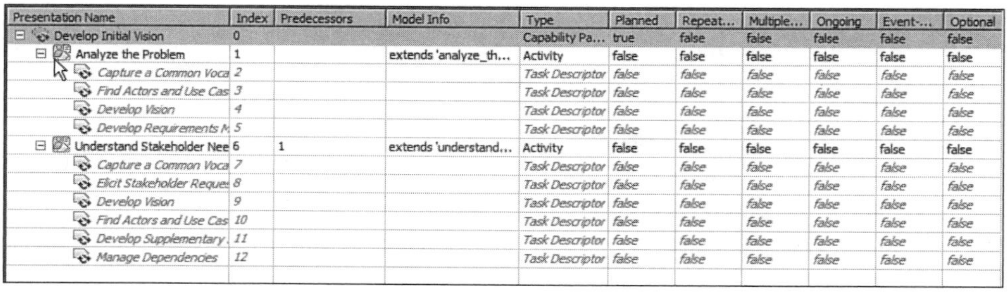

Presentation Name	Index	Predecessors	Model Info	Type	Planned	Repeat...	Multiple...	Ongoing	Event-...	Optional
Develop Initial Vision	0			Capability Pa...	true	false	false	false	false	false
Analyze the Problem	1		extends 'analyze_th...	Activity	false	false	false	false	false	false
Capture a Common Voca	2			Task Descriptor	false	false	false	false	false	false
Find Actors and Use Cas	3			Task Descriptor	false	false	false	false	false	false
Develop Vision	4			Task Descriptor	false	false	false	false	false	false
Develop Requirements M	5			Task Descriptor	false	false	false	false	false	false
Understand Stakeholder Nee	6	1	extends 'understand...	Activity	false	false	false	false	false	false
Capture a Common Voca	7			Task Descriptor	false	false	false	false	false	false
Elicit Stakeholder Reques	8			Task Descriptor	false	false	false	false	false	false
Develop Vision	9			Task Descriptor	false	false	false	false	false	false
Find Actors and Use Cas	10			Task Descriptor	false	false	false	false	false	false
Develop Supplementary	11			Task Descriptor	false	false	false	false	false	false
Manage Dependencies	12			Task Descriptor	false	false	false	false	false	false

Figure 16-13   RMC work breakdown structure

For project planning and managing purposes, you can export the WBS structures from RMC and potentially import them into other project or portfolio management tools.

Through the use of work breakdown structures, process engineers can rearrange certain process elements and alter the flow when activities or tasks are scheduled to be executed. Every WBS can also be visualized through an Activity Diagram. Figure 16-14 maps the WBS of the capability pattern Develop Initial Vision to an activity diagram.

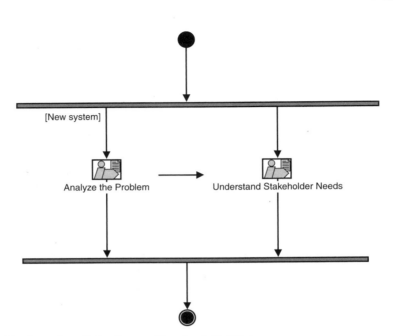

Figure 16-14   Sample activity diagram Develop Initial Vision

As you may have noticed in our small tailoring scenario, RMC not only has major method authoring advantages over MyRUP, but it also generates MyRUP during the publication steps and adds it to the finally released process. That means RMC does not exclude MyRUP, enabling process engineers to release strategic processes through RMC enterprise wide, while MyRUP coexists for local tailoring.

Equipped with RMC, process engineers have access to a state-of-the-art method authoring tool, which enables them to not only modify RUP but to also create new processes from scratch.

Summary

This chapter introduced the two tools available to manage existing RUP content for organizational use, project use, and personal use. It first looked at MyRUP, with its quick and easy approach to filtering and creating personal views on RUP. Then it considered RMC, a highly flexible and powerful method authoring tool for professional process engineering. This chapter stepped through typical RUP tailoring scenarios for MyRUP and RMC and worked out the pros and cons of each tool that have to be evaluated when considering them for use in a certain situation.

References

Bergstrom, S., & Raberg, L. (2003). *Adopting the rational unified process—Success with RUP*. Boston: Addison-Wesley.

Haumer, P. IBM Rational Method Composer—Authoring method content and processes. *The Rational Edge*. Retrieved January 2006 from http://www-128.ibm.com/developerworks/rational/library/jan06/haumer/index.html.

Haumer, P. IBM Rational Method Composer—Key concepts. *The Rational Edge*. Retrieved December 2005 from http://www-128.ibm.com/developerworks/rational/library/dec05/haumer/index.html.

IBM Rational Unified Process v7.0.

Kroll, P. Introducing IBM Rational Method Composer. *The Rational Edge*. Retrieved November 2005 from http://www-128.ibm.com/developerworks/rational/library/nov05/kroll/index.html.

Maréchaux, J. L. Method content authoring: Creating a customized work product with IBM Rational Method Composer. *The Rational Edge*. Retrieved November 2006 from http://www-128.ibm.com/developerworks/rational/library/nov06/marechaux/index.html.

PART V

Certification, Examination, and Practice

The Value of RUP Certification

By Jochen Krebs

Being certified is like having a key to a door that opens a room filled with colleague specialists. Typically, the questions on the RUP certification exam are carefully selected to ensure that in a small period of time, the candidate can prove his knowledge—knowledge that is consistent with the standards in the area of expertise. Jumping over the hurdle of certification is in the interest of both parties: the organization that sets the standards and welcomes new members and the individuals who want to become members and deserve the amenities that such membership affords them. This chapter takes a closer look at the motivations and benefits of the RUP certification.

Standards, Consistency, and Compliance

When you undertake a construction project on your home, it is important to ask the contractor, "Are you licensed?" Beyond the cost and schedule associated with the work, knowing you're dealing with a qualified professional gives you peace of mind with respect to the quality of the result. Further, the licensure of contractors serves as an instrument through which municipalities ensure that building codes are communicated and adhered to. Structural, electrical, and final inspections by a building inspector monitor the contractor's compliance with codes and professional quality standards.

Of course, there is no guarantee that a licensed contractor will work more efficiently, in terms of cost and schedule, than an unlicensed one. But the fact that he holds a license shows that he has acquired and demonstrated the necessary on-the-job experience and skill to undertake the work.

The role of the homeowner in the preceding scenario is analogous to that of an IT organization with respect to software development professionals. Imagine that you are being asked to hire an individual or third-party vendor for a project. The goal of the project is either to tailor RUP to your environment or develop a large-scale software solution in accordance with the RUP process framework. A number of applicants for the position have the necessary work experience, but a few of them also are certified in RUP by IBM. Which candidates would you rank higher: those with or without certification?

Recently I read submission guidelines for a conference whose presentations were grouped according to several different tracks. Guidelines for presenters in the project management track indicated that only applications from individuals with a specific certification would be considered. Although some good speakers might have been neglected due to this prerequisite, the conference organizers valued the particular certification highly and wished to guarantee that every speaker would be able to relate to his audience via the same terminology and process. Every speaker would thus be able to put questions into the proper context and answer them in relation to that particular project management standard.

In our professional and personal lives, we are often required to comply with formal standards. We need a driver's license to legally operate a motor vehicle on public roads. Restaurants must display health inspection certificates to serve food, and umpires and referees need to demonstrate the skills necessary to oversee sporting events. I don't think many people would argue against the claim that these and similar standards are useful outside the realm of software development, as well as within it.

Personal Rewards of RUP Certification

Picture a salary negotiation with an employer who has deployed or wants to deploy RUP within the organization. Your RUP certification is more than a snapshot in time about your skills and knowledge; it shows your ongoing commitment to the process. Some software development professionals might believe that they have substantial experience with RUP after participating in their first and only RUP project. However, it is often the case that team members play only one or a few RUP roles over the course of a single project. For example, a subject matter expert (SME) who is assigned the role of System Analyst might work solely within the requirements discipline. This SME might have little opportunity to experience the "big picture" of how the different disciplines, roles, and work products function and are connected.

The RUP certification randomly tests skills across all subject areas, ensuring that a certified RUP Solution Designer has considerable knowledge of the entire process framework, not just part of it. A RUP-certified SME is able to look beyond his own area of concern to put other aspects of the process into context from different perspectives.

Because a certified RUP Solution Designer has demonstrably more value to the organization, he might well expect to be compensated for that greater value with more money. Of course, I cannot guarantee that a RUP certification will earn you more money. However, studies do show that achieving other certifications results in substantial monetary compensation, at least within some companies. The relatively low cost of obtaining the certification is therefore easily balanced out.

Monetary rewards notwithstanding, a RUP certificate on the wall of an office conveys professional pride and confidence that reflects back positively onto the work ethic of those in the surrounding work environment. Certified RUP Solution Designers, having devoted considerable time and energy to thoroughly studying RUP, are likely to identify strongly with "core" RUP values such as a quality focus, a disciplined approach, adaptability to the needs of the organization, and a willingness to appreciate other stakeholders' perspectives. When key team members hold these values, it supports the team as a whole to embody them. Equipped with the certification, such individuals who understand and exhibit these core values are often rewarded with more visible and challenging projects in their organization.

The Value of the RUP Certification to Organizations

Following a software engineering process inherently implies a commitment to consistency and standardization. In this context, certification is simply a guarantee to the consumer regarding compliance with a well-defined process and its terminology and deliverables. With a RUP certification in your pocket, you can demonstrate that you can talk the lingo and put things in context while collaborating with others. Being able to provide consistent, articulate answers to questions like, "What is an activity?", "What belongs in a vision document?", or "Who is responsible for the risk list?" serves to reduce ambiguity and support the process as a whole.

Moreover, the RUP certification verifies that the certified RUP Solution Designer will demonstrate considerable skill in applying the RUP process framework. Candidates for certification must provide satisfactory answers to a wide range of questions about the underlying process architecture and tools for customization. RUP certification, therefore, shows that the Solution Designer can tailor the process framework according to the real-life needs of an IT organization, which is a critically important factor in applying RUP successfully.

From an organizational perspective, employing RUP-certified Solution Designers creates a consistent environment for communication and collaboration between project team members and other stakeholders, which is the basis for efficiency and productivity. Further, if an organization can execute a project following RUP, repeat the process across multiple projects consistently, and constantly improve the process as it goes, then that organization is not only likely to achieve regular success with its projects, but it also has what it takes to demonstrate and reach higher Capability Maturity Model Integration (CMMI) levels. It is not uncommon for IT organizations to reach CMMI levels of 3 or 4 after they have successfully deployed RUP.

IT consulting companies working exclusively with RUP-certified Solution Designers could have an advantage in contract negotiation and staffing with their customers. They can demonstrate their commitment but also underline their expertise in this field.

Content and Objectivity of the Certification Process

The RUP certification process is well established and has a reputation for being quite challenging. It includes a formal, written exam, the content and structure of which has been kept up-to-date to cover and reflect the latest industry practices. Not all the players in the game of software methodologies certification require a comparable certification process. For example, some certifying organizations hand candidates a certificate after they sit through a training·course, without requiring validation that the student has successfully learned the information presented in the training.

The content of the examination overall emphasizes applying Classic RUP for large projects, which is broadly applicable across much of the software development industry. And although many organizations and projects tailor RUP to their own needs, the standard RUP framework is the subject of the certification.

Although IBM creates the questions for the certification exam, the RUP certification process is conducted by Prometric, Inc., an independent, worldwide testing service that handles all administrative aspects of the certification. The set of questions is fixed and is developed by a team of RUP Solution Designers. The ratio of questions targeting a specific topic is carefully balanced so that examinees must demonstrate knowledge in a broad range of different subject areas.

Prometric interacts with examinees directly and keeps exam results confidential. In particular, Prometric does not inform examinees' organizations about whether they have passed or failed the test. It does, however, inform IBM about who has successfully gained the certification. (Beyond that, all Prometric shares with IBM is generalized statistical information about testing outcomes.) This anonymity is useful to shield individuals from any potential negative ramifications with their current employer.

RUP certificates are issued via e-mail. Candidates can attempt the certification as often as they wish without any issues beyond what it costs to take the test. Once obtained, the RUP certification does not expire, and recertification is not necessary.

Summary

The RUP certification process is a formalized, reliable way of demonstrating that an individual has acquired the skills and experience necessary to carry the title of IBM Certified Solution Designer - Rational Unified Process v7.0.

IBM's stringent certification process means that turning a self-declared RUP practitioner into a certified RUP Solution Designer requires more than sitting through a training course. It demands that each person actively pursues the certification by leaving his comfort zone, preparing for, enrolling in, and successfully completing the certification process. Certified RUP Solution Designers can be justifiably proud of their accomplishment.

References

Krebs, J. The value of RUP certification. *The Rational Edge*. January 2007.

CHAPTER 18

Sample Examination

By Jochen Krebs

The sample examination in this chapter is for the purpose of self-assessment. You have worked through the book and the content of RUP. It is now time to test yourself and see if you would pass this sample examination. We highly recommend that you do not use this sample examination too early in your preparation. Work through the book twice before attempting this sample exam. Using this exam too early or repeatedly using this examination will prevent you from receiving a reliable and valid assessment. This could lead you to overestimate your readiness for the real examination.

Overview

In the next section, you will be presented with a sample examination that addresses the same categories of the official certification exam. To practice this examination as accurately as possible, set a timer to 75 minutes when you begin answering the sample questions. After completion, compare your answers to the correct answers given in the Appendix, "Answers to Sample Questions." If you answered 39 or more of the total 52 questions correctly, you have passed this sample examination. As in the official examination, you will be given the following number of questions in one of the following five categories:

- Iterative Development (~17 percent of questions)
- Iterative Development Work-Products (~17 percent of questions)
- Basic Method Elements and their Relationships (~17 percent of questions)
- Basic Process Elements and their Relationships (~17 percent of questions)
- Basic Content of Disciplines (~32 percent of questions)

As in the real examination, the questions are presented randomly, not grouped in the preceding categories. The inclusion of the categories and the relative percentages of questions from those categories is intended to give you an overview of the scope and focus of the examination.

Sample Examination

1. Which of the following concepts is the most coarse-grained element of the four that follow?
   a. Step
   b. Activity
   c. Task
   d. Task Descriptor

2. The team is developing use cases that are not critical to the architecture. Which phase is the project in?
   a. Testing
   b. Elaboration
   c. Collaboration
   d. Construction

3. Which of the following work products is part of the project management discipline? (Select all that apply.)
   a. Project Repository
   b. Business Case
   c. Glossary
   d. Review Record

4. An inexperienced Project Manager makes four different statements about iterations. Which ones are correct? (Select all that apply.)
   a. Every project consists of four phases, and each phase always consists of only one iteration.
   b. An iteration can include all disciplines.
   c. Iterations are optional and are only needed when stakeholders ask for them.
   d. Iterations should be between 2 and 8 weeks long.

5. On which concepts does iterative development have a positive impact? (Select all that apply.)
   a. Syntax
   b. Risks
   c. Customer Feedback
   d. Quality

6. Which of the following is a RUP discipline? (Select all that apply.)

   a. Environment

   b. Configuration and Change Management

   c. Quality Assurance

   d. Quality Control

7. Which of the following is true about risks in iterative development?

   a. They increase over time and peak at the end of the project.

   b. Architectural risks are addressed early in the project.

   c. Risks are transferred during transition.

   d. Without any high risks, iterative development is not necessary.

8. Which of the following is a "type" of test in RUP?

   a. Stress

   b. Safety

   c. Refactoring

   d. Load

9. For which of the following work products is the RUP Project Manager responsible? (Select all that apply.)

   a. Every work product

   b. Business Vision

   c. Business Case

   d. Iteration Plan

10. Configuration management tools support project team members with doing which of the following? (Select all that apply.)

    a. Performing version control

    b. Eliciting change requests

    c. Enabling human collaboration

    d. Creating a baseline

11. Who is responsible for the Requirements Management Plan?

    a. System Analyst

    b. Project Manager

    c. Change Control Manager

    d. Configuration Manager

12. What artifact references the iteration plan, the iteration objectives, and the evaluation criteria of an iteration?

    a. Status Assessment

    b. Risk List

    c. Deployment Plan

    d. Software Development Plan

13. You are playing the role of a project manager, and you have estimated the length of the entire project. Now you need to allocate a length to each phase. Without prior project experience, you want to apply the template recommendation of RUP. Which one would you choose?
    a. Inception (10%), Elaboration (30%), Construction (50%), Transition (10%)
    b. Inception (5%), Elaboration (20%), Construction (65%), Transition (10%)
    c. Inception (20%), Elaboration (20%), Construction (40%), Transition (20%)
    d. Inception (25%), Elaboration (25%), Construction (25%), Transition(25%)

14. Who is responsible for the Deployment Plan?
    a. Deployment Architect
    b. Deployment Manager
    c. Configuration Manager
    d. Technical Writer

15. The Risk-List contains high-ranked architectural risks, and the Software Architect is leading a team of developers to create an architectural prototype for a use-case scenario. What RUP phase is this project in?
    a. Elaboration
    b. Inception
    c. Construction
    d. Prototyping

16. Use cases are a basis for which of the following? (Select all that apply.)
    a. System Modeling
    b. Iteration Planning
    c. Process Planning
    d. Test Planning

17. How many iterations would a RUP project have during the Construction phase when the "Grand Design" strategy for iterative development was chosen?
    a. 4
    b. 1
    c. One more than Elaboration
    d. Not possible to determine.

18. Which of the following statements best defines the relationship between roles and a team member?
    a. Roles might or might not be assigned to team members.
    b. A team member fills one role, and a role is filled by exactly one team member.

     c. A team member can fill one or more roles, and a role can be filled by one or more team members.

     d. A team member can fill one role only, but a role can be filled by one or more team members.

19. Which of the following is a phase in a RUP development project? (Choose two.)

     a. Test

     b. Transition

     c. Collaboration

     d. Construction

20. Which of the following terms characterizes a role? (Select all that apply.)

     a. Competency

     b. Skills

     c. Integrity

     d. Responsibility

21. Which of the following statements is true about the software development plan? (Select all that apply.)

     a. It is only useful for inexperienced Project Managers.

     b. It describes all iterations in depth from project start to end.

     c. It contains the Risk Management Plan .

     d. It outlines the phases and major milestones of the project.

22. A customer asks you to assemble and publish a process that is similar to the existing one but only slightly different in one area. Which elements do you focus your attention on first?

     a. Delivery Processes

     b. Capability Patterns

     c. Reusable Assets

     d. Practices

23. Which of the following is a work product type? (Select all that apply.)

     a. Package

     b. Deliverable

     c. Outcome

     d. Artifact

24. Which of the following is correct about the primary and the secondary performer of a task?

     a. The primary performer is supposed to do the work; the secondary performer is the backup.

     b. The primary performer does the planning of the work; the secondary executes.

    c. The primary performer is responsible for the task; the secondary assists.

    d. There is no difference. It is useful only for senior management to have a point of contact for each task.

25. A project is considered low ceremony. What characteristics apply to it? (Choose two.)

    a. Large project

    b. Small project

    c. Few stakeholders

    d. Distributed teams

26. Which of the following elements contains a practical explanation of how to create or revise a work product?

    a. Concept

    b. Template

    c. Guideline

    d. Roadmap

27. A content page provides a general purpose, primary, and additional performer, optional and mandatory input work products, output work products, and steps. Which content element is described?

    a. Task

    b. Checklist

    c. Work-Product Descriptor

    d. Activity

28. What is the benefit of the key principle Balance Stakeholder Needs?

    a. Perform version control.

    b. Forecast future change requests.

    c. Align applications with business and user needs.

    d. Get agreement of the acceptance test.

29. Which of the following is a process element?

    a. Capability Pattern

    b. Role Descriptor

    c. Practice

    d. Task

30. Which of the following statements is correct about a Capability Pattern? (Select all that apply.)

    a. It allows reuse of common process fragments.

    b. It is used to compose delivery processes.

    c. It shows the capabilities assigned to a role.

    d. It is a mandatory process element.

31. A process engineer wants to organize Capability Patterns. Which folder could she group them in? (Select all that apply.)
    a. Process Package
    b. Parcel
    c. Content Package
    d. Capability Pattern

32. Which statement is true about the relationship between Capability Pattern, Activities, and Tasks?
    a. Activities assemble Tasks, Tasks assemble Capability Patterns.
    b. Tasks assemble Capability Patterns, Capability Patterns assemble Activities.
    c. Tasks assemble Activities, Activities assemble Capability Patterns.
    d. There is no relationship.

33. Which process element is synonymous with RUP for large projects?
    a. Delivery Process
    b. Capability Pattern
    c. Milestone
    d. Discipline

34. Who is responsible for the Vision document?
    a. Business Analyst
    b. System Analyst
    c. Project Analyst
    d. Business Process Analyst

35. What type of process element is the Product Release or Initial Operation Capability?
    a. Milestone
    b. Reusable Asset
    c. Roadmap
    d. Practice

36. Which of the following statements best describes the term *Discipline* ?
    a. A collection of activities that are all related to a major area of concern
    b. A collection of capabilities that are all related to a minor area of concern
    c. A collection of delivery processes that are all related to a major area of concern
    d. A collection of tasks that are all related to a major area of concern

37. Which work product captures requirements of the type Feature?
    a. Functional Requirements
    b. Supplementary Specification
    c. Use Case
    d. Vision

38. Which discipline will result in the definition of a system boundary?

    a. Requirements

    b. Analysis and Design

    c. Project Management

    d. Deployment

39. What is a scenario?

    a. Just another term for use case

    b. An instance of a use case

    c. A problem for Project Managers

    d. Another term for change control

40. What elements are illustrated in a use case diagram? (Select all that apply.)

    a. Actor

    b. Scenario

    c. Use case

    d. Non-functional Requirements

41. Which discipline is considered an optional discipline prior to the Requirements discipline?

    a. Environment

    b. Analysis and Design

    c. Business Modeling

    d. Testing

42. The following three elements have something in common: Whitepaper, Example, Reusable Asset. They are which type of element?

    a. Subactivity

    b. Deliverable

    c. Outcome

    d. Guidance

43. Which of the following roles is responsible for promoting baselines?

    a. Integrator

    b. Baseline Manager

    c. Supervisor

    d. Configuration Manager

44. Which of the following can be said about a task? (Select all that apply.)

    a. Describes a unit of work

    b. Serves as the basis of planning

    c. Performed by a role

    d. Is usually coarse grained

45. Why are tool mentors useful? (Select all that apply.)

    a. They keep the task content independent from vendor-specific details.

    b. They provide immediate online assistance with tech support from the tool vendor.

    c. They increase maintainability of the content when software tools update.

    d. They provide just-in-time technical details for administrator and team members when the tool is being used.

46. Which of the following work products is part of the Environment discipline? (Select all that apply.)

    a. Development Process

    b. Target Organization Assessment

    c. Development Case

    d. Test Environment Configuration

47. Select the key principles of business-driven development from the following choices. (Select all that apply.)

    a. Demonstrate value iteratively

    b. Adapt the process

    c. Communicate among team members

    d. Elevate level of generalization

48. Who is responsible for the work product Developer Test?

    a. Integrator

    b. Implementer

    c. Any Role

    d. Software Architect

49. Which "level" of process element is used to publish a process to a consumer?

    a. Task

    b. Capability Process

    c. Activity

    d. Delivery Process

50. Which type of information would you find in a Risk-List? (Select all that apply.)

    a. Mitigation Strategy

    b. Magnitude

    c. Ranking

    d. Requirements Traceability

51. Your customer does *not* like the idea of frequent checkpoints throughout the project. In previous projects, she got used to signing off on requirements specification and acceptance testing. Which type of project was she exposed to?

    a. Iterative

    b. Incremental

    c. Waterfall

    d. Upstream

52. Which of the following is a factor that affects process rightsizing? (Choose two.)

    a. Project size

    b. Compliance requirements

    c. Version of RMC

    d. Skill level of stakeholders

Summary

The intent behind this chapter was not only to give you another chance to assess your knowledge but to provide you with an experience similar to that of the real examination situation. The questions in this practice exam are in the same ratio as the categories of questions that you will receive in the real examination. Treat the wrong answers as your to-do list to revisit those sections in the book that covered that material. Your review of that material will fill the gaps.

CHAPTER 19

Before, During, and After the Examination

By Jochen Krebs

This chapter provides important information for preparing for the final examination. It also gives you advice for the hour you're taking the examination and the time after you've completed certification.

Before the Examination

This section covers pre-exam preparation.

Preparing for Success

Perhaps one of your biggest motivations for purchasing this book was to prepare for the examination and become a member of a group of individuals who share the title IBM Certified Solution Designer - IBM Rational Unified Process. Based on our experiences and the fact that only 30 percent of those who take the exam pass on their first attempt, this certification requires careful preparation.

Verifying that an individual has intermediate skills in the RUP is not easy. In other technical examinations where the answers are more black and white, it is much easier to create valid testing. We can argue about whether certification in such a topic is fair and justified, but what is not arguable is that the preparation for the examination will deepen your understanding of RUP and strengthen your skills. The examination will validate your skills in this subject to some extent. Whether you like it or not, the form of this examination remains the most effective way to validate your knowledge of RUP.

There are two ways to successfully prepare for the RUP certification. You can do either of these or both together.

- Participating in the two-day course *Essentials of Rational Unified Process*
- Studying the *IBM Rational Unified Process Reference and Certification Guide* (this book)

An interesting fact, however, is that most participants who attend the related IBM Rational instructor-led courses do not pursue the certification afterward. At this point, time and money have already been invested, and the individual could not be in a better position to drive his certification to closure. Many course participants who were sent by their company were not even aware that the RUP certification examination actually existed. Certification could be an important achievement for you, because the certificate is issued in your name and never expires. Therefore, we hope that our book will give you the necessary details about transitioning from a self-declared to an *officially recognized* RUP expert. We also hope it gives you the motivation to follow through and take the exam.

Currently, the RUP Certification examination is available only in English. The examination consists of multiple choice questions, with one or more correct answers. The layout and the format of the questions are like the sample review questions at the end of each chapter in this book. True/false questions are not part of this test. There are, however, multiple choice questions that ask you to assess a situation or statement and select the answer(s) that the question applies to, such as, "Which of the following statements is true of iterative development?"

Some answers differ by just one word. They are written that way for a reason. The intent is not to trick anybody but to be able to measure if the test-taker has a clear understanding of the subject. For example, "The Project Manager must…" is clearly different from an answer starting with "The Project Manager should…" Being able to notice the important differences in such questions and proposed answers demonstrates that you have a clear understanding of the subject matter.

Courses

IBM Rational offers a two-day instructor-led training course, called *Essentials of IBM Rational Unified Process v7.0* (Code PRJ270 Version 2). During the first one and a half days, you will learn the fundamentals and the key principles of business-driven development, the RUP process framework, and tooling. The second half of the second day is dedicated to a competitive RUP simulation game, which will tie all the concepts together. That project simulation will enable you to internalize the characteristics of RUP, especially during the Elaboration and Construction phases. Through learning by doing, you will maximize your learning experience. It is important, however, to point out that the course does not make references to the examination and does not cover sample questions. Therefore, the best preparation for the examination is to use the combination of the two-day course and this book.

A shorter alternative to the instructor-led course is *Principles of IBM Rational Unified Process* (Code PRJ110). This is a Web-based training course that allows you to learn at your own pace. Compared to the two-day instructor-led training course, this lecture course provides the fundamentals of RUP within the 4-hour timeframe, but it has no hands-on exercises.

Considering the number of available courses that various vendors offer in RUP-related training, it is impossible to evaluate the quality of each one and judge its usefulness regarding preparation for the examination. Therefore, we make no attempt to do so here.

Books

As mentioned earlier, this book serves two key objectives: a highly distilled RUP reference of classic RUP and a RUP certification guide. The sample questions at the end of the chapters help you assess your understanding of the chapter material, give you feedback about your progress in preparing toward certification, and help reinforce what you learned from the chapter.

We do not want to miss the opportunity to recommend a few books that are up-to-date and useful to consider as additional reading during preparation:

- Kroll, P., & Kruchten, P. (2003). *The Rational Unified Process Made Easy*. Addison-Wesley: Boston.
- Kruchten, P. (2003). *The Rational Unified Process: An Introduction* Addison-Wesley: Boston.
- Kroll, P., & MacIsaac, B. (2006). *Agility and Discipline Made Easy*. Addison-Wesley: Boston.

Internet

With search engines, you are often just one mouse-click away from RUP information. You will find a lot of useful resources when browsing for RUP information. With respect to the examination, however, keep in mind that the information might be outdated and therefore incorrect. Especially for the purpose of certification, examine Internet content carefully and distinguish between official resources and individual opinions. Also remember that the content of the RUP certification focuses on the RUP process framework and disregards subjects like plug-ins, customization, and the technical knowledge around Rational Method Composer. The Rational Edge e-magazine (www.therationaledge.com) often features RUP-related articles and offers an archive of the past articles organized by subject. The official RUP examination Internet site (www-03.ibm.com/certify/certs/ 38008003.shtml) provides a good starting point for supplementary insights into the exam.

Sample Examination

Considering how many candidates spend time and money on unsuccessful attempts to pass the RUP certification, we thought it would be a good idea to provide a sample exam as a part of this book before you go to one of the test centers. Chapter 18, "Sample Examination," provides such an exam and another chance for you to assess your readiness for the exam. Because it is a self-administered test, it requires your self-discipline to make the sample exam as effective as possible.

The only person who is monitoring you in this scenario is yourself. We recommend an approach to it as outlined in Figure 19-1.

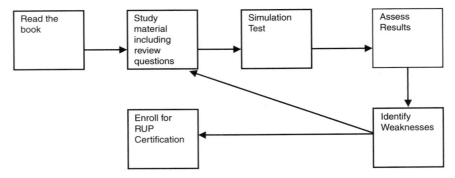

Figure 19-1   Simulation test as integral part of the preparation process

It was our goal to create a sample test that mimicked the real exam as closely as possible. Of course, the questions are not identical to those in the real exam, but the sample exam covers the same content, is in the same style, lasts the same amount of time, and has an identical pass score as the real exam. We do not recommend that you "waste" the simulation test by approaching it when you are still studying the content of the book. Approach the simulation test when you feel ready to attempt the real test, and use it to assess your knowledge. We also recommend, even though we know that is not always feasible, that you simulate the test environment at home or in your office. Remove all distractions (phone, music, TV), use a clock, and remove items that you will not be allowed to bring into a test facility, including this book. You can take the sample exam only once and expect to get valid results from it. After that, it can serve as review material, but you obviously won't get a valid score on subsequent retests since you will begin to memorize which answer is correct instead of making choices based solely on your knowledge of RUP.

Enrollment

For the RUP Certification, IBM Rational has partnered with Prometric Inc. (http://securereg3.prometric.com/), which executes and proctors the examination. The closed environment of Prometric is currently the only way to receive RUP certification worldwide. Taking the examination on your premises or receiving discounts for a large number of enrollments is not possible. In addition, Prometric handles all the administrative tasks, including enrollment, scheduling /rescheduling, or canceling appointments. When you are ready for the examination, you can quickly and easily enroll on the Internet.

When you log on to the Prometric site, choose IBM as the vendor and choose the country of your choice. In the Thompson Prometric main menu that follows, you see the most typical functions that test takers are looking for. Let's assume that you want to enroll. Follow the link Schedule Appointment until you see all examinations sorted by examination numbers. For RUP certification, select 000-839—IBM Certified Solution Designer - IBM Rational Unified Process. Notice that the language of the examination is English only. The price is indicated automatically; for example, in the U.S., it is $200 every time you attempt the test. Prometric has a large network of test facilities and, with little effort, you should be able to locate test centers in many countries around the world. Keep in mind that even though the list of countries is quite diverse, the actual test is given in the English language only.

Tips and Advice

Prometric facilities do not allow you to bring any material from outside into the test area. That includes pens, papers, cell phones, and so on. The facilities usually offer a locker where you have to leave all your extra belongings behind before you are seated in the test area. If you bring too many items, or the facility does not provide storage capabilities, Prometric might ask you to come back some other time. If you are not sure what is allowed, contact the local Prometric facility and inquire about any special requirements prior to the test. Also, keep in mind that the facility is not just for those taking the RUP exam; people are there to take many different tests on various schedules. Request headphones at the Prometric site if you need a more quiet atmosphere.

Some things are just common sense, but if you have not had to take any examinations for a long time, keep the following in mind. Dedicate enough time for the test; do not squeeze it into an already packed business day. (For example, don't try to do it on your lunch break.) Familiarize yourself with the location of the test center, and find out how you get there, where to park your car, and how long it will take you to get there.

Watch your own biorhythm, and take the test at your most productive time of the day. For most people, that is between 10 a.m. and 12 p.m. and 2 p.m. and 4 p.m. Food and beverages are prohibited in the test center. You will not have a lot of time to eat anyway.

Depending on the time of day you plan to take the test, shortly before the exam, run through the sample questions and the sample examination in this book one more time. For example, let's say you chose to take the exam in the afternoon. Walk through the sample questions and the sample examination in the morning of the same day. That can revitalize your short-term memory and help you become focused for the exam.

During the Examination

At this point, all the preparation for the examination is behind you, and the actual examination is in front of you. This section contains advice on what to do in the test situation and offers tips on approaching the questions and managing your time effectively during the examination.

Pick a Seat

Prometric hosts examinations for many different vendors and on many different topics. Even though Prometric employees try to seat you at the best possible workstation, there are a few things you might want to consider. For example, think about how sunlight affects your ability to see the screen and how many people around you are taking other tests and might distract you. Keep in mind that after the test has started, you can't relocate to another seat. Speak up to the

Prometric assistant before he starts the examination. Sometimes it might be useful to take a time-out and wait a few minutes until the test center becomes quiet again.

You might think that it sounds unreasonable to worry about all these things for a short test like this, but whether you achieve the certification is often decided by only a few questions (often just one question). One distracting neighbor or difficulty seeing the screen could determine success or failure despite all the preparation you have done.

Examination Questions

During the 75 minutes of the exam, you will answer 52 multiple choice questions that reflect the following five learning objective categories:

- Iterative Development Principles
- Iterative Development Work-Products
- Basic Method Elements and their Relationships
- Basic Process Elements and their Relationships
- Basic Content of Disciplines

Each category provides the same number of questions to the test, except Basic Content of Disciplines, which contributes more questions due to its importance to the overall understanding of RUP. Therefore, nine chapters in this book address the disciplines. The good news here, however, is that nearly 50 percent of the questions have a strong focus on RUP discipline content. If you get all the Basic Content of Disciplines questions correct, you are well on your way to having enough correct answers to earn the certification.

The questions from the learning objective categories are presented in random fashion; there is no structure in the test. The sample examination in this book also reflects questions shuffled in this manner.

As with the sample questions and the sample examination, you aren't asked to assess true or false questions. The questions ask you to pick the correct answer(s) out of a list of provided choices; typically four answers are provided, with one or more of them being correct answers. The format and wording of the question indicate whether the question requires you to choose a single answer or multiple answers.

All questions and answers are weighed the same. Therefore, difficult questions count the same as easy ones. That could be an important piece of information for developing your strategy for the test. The RUP certification test allows you to mark questions for later review. By using this feature, you can move on to other questions and prevent getting stuck on one difficult question. Then, just before you submit the final results for grading, you can revisit the marked questions if time allows.

The passing score is 62 percent

Time Management

You have 75 minutes for 52 questions, which means roughly 85 seconds for each question, not counting the ones marked for revisiting. That is a lot of time if you approach a question you know immediately. Experience shows, however, that everybody struggles in at least one area of the test, usually covering a few questions. Sometimes the difficulty is with the wording of the question rather than the topic. Unfortunately, nobody from Prometric can help you with that. Please do not spend valuable time by trying to get in touch with someone to clarify the question. You only waste time by doing so. To successfully pass the overall certification, your buffer is 19 wrong out of 52 total questions. Time is of the essence; note that your stress level might increase toward the end of the test when you start monitoring the time that is always visible on the screen.

You can also use the time constraint and make it work in your favor. Your first reaction on reading the question is typically going to be the right reaction. You don't have the time to pore over each question, think it over, and then rethink it. It's good you don't. Most often, a test taker's original answer is correct. Whether you receive the certification or not should not be about the speed of execution but about your knowledge and skills. But realize that the limited time will actually work to your advantage rather than be a disadvantage.

It is nobody's intention to mislead people and to get them to choose the wrong answers, but there are hurdles in the test that you have to be aware of. If we can give you one piece of advice to use during the examination, it would be not to get bogged down at one question, but rather take a guess, mark the question for later review, and revisit the question at the far end from a new angle.

Technical Issues

When you encounter technical problems during the test that are not related to the content of the actual test, approach a Prometric representative immediately. The representative can work with you on a fair solution, which might require restarting the test or asking you to come back another time. We highly recommend that you approach the Prometric staff during the test only for technical issues that prevent you from executing your test. Any organizational or content-related question can only lead to a loss of your time.

After the Examination

After you finish and submit the examination, Prometric compiles your results and forwards them to IBM Rational for statistical and administrative purposes. This section covers what happens after the certification is submitted.

Results

Your examination results are brutally honest. As soon as you submit the examination, Prometric generates the overall result and presents your percentage score on your screen. It is especially nerve racking if your receiving or not receiving the certification is decided by a single question. After your work with this book, we hope, of course, that you answered that single question correctly and to your advantage. The results for RUP certification are black and white. You pass or you fail.

If you pass, you receive a congratulations page. Despite your excitement at this point, please celebrate the certification somewhere else other than the test center. Just imagine if someone else is jumping around in excitement when you are in the middle of your test. Please respect the work of others. On the way out, the Prometric examination coordinator is automatically notified about your results and prints your test results as a record. If you were successful, the record is proof that you are now officially certified in the RUP, albeit at this point just with a temporary certificate. Then Prometric forwards your results to IBM, which issues the official certificate.

The certificate is issued as a PDF document, electronically transmitted (see Figure 19-2). Monitor your e-mail box for an e-mail coming from the IBM certification team; it carries your official certificate as a PDF document. If you have not received an e-mail with the certificate within 2 weeks after you passed the examination, please send a quick e-mail to certify@us.ibm.com. You can also use this address to request a copy of the certificate in case you lost it, but that might take some time.

Figure 19-2   The official IBM Rational Solution Designer - IBM Rational Unified Process Certificate

Summary

Being prepared for the examination is the most important thing during the RUP Certification process. But being prepared for the time during the exam, due to the time constraint, is nearly as important. We shared our advice with you for preparing for the exam and dealing with the examination questions and time. We also gave you recommendations for the time after you passed the examination. All we can do now is wish you good luck.

Answers to Sample Questions

This appendix provides the correct answers to the sample questions at the end of each chapter and to the questions in Chapter 18, "Sample Examination."

Answers to Sample Questions

Chapter 1

1. b
2. a
3. b
4. a, b, c
5. c, d
6. a
7. a, c, d
8. a, b
9. a, b, d
10. a, b, c
11. a, b, c, d
12. b
13. b
14. a, b

15. a, c
16. a, b, d
17. a, b
18. a, b, c, d
19. a, b, c, d
20. a
21. a

Chapter 2

1. a, c, d
2. a, c, d
3. c, d
4. a, c, d
5. a, b, d
6. a, c, d
7. a, c
8. a, d
9. a, c
10. a, c

Chapter 3

1. a, c, d
2. a, b, d
3. b, d
4. c
5. a, b
6. d
7. c
8. a, b, c
9. c
10. a

Chapter 4

1. c
2. a, b, d
3. a
4. a, b, d
5. a, c
6. a, b
7. b
8. a, b, c
9. b, c
10. a, d

Chapter 5

1. a, b ,c
2. a, b, d
3. b, c, d
4. c
5. d
6. c
7. c
8. a
9. a, c, d
10. b

Chapter 6

1. a, b, c
2. a, b
3. a, b
4. b
5. a, c
6. a, c

7. a

8. a

9. a, b, c

10. a, b, c, d

11. b, c, d

12. a, c, d

13. b, d

14. a, b, c, d

Chapter 7

1. a, b, c

2. b

3. a

4. a

5. a, b, c

6. c

7. c, d

8. a, b, c, d

9. b

10. b

11. a, d

12. a, c, d

13. a

14. a, b, c, d

Chapter 8

1. a

2. b

3. c

4. c

5. a

6. a, b, c, d

7. a, b, d

8. a
9. c
10. a, b
11. d

Chapter 9

1. b, d
2. a, b, c
3. a
4. b
5. b
6. a, c, d
7. a
8. a
9. a, b, c, d
10. a, b, c, d

Chapter 10

1. a, d
2. a, b, c, d
3. a
4. d
5. a
6. a, b
7. a, d
8. d
9. a, b, c
10. a, b, d

Chapter 11

1. a, c
2. a
3. a, b, c

4. a, d

5. c

6. a

7. b, d

8. a, b, c, d

9. a, b, d

10. b

11. c, d

12. a

13. b

14. c

Chapter 12

1. a, b, c

2. a, b, c

3. a, b, c, d

4. a, b, d

5. a, b, c

6. a, b, d

7. c

8. a, b, c

9. b, c, d

10. a, b

11. a, c, d

12. a, b

13. a, b

14. c

15. a

16. a

Chapter 13

1. a, c

2. b, c

3. b
4. b, c, d
5. a, b, c
6. a, b, c
7. b, c
8. d
9. a, b
10. a, d

Chapter 14

1. a, c
2. b, c, d
3. c
4. d
5. a
6. c
7. b, c
8. d
9. a, c
10. c

Answers to Sample Examination Questions (Chapter 18)

1. b
2. d
3. b, d
4. b, d
5. b, c, d
6. a, b
7. b
8. d
9. c, d
10. a, d
11. a

12. d

13. a

14. b

15. a

16. a, b, d

17. b

18. c

19. b, d

20. a, b, d

21. c, d

22. b

23. b, c, d

24. c

25. b, c

26. c

27. a

28. c

29. a

30. a, b

31. a, d

32. c

33. a

34. b

35. a

36. d

37. d

38. a

39. b

40. a, c

41. c

42. d

43. a

44. a, c

45. a, c, d
46. a, c
47. a, b
48. b
49. d
50. a, b, c
51. c
52. a, b

Index